Nehemiah
Becoming a Godly Leader

The Bible Teacher's Guide

Gregory Brown

BTG
Publishing

3

Endorsements

"*The Bible Teacher's Guide* ... will help any teacher study and get a better background for his/her Bible lessons. In addition, it will give direction and scope to teaching of the Word of God. Praise God for this contemporary introduction to the Word of God."

—Dr. Elmer Towns
Co-founder of Liberty University
Former Dean, Liberty Baptist Theological Seminary

"Expositional, theological, and candidly practical! I highly recommend The Bible Teacher's Guide for anyone seeking to better understand or teach God's Word."

—Dr. Young–Gil Kim
Founding President, Handong Global University

"Helpful to both the layman and the serious student, The Bible Teacher's Guide, by Dr. Greg Brown, is outstanding!"

—Dr. Neal Weaver
President, Louisiana Baptist University

"Whether you are preparing a Bible study, a sermon, or simply wanting to dive deeper into a personal study of God's Word, these will be very helpful tools."

—Eddie Byun
Missions and Teaching Pastor, Venture Christian Church, Los Gatos, California
Author of Justice Awakening

"I am happy that Greg is making his insights into God's truth available to a wider audience through these books. They bear the hallmarks of good Bible teaching: the result of rigorous Bible study and thoroughgoing application to the lives of people."

—Ajith Fernando
Teaching Director, Youth for Christ
Author of A Call to Joy and Pain

"The content of the series is rich. My prayer is that God will use it to help the body of Christ grow strong."

—Dr. Min Chung
Senior Pastor, Covenant Fellowship Church, Urbana, Illinois
Adjunct Professor, Urbana Theological Seminary

"Knowing the right questions to ask and how to go about answering them is fundamental to learning in any subject matter. Greg demonstrates this convincingly."

—Dr. William Moulder
Professor of Biblical Studies, Trinity International University

"Pastor Greg is passionate about the Word of God, rigorous and thorough in his approach to the study of it... I am pleased to recommend The Bible Teacher's Guide to anyone who hungers for the living Word."

—Dr. JunMo Cho
Professor of Linguistics, Handong Global University
Contemporary Christian Music Recording Artist

"I can't imagine any student of Scripture not benefiting by this work."

—Steven J. Cole
Pastor, Flagstaff Christian Fellowship, Flagstaff, Arizona

Author of the Riches from the Word series

"Greg deals with the principles, doctrines, and applications of the text in a practical way which is useful for both individual growth or for help in preparation for teaching."

—Bob Deffinbaugh
Ministry Coordinator, Bible.org
Pastor, Community Bible Chapel, Richardson, Texas

Contents

Preface

And entrust what you heard me say in the presence of many others as witnesses to faithful people who will be competent to teach others as well.
2 Timothy 2:2 (NET)

Paul's words to Timothy still apply to us today. There is a need to raise up teachers who clearly and fearlessly teach the Word of God. It is with this hope in mind that The Bible Teacher's Guide (BTG) series has been created. The series includes both expositional and topical studies. This guide will be useful for teachers who are preparing to lead small groups or give sermons, or for an individual's devotional study.

Each lesson is based around the hermeneutical principle that the original authors wrote in a similar manner as we do today—with the intention of being understood. Each paragraph and chapter of Scripture is centered on one main thought often called the Big Idea. After finding the Big Idea for each passage studied, the Big Question was created, which will lead the small group through the entire gamut of the text. Alongside the Big Question, hermeneutical questions such as Observation Questions, Interpretation Questions, and Application Questions have been added. Observation questions point out pivotal aspects of the text. Interpretation questions lead us into understanding what the text means through looking at the context or other Scripture. Application questions lead us to life principles coming out of the text. It was never the intent for all these questions to be used, but they have been given to help guide the teacher in the preparation of his own lesson.

The purpose of this guide is to make the preparation of the teacher easier, as many commentaries and sermons have been used in the development of each lesson. After meditating on the Scripture text and the lesson, the small group leader can follow the suggested teaching outline, if preferred:

1. The leader would introduce the text and present the big question in the beginning of the study.

11

2. He would allow several minutes for the members to search out answers from within the text, questions, or ways God spoke to them.

3. Then the leader would facilitate the discussion of the findings and lead the group along through observation, interpretation, and application questions provided in the guide.

The leader may find teaching part or the entire lesson preferred and then giving application questions. The leader can also choose to use a "Study Group" method of facilitation where each member prepares beforehand and shares teaching responsibility (see Appendices 1 and 2). Some leaders may find that corporately reading each main section in a lesson, followed by a brief discussion of the topic and an application question, as the most effective method.

Again, The Bible Teacher's Guide can be used as a manual to follow in teaching, a resource to use in preparation for teaching, or simply as an expositional devotional to enrich one's own study. I pray that the Lord may bless your study, preparation, and teaching, and that in all of it you will find the fruit of the Holy Spirit abounding in your own life and the lives of those you instruct.

A Word on Leadership

Look, the sovereign Lord who commands armies is about to remove from Jerusalem and Judah every source of security, including all the food and water, the mighty men and warriors, judges and prophets, omen readers and leaders, captains of groups of fifty, the respected citizens, advisers and those skilled in magical arts, and those who know incantations. The Lord says, "I will make youths their officials; malicious young men will rule over them. The people will treat each other harshly; men will oppose each other; neighbors will fight. Youths will proudly defy the elderly and riffraff will challenge those who were once respected. Indeed, a man will grab his brother right in his father's house and say, 'You own a coat—you be our leader! This heap of ruins will be under your control.' At that time the brother will shout, 'I am no doctor, I have no food or coat in my house; don't make me a leader of the people!'"
Isaiah 3:1-7 (NET)

In this text, God is about to judge the nation of Israel for their unfaithfulness to him, and one of the ways he judges this nation is by removing its leaders. It says, "The sovereign Lord who commands armies is about to remove from Jerusalem... the mighty men and warriors, judges and prophets, omen readers and leaders, captains of groups of fifty, the respected citizens, advisers and those skilled in magical arts, and those who know incantations." One of the implications we can take from this passage is that leadership is a gift from the Lord. When Israel needed a godly leader, God gave them prophets, judges, and kings. He gave them Samuel, David, Elijah, Isaiah, etc., to bless the people and lead them into righteousness. However, when a community or a nation is in rebellion towards God, God often removes their leadership or gives them unsuitable leadership (v. 4).

It is no surprise that when we look at many of our national and local elections, we often find ourselves not voting for a person we want but voting for the lesser of evils. The world is in a leadership crisis, and the answer is not

13

more training or more education. The answer is God. God is the ultimate leader and the reproducer of leaders. In fact, Scripture declares that there is no authority but that which comes from God (Romans 13:1). Leadership comes from the Lord and godly leadership is a gift from him.

Therefore, if we are going to fix the leadership crisis in our churches, our schools, our homes, and our nations, we must start with God. He is the giver of authority and leadership, and he is the one who takes them away. Therefore, the primary way that we can learn about leadership and, specifically, how to become a godly leader is by studying God's Word. Second Timothy 3:17 says that the Word of God is useful for equipping the man of God for all righteousness. Leadership is a righteous act that Scripture is more than suitable to equip us for.

And, possibly the greatest book in the Bible that we can learn about leadership from is the book of Nehemiah. When somebody wants to learn about worship, they go to the Psalms. When somebody wants to learn about wisdom, they go to Proverbs. But where should a person go to learn about leadership? Most would say that we should go to the book of Nehemiah.

Nehemiah, the cupbearer to the king of Persia, persuaded the king to support the rebuilding of the city of Jerusalem (Neh 2:5) and motivated Israel to rebuild ruins that had been abandoned for more than 140 years (586 BC-445 BC). He led the rebuilding project while under the constant threat of attack by Israel's antagonistic neighbors. He completed the rebuilding of the walls around Jerusalem within only fifty-two days. If this were not enough, Nehemiah demonstrated great humility and wisdom as he enabled Ezra and the Levites to help bring spiritual revival to the nation of Israel. The book of Nehemiah is a tremendous narrative on godly leadership. Let us drink deeply from it, and may God use us to be the answer to this leadership crisis in our communities and ultimately in our world today.

May God richly bless your study.

Introduction

Authorship

Who is the author of the book of Nehemiah? The original book is anonymous and does not carry any name.[1] Therefore, there is some controversy over the authorship. Traditionally, both Christians and Jews recognize Ezra, the scribe, as the author.[2] This is based primarily on external evidence, as the books Ezra and Nehemiah are one book in the Hebrew Bible and probably were initially written that way. Because of this, both the Septuagint (the Greek translation of the Old Testament) and the Latin Vulgate also made them one book, calling Nehemiah "Second Ezra."[3] The book of Ezra details the first and second return of the Israelites from exile in Babylon. It talks about the rebuilding of the temple in Israel and the restoration of the ceremonies led by Ezra. The book of Nehemiah details the third return of the Jews, the rebuilding of the walls, and the restoration of covenant life led by Ezra.

The book of Nehemiah is a compilation of works. There are memoirs and lists in the letter. Though a compilation, it is very clear that Nehemiah, the cupbearer of King Artaxerxes, wrote large portions of the book. Verses 1:1-7:5, 12:27-43, 13:4-31 are Nehemiah's personal memoirs, as they are written in first person.[4] Other sections were probably written by another author, most likely Ezra. Therefore, the book of Nehemiah was written by both authors; however, it seems like Ezra was the compiler of the contents. He compiled the writings sometime after 432 BC but no later than 400 BC.[5]

What do we know about Ezra and Nehemiah? Ezra was a priest and scribe; Nehemiah was a layman and cupbearer to the king of Persia. Scripture teaches that Ezra devoted himself to the study and observance of the law and the teaching of its decrees to Israel (Ezra 7:10). We see his devotion to Scripture by looking at how he led Israel into spiritual revival both in the book of Ezra and Nehemiah. In Nehemiah 8, he led Israel in the reading of Scripture from morning till noon. During this time of observance, Ezra and some of the Levites also explained the meaning of the Scriptures to the people (8:8). Then the next day, Ezra met the fathers of the households, the Levites, and the priests to help them

15

further understand the words of the Law (8:13). This led to a great spiritual revival in Israel and eventually to their recommitment to the Mosaic covenant as they bound themselves with a curse and an oath to obey its laws (10:29).

As for the person of Nehemiah, we don't know much about him. He is only mentioned in the book of Nehemiah. He was probably born during the exile in Persia. He was a trusted cupbearer to King Artaxerxes. He, obviously, was a devout person of prayer as he prays eleven times throughout the book. He also had a strong awareness of God's sovereignty over all events. After the king listened to Nehemiah's plan and granted his request to go and rebuild Jerusalem, he did not boast in his business plan or favor with the king but humbly recognized God's gracious hand over the whole situation (Nehemiah 2:8). In addition, He clearly was a man of great integrity. While he served as governor of Israel for twelve years, he never abused the people or even used the governor's allowance for food. He declared that the reason he did not abuse his authority, as the previous governors had, was because of his "fear of God" (Nehemiah 5:15). He was a man of great integrity who feared the Lord.

Nehemiah and Ezra were great leaders who God called to work together. Nehemiah handled the practical aspects, while Ezra handled the spiritual. As we consider them, we cannot but remember other great leaders who God called to work together throughout the narrative of Scripture. God called Moses and Aaron, David and Nathan, Hezekiah and Isaiah, Paul and Barnabas, and many others to help lead his people in reform. Nehemiah and Ezra had a lasting impact on the post-exilic community, and they are still having a great impact today.

Background

What is the background of the book of Nehemiah? The background is God's faithfulness to his covenant promises with Israel. In the Mosaic Law, God promised Israel that if they obeyed his commands and worshiped him alone that he would bless them, but if they disobeyed him, he would bring nations to destroy Israel and exile them from the promised land (Deuteronomy 28). In the book of Kings, King Solomon led the nation into idolatry as he worshiped the gods of his foreign wives. This resulted in God judging the nation by splitting it in two. It split into the Northern Kingdom (Samaria), which had Jeroboam as king, and the Southern Kingdom (Judah), which followed Rehoboam, the son of Solomon.

The Northern Kingdom had many ungodly kings who continued to worship foreign gods in disobedience to God's law, and as a consequence, the nation was conquered and scattered by the Assyrians in 722 BC. The Southern

Kingdom fared a little better as they had more good kings, but they also fell into spiritual adultery, leading to God's discipline. They went through several deportations by the nation of Babylon from 605 to 586 BC (2 Kings 25).[6]

The deportees from Israel lived in Babylon for seventy years (cf. Jeremiah 25:11), and the first return to Israel happened in 539 BC. This return, which resulted in the rebuilding of the Jewish temple, was led by Zerubbabel and Joshua. The details of this return and rebuilding are documented in Ezra chapters 1-6. The second return was led by the priest Ezra in 458 BC.[7] Ezra, then, led Israel into the restoration of the covenant and the worship of God (Ezra 7-10). However, this renewal of worship was short lived. The final return happened in 445 BC and was led by Nehemiah, the cupbearer to King Artaxerxes of Persia.[8] Nehemiah became the governor of Israel and accomplished the rebuilding of the walls of Jerusalem, as seen in Nehemiah chapters 1-7. In chapters 8-12, Ezra again led Israel into revival and covenant renewal. In chapter 13, it is clear that Nehemiah left for some unspecified amount of time to again serve the king in Persia (13:6); however, Nehemiah returned only to find Israel again in spiritual turmoil. They had married foreign wives and were no longer practicing the Sabbath. The book ends on a sour note. Israel would not be faithful to their covenant God, which was a foreshadowing of the later rejection of the messiah in the Gospels.

Purpose

What is the purpose of the book of Nehemiah? The primary purpose is to show God's covenant faithfulness to Israel. Even though they had disobeyed God and were exiled from the land, God remained faithful to his covenant with Abraham. In Genesis 13, God promised to give Abraham's seed the land of Israel "forever" (v. 15). Though Israel was unfaithful, the faithful God brought them back from exile, first by Zerubbabel, then by Ezra, and finally by Nehemiah. The book of Nehemiah documents the rebuilding of the walls amidst turmoil and persecution. It then documents a revival and restoration of Israel to God's covenant. God still had plans for Israel. He was faithful, even when they were not.

The major themes of this letter include Nehemiah's obedience. Nehemiah, who was serving in Persia under the king, developed a burden for the nation of Israel which was in turmoil. He gained favor from the king and returned to rebuild the walls around Jerusalem, the capital city. After rebuilding the wall, Nehemiah developed a plan to repopulate Jerusalem. He attributed this to God as he said, "Now the city was spread out and large, and there were not a lot of people in it. At that time houses had not been rebuilt. My God placed it on my heart to gather the leaders, the officials, and the ordinary people so they could be enrolled on the basis of genealogy" (7:4-5). Nehemiah was faithful to God's plans throughout the narrative.

Another major theme in the book is opposition. As soon as Nehemiah came to Jerusalem to rebuild the walls, those who were profiting from Israel's misfortune began to antagonize Nehemiah. They mocked him and the Israelites. They sent out rumors that Nehemiah was rebelling against the king of Persia. They plotted to come against Israel in battle. In fact, there was even division amongst the leaders of Israel, as the nobles in the tribe of Judah partnered with the enemy. Nehemiah received some type of opposition or persecution seven times throughout the book (Nehemiah 2:19; 4:1-3; 4:7-23; 6:1-4; 6:5-9; 6:10-14; 6:17-19).[9] Faithfulness to God will always bring persecution and trials. However, Nehemiah and Israel still completed the rebuilding of the walls in only fifty-two days.

God's sovereignty over Israel is also a resounding theme throughout the book. Nehemiah seeks favor from the king in chapter 2 in order to go and rebuild the wall. When the king granted his request, Nehemiah attributed this to God's gracious hand over his life (Nehemiah 2:8). He says, "so the king granted me these requests, for the good hand of my God was on me." Also, when Nehemiah told the Israelites about his plan to rebuild the wall, he again attributed his success to God's gracious hand guiding the process (2:18). Throughout the narrative, God continued to graciously prosper the restoration of Israel.

In addition, prayer is a major theme in the book of Nehemiah. Eleven times Nehemiah prays in this book (cf. 1:5-11; 2:4; 4:4, 9; 5:19; 6:9, 14;13:14, 22, 29, 31). In chapter 1, it was Nehemiah's fasting and prayer which led to his plan to seek favor from the king. In chapter 2, when Nehemiah approached the king for permission to go to Israel, the text says that Nehemiah prayed right before asking the king (v. 4-5). Nehemiah records, "The king responded, 'What is it you are seeking?' Then I quickly prayed to the God of heaven and said to the king" Nehemiah was a man of prayer, and it was prayer that led to the rebuilding of the walls and the restoration of the people.

Finally, another major theme of the book is obviously leadership. Nehemiah coordinated and made plans on how to get to Israel and what would be needed for the building project before he left Persia. He motivated the Israelites to rebuild the wall that had been down for over 140 years. He encouraged them to be faithful in the midst of persecution from without and turmoil from within. Nehemiah even stands up to the Jews who were sinning against God by neglecting the house of God, breaking the Sabbath, and marrying foreign wives (Nehemiah 13). From Nehemiah's example, we can learn a great deal about leadership.

Characteristics of Godly Leaders

These are the words of Nehemiah son of Hacaliah: It so happened that in the month of Kislev, in the twentieth year, I was in Susa the citadel. Hanani, who was one of my relatives, along with some of the men from Judah, came to me, and I asked them about the Jews who had escaped and had survived the exile, and about Jerusalem. They said to me, "The remnant that remains from the exile there in the province are experiencing considerable adversity and reproach. The wall of Jerusalem lies breached, and its gates have been burned down!" When I heard these things I sat down abruptly, crying and mourning for several days. I continued fasting and praying before the God of heaven.
Nehemiah 1 (NET)

What are characteristics of godly leaders?

Second Timothy 3:17 says that Scripture is given to equip the man of God for "every good work". Every good work includes things like marriage, being a good employee, and even being a great leader. The Bible is full of stories about leadership but none may be as instructive as the book of Nehemiah.

Nehemiah, who was a cupbearer for the king of Persia, gained favor with the king to leave his post and rebuild the walls of Jerusalem. He inspired the Israelites to rebuild the walls and also to restore the worship of God. He was a tremendous leader.

The story behind the rebuilding of the walls is that Israel had rebelled against God during the times of the kings, and God judged them by exiling them to Babylon for over 140 years (586 BC-445 BC). After seventy years in exile, bands of Israelites started to return to Israel. In fact, there were three returns. The first was led by Zerubbabel—a descendant of David who rebuilt the temple in Israel. The second was led by Ezra—the priest who brought an initial spiritual revival in Israel. The third return was led by Nehemiah, as told here.

Nehemiah began to rebuild both the walls and the spiritual lives of the people, as he became their governor. As we look at Nehemiah, we will learn a lot about godly leadership.

I say godly leadership because godly leaders have character and they commonly tackle God-sized problems. This work was beyond Nehemiah's power, and it virtually seemed impossible to complete.

God's leaders are always confronting impossible problems. Moses had to set Israel free from the slavery of Egypt; he had to cross the Red Sea with the angry Egyptians following right behind him. Here in this text, Nehemiah was over 800 miles away from the problem.[10] Israel was in ruins, and the people were being harassed by their neighbors. He had an impossible problem. However, he did not only confront it but also was successful.

God wants to develop leaders today in his church to help rebuild nations, churches, families, and individuals who have fallen away from God or never known him. In ancient societies, walls were very important because they protected the people from the attack of looters and other enemies.

In the same way, for many Christians, their walls have been broken down by allowing sin to infiltrate them both individually and corporately. Many churches and Christian organizations have been affected by doctrinal liberalism. Many young Christians have started to look and walk like the world. There is a need to rebuild the walls in order to protect God's people.

This is what Galatians says about a brother in sin: "Brothers and sisters, if a person is discovered in some sin, you who are spiritual restore such a person in a spirit of gentleness. Pay close attention to yourselves, so that you are not tempted too" (Galatians 6:1).

Godly leadership brings one in contact with the sinful and the broken in order to help rebuild, but it also exposes one's life to dangers and temptations. We see this with Nehemiah as he was confronted by many detractors because he sought to help Israel. In this text, we will see many characteristics of godly leadership.

Big Question: What characteristics of godly leadership do we find in chapter 1?

Godly Leaders Are Concerned and Responsive to Problems

Hanani, who was one of my relatives, along with some of the men from Judah, came to me, and I asked them about the Jews who had escaped and had survived the exile, and about Jerusalem. They said to me, "The remnant that remains from the exile there in the province are experiencing considerable adversity and reproach. The wall of Jerusalem lies breached, and its gates have been burned down!" When I heard these things I sat down abruptly, crying and mourning

for several days. I continued fasting and praying before the God of heaven.
Nehemiah 1:2-4

Nehemiah was the cupbearer to the king; he tasted the king's food and lived in the king's palace. Even though the position doesn't sound very impressive, it was. One scholar said that the cupbearer "was often chosen for his personal beauty and attractions, and in ancient oriental courts was always a person of rank and importance. From the confidential nature of his duties and his frequent access to the royal presence, he possessed great influence."[11]

Certainly, this was an easy position for a person to be unconcerned about the situation in Israel. Nehemiah was completely taken care of.

He first shows his concern by asking questions of Hanani, his brother, who had just come from Judah. Godly leaders are concerned and informed. However, it is one thing to be concerned and to gather information, and it's another thing to be responsive. He immediately wept and began to pray for the nation.

His response was very similar to that of Christ when he saw the large crowds in Matthew 9. This is what Matthew said:

When he saw the crowds, he had compassion on them because they were bewildered and helpless, like sheep without a shepherd. Then he said to his disciples, "The harvest is plentiful, but the workers are few. Therefore ask the Lord of the harvest to send out workers into his harvest."
Matthew 9:36-38

Christ was concerned about the needs of the people and so was Nehemiah. They both responded in prayer.

Application Question: Why is it so easy to not be concerned about the spiritual temperature of others or the problems of others?

There are many reasons:

- People are unconcerned sometimes simply because of apathy. It is easy to care only about ourselves and not about others, especially when the problem doesn't affect us.

21

- People are unconcerned sometimes because they feel like they cannot help. The problem is too big. We say to ourselves we cannot do anything about it.

- People are unconcerned sometimes because they fear responsibility. The more we know; the more we are responsible for. Solomon said with knowledge comes more pain (Ecc 1:18).

- People are unconcerned sometimes because they are too busy with other things.

- People are unconcerned sometimes because they suffer from the "bystander effect." This means we say to ourselves that somebody else will take care of it.

Nehemiah was wealthy and living in the house of the king of Persia. He had many reasons to not care about or get involved with the problems in Israel. Yet, when his brother came back from Israel, he asked how things were going there because he cared. But not only did he care enough to ask questions, he also cared enough to get involved.

The Danger of Knowing but Not Responding

Even worse than the uninformed are those who know but are not willing to get involved and serve. Let me tell you the story about a man whom God judged for not responding to his knowledge. His name is Eli. Look at what 1 Samuel 3:11-13 says:

> The Lord said to Samuel, "Look! I am about to do something in Israel; when anyone hears about it, both of his ears will tingle. On that day I will carry out against Eli everything that I spoke about his house—from start to finish! You should tell him that I am about to judge his house forever because of *the sin that he knew about*. For his sons were cursing God, and he did not rebuke them.

See, Eli knew about his sons' sins. They were sleeping with the women who came to the temple and not properly leading Israel into worship. For that reason God judged him. He knew, but he failed to restrain them. What areas are we neglecting? Is it family? Is it problems in the church or work? Is it our devotional lives? Is it our private thought patterns that are ungodly?

Ignorance is not always bliss. God cares about our homes, our churches, and our friends. And, we are responsible to minister to them as well. He cares about every area of leadership he gives us. Romans 13:1b says, "for there is no authority except by God's appointment." Therefore, whatever area of influence God has given us, he requires us to be good stewards in it.

Listen to what God told Ezekiel about his knowledge and his responsibility to it:

> When I say to the wicked, "You will certainly die," and you do not warn him—you do not speak out to warn the wicked to turn from his wicked deed and wicked lifestyle so that he may live—that wicked person will die for his iniquity, but I will hold you accountable for his death.
> Ezekiel 3:18

Essentially, he says, "Ezekiel, if I tell you to warn and you do not, I will hold their blood on your hands." God told Ezekiel that he was responsible.

Godly leaders are concerned, and they are willing to get involved. They are not apathetic as so much of the church is. They are not too busy, and they do not say, "Somebody else will do it." Nehemiah was willing to ask questions and get involved.

In what ways is God calling you to get involved? Maybe he is calling you to serve by responding to a need in your church with the children's ministry or to develop a ministry to reach the college students. He may be calling you to get involved in your community with a project. Maybe, the first step he would have you take is simply asking a question so you can become more informed.

Application Questions: For what area(s) is God burdening your heart? How can you take steps in order to be more informed and ready to serve?

Godly Leaders Are Constant in Prayer

> Then I said, "Please, O Lord God of heaven, great and awesome God, who keeps his loving covenant with those who love him and obey his commandments, may your ear be attentive and your eyes be open to hear the prayer of your servant that I am praying to you today throughout both day and night on behalf of your servants the Israelites. I am confessing the sins of the Israelites that we have committed against you—both I myself and my family have sinned.
> Nehemiah 1:5-6

23

What do we see next? Certainly, we can't miss the fact that Nehemiah began to pray for Israel.

Nehemiah faced a big problem, one that seemed impossible to fix. His nation had been in reproach for over 140 years, and he was 800 miles away from the problem. However, even though the problem seemed impossible to fix, he immediately brought it to God. Listen to his prayer: "Please, O Lord God of heaven, great and awesome God, who keeps his loving covenant with those who love him and obey his commandments" (Nehemiah 1:5).

What problems are you facing that are too big and overwhelming? Are there any problems that you have not yet brought to God? We all face problems that seem unsolvable like trafficking, abortion, corruption in the government, sin in the church, sin in our own lives, etc. We might be tempted to look at the problem and not even bring it to God.

Nehemiah responds to this impossible problem by praying and fasting night and day (Neh 1:4). He constantly brings the situation to God. This is a characteristic of a godly leader.

One of the things that Scripture commonly does is let us in on the prayer life of those God used greatly. Moses was constantly praying for Israel, asking God to remove his wrath from them (Exodus 32:10-14). Daniel is shown as a man who prays three times a day (Daniel 6:10): morning, noon, and night. When the king's wise men wanted to bring a charge against him, they knew to trap him during his prayer time.

God also has chosen to show us Christ's prayer life in Scripture. He was always sneaking away to meet with God (Mark 1:35). He went to the mountain to pray alone, and his disciples got up in the morning to look for him.

Godly leaders are prayer warriors who constantly bring their seemingly impossible problems to the Lord. They pray to the Lord about their superiors, those they lead, and their families. They are a blessing to whatever community they serve because of their commitment to prayer. Consider what Paul commanded in 1 Timothy 2:1-3:

> First of all, then, I urge that requests, prayers, intercessions, and thanks be offered on behalf of all people, even for kings and all who are in authority, that we may lead a peaceful and quiet life in all godliness and dignity. Such prayer for all is good and welcomed before God our Savior.

Paul calls for us to pray for "all people" with all kinds of prayers. This type of lifestyle pleases God.

Similarly, Nehemiah was constant in prayer, even for people who were far away from him. He heard about the problems in Israel and interceded, and, no doubt, God was pleased.

Application Question: What are the benefits of bringing such big problems first to God?

- A benefit of bringing our problems first to God is that it makes us wait. Sometimes we are prone to act too quickly, but it is almost always best to first spend time in prayer.

- A benefit of bringing our problems first to God is that it gives us a proper perspective. Praying first puts things in perspective as problems get smaller in view of the "great and awesome God" (v.5). I believe that is why the Lord's Prayer starts with God and his kingdom before it gets to our request—"give us our daily bread."

- A benefit of bringing our problems first to God is that it brings the resources of God into our situation: his wisdom, his power, his comfort, etc.

- A benefit of bringing our problems first to God is that it quiets our hearts. Philippians 4:6-7 promises the peace of God to those who pray and give thanks in everything.

- A benefit of bringing our problems first to God is that it activates our faith. Prayer is an act of trusting in God, and therefore, it allows us to trust God more in the situation. It helps our belief.

Application Question: What situation or person is God calling you to intercede for as Nehemiah did?

Godly Leaders Can Identify with Others' Failures

May your ear be attentive and your eyes be open to hear the prayer of your servant that I am praying to you today throughout both day and night on behalf of your servants the Israelites. I am confessing the sins of the Israelites that we have committed against you—both I myself and my family have sinned.
Nehemiah 1:6

What other characteristics of a godly leader can we see as we look at Nehemiah's prayer?

Nehemiah's considering himself a sinner just like the rest of the nation of Israel should stand out in verse 6. He says, "I am confessing the sins of the Israelites that we have committed against you—both I myself and my family have sinned."

Many leaders only see other people's failures and never see their own, which affects how they minister to and lead others. This is what we saw with the leadership style of the Pharisees. One Pharisee cried out, "God, I thank you that I am not like other people: extortionists, unrighteous people, adulterers—or even like this tax collector. I fast twice a week; I give a tenth of everything I get" (Lk 18:11-12). The Pharisee could not see his own sin, and therefore, could never minister to not only the tax collector, but also the robber, the evil doer, and the adulterer. For this reason, these leaders often become very judgmental and self-righteous, especially in the area of discipline. However, godly leaders can identify sin in their own lives, and it helps them deal with others graciously even in discipline.

A godly leader can say, "I have lusted," "I have hated," "I have lied." "I have at times struggled with pride, apathy, and lack of self-discipline." "The same root that causes murder, rape, bribery, and other injustices are all in me." This kind of leader can minister to people because he sees his own sin and can empathize.

Interpretation Question: How do we see this trait of identifying with others' sins in other ministers throughout Scripture?

In a sense, we see this with Christ. He became a man for this very purpose. He may not have sinned, but he was tempted and felt the weakness of man so he could relate to us. Hebrews 4:15-16 says this:

> For we do not have a high priest incapable of sympathizing with our weaknesses, but one who has been tempted in every way just as we are, yet without sin. Therefore let us confidently approach the throne of grace to receive mercy and find grace whenever we need help.

Do we not see this in other great leaders? Paul called himself the chief of sinners (1 Tim 1:15), the least of all God's people (Eph 3:8), and the least of the apostles (1 Cor 15:9). He also said in Romans 7 that the things he would do, he did not do, and things he would not do, he did; "who will rescue me from this body of death?" (v. 24). That passage alone makes it easier to read and digest Paul's writings because it says that he can understand and relate to us.

We saw this in the prophet Isaiah. He was a man who had struggles, and yet he was called to lead and minister to others. Hear his response to God. Isaiah 6:5 says, "I said, 'Too bad for me! I am destroyed, for my lips are contaminated by sin, and I live among people whose lips are contaminated by sin. My eyes have seen the king, the Lord who commands armies.'"

Peter, the leader of the apostles, said to Christ at his calling, "Go away from me, Lord, for I am a sinful man!" (Lk 5:8). Peter had a strong awareness of his sin, just as Nehemiah did, which made him a more than suitable candidate for ministry. He would be able to identify with those he was seeking to save.

Christ taught this awareness of sin was needed to do any type of effective ministry. In Matthew 7:1-5, he taught that in order to pluck the speck out of somebody else's eye, we must first take the log out of our own eye. In order to minister to people and help them be free from sin, we must be aware of our sin and constantly repenting of it. A person who is unaware of his great sinfulness will only harm people in ministry. The Pharisees harmed people and put yokes on their necks that they themselves could not bear. A godly leader has a strong awareness of his own sin, and it enables him to empathize with his flock and better minister to them.

Application Question: How can we develop a greater sense of our own sin so we can better identify with the sins and failings of others?

- We must develop a greater awareness of God by spending more time with him. Isaiah saw God which clearly revealed his sins and the sin of others (Isaiah 6:1-5).

- We must expose ourselves to the Word of God more. James compared studying the Word of God to a mirror which shows our faults so we can correct them. He said:

  For if someone merely listens to the message and does not live it out, he is like someone who gazes at his own face in a mirror. For he gazes at himself and then goes out and immediately forgets what sort of person he was. But the one who peers into the perfect law of liberty and fixes his attention there, and does not become a forgetful listener but one who lives it out—he will be blessed in what he does.
  James 1:23-25

- We must develop healthy accountability relationships with people who will challenge us when we are in sin.

Proverbs 27:17 says, "As iron sharpens iron, so a person sharpens his friend." We must have relationships that challenge and sharpen us. Certainly, we see this with David while he was living in unrepentant sin with Bathsheba. It was the prophet Nathan who confronted his sin and helped bring him to repentance. We need these types of relationships to help us stay humble and aware of our sin.

A lack of time with God through prayer, a lack of time in the Word, and a lack of accountability relationships will create prideful and self-righteous leaders who do not understand the people they are leading. Godly leaders have the ability to identify with their people even in their failures.

Application Questions: Why is it important for a leader to be able to see his own sin and identify with the failings of others? Give examples or experiences which demonstrate its importance.

Godly Leaders Are Motivated and Strengthened by the Promises of God

Please recall the word you commanded your servant Moses: 'If you act unfaithfully, I will scatter you among the nations. But if you repent and obey my commandments and do them, then even if your dispersed people are in the most remote location, I will gather them from there and bring them to the place I have chosen for my name to reside.
Nehemiah 1:8-9

Observation Question: What characteristics of a godly leader can we discern from verses 8 and 9?

Nehemiah quotes from Leviticus 26 and Deuteronomy 30 which says that God would scatter Israel if they were unfaithful and that he would restore the nation from their exile if they returned to him. Essentially, Nehemiah was saying, "God, I believe you will restore us because your Word says so." Look at Deuteronomy 30:1-3:

When you have experienced all these things, both the blessings and the curses I have set before you, you will reflect upon them in all the nations where the Lord your God has banished you. Then if you and your descendants turn to the Lord your God and obey him with your whole mind and being just as I am commanding you today, the Lord your God will reverse your captivity and have pity on you. He will turn and gather you from all the peoples among whom he has scattered you.

Nehemiah was both motivated and strengthened by the promises of God. These promises, no doubt, gave him the encouragement and confidence to eventually become the leader of Israel. If they returned to God, Scripture promised that God would bless the nation.

In fact, we see this same faith in many leaders in the Bible. Listen to what Paul said about Abraham in Romans:

He did not waver in unbelief about the promise of God but was strengthened in faith, giving glory to God. He was fully convinced that what God promised he was also able to do.
Romans 4:20-21

When God told Abraham he was going to have a child at a hundred years old, he was strengthened by the promise of God. In the same way, godly leaders find encouragement to pray, to act, and to persevere because of the promises of God.

Remember what Paul told Timothy: "I put this charge before you, Timothy my child, in keeping with the prophecies once spoken about you, in order that with such encouragement you may fight the good fight" (1 Timothy 1:18).

Timothy was to fight based on the prophecies or promises given from God. Godly leaders know the promises of God and fight based on them. God has given us many promises to hold onto in Scripture.

Application Question: What are some promises God has given us in Scripture in order to strengthen and motivate us, especially while serving in roles of leadership?

Look at some of these: Galatians 6:9 says this: "So we must not grow weary in doing good, for in due time we will reap, if we do not give up." God promises that in our labor for good we will reap a harvest if we remain faithful. Matthew 5:10-12 says this:

29

Blessed are those who are persecuted for righteousness, for the kingdom of heaven belongs to them. Blessed are you when people insult you and persecute you and say all kinds of evil things about you falsely on account of me. Rejoice and be glad because your reward is great in heaven, for they persecuted the prophets before you in the same way.

God promises heavenly reward when we are persecuted for righteousness sake.

Matthew 5:6 says this: "Blessed are those who hunger and thirst for righteousness, for they will be satisfied." God promises that if we really hunger to be used by God and to be a blessing to others, we will be filled with that righteousness. The question only is whether we really hunger for it.

Godly leaders are strengthened and many times motivated by the promises of God. They take hope from them, no matter the discouragements that come their way.

Application Question: In what ways have you found encouragement in the promises of God while facing a trial or an opportunity to lead? What specific Scriptures or promises of God have you found most helpful in your spiritual life?

Godly Leaders Are Assertive

Please, O Lord, listen attentively to the prayer of your servant and to the prayer of your servants who take pleasure in showing respect to your name. Grant your servant success today and show compassion to me in the presence of this man." Now I was cupbearer for the king. Nehemiah 1:11

Nehemiah did not just pray. He volunteered. Listen to what he said in v. 11: "Grant your servant success." Leaders not only pray but they are willing to volunteer. After praying for his nation for some extended amount of time, he asked God for favor with the king in order to be used in the restoration of Israel.

What do you feel God is calling you to volunteer for? How do you feel he wants you to step up and meet the needs of others?

One of the greatest problems with leadership is apathy. We often don't care enough about a problem or a situation. When a person is truly passionate, assertiveness is a normal response. When you are invested in something, it is normal to be assertive.

Application Question: How do we develop this assertiveness that Nehemiah had in his leadership?

One thing that must jump out to us in this scenario is how this petition to be successful (to be used) came at the end of a prayer and intimacy with God.

Intimacy Precedes Service

It is interesting to see that intimacy often precedes a willing heart and sometimes even a call from God. We see this with Isaiah. Look again at his story in Isaiah 6:5-8.

> I said, "Too bad for me! I am destroyed, for my lips are contaminated by sin, and I live among people whose lips are contaminated by sin. My eyes have seen the king, the Lord who commands armies." But then one of the seraphs flew toward me. In his hand was a hot coal he had taken from the altar with tongs. He touched my mouth with it and said, "Look, this coal has touched your lips. Your evil is removed; your sin is forgiven." I heard the voice of the sovereign master say, "Whom will I send? Who will go on our behalf?" *I answered, "Here I am, send me!"*

Isaiah was praying, confessing his sin before God, and spending time in God's presence which led to his volunteering for his future ministry as a prophet to Israel. It began first with prayer and time with God; then it led to volunteering. Intimacy with God preceded service.

Similarly, in Matthew 9:39, Christ called the disciples to pray for laborers to go into the harvest, and, in Matthew 10 he sent them out into the fields to minister. Often prayer and intimacy come right before a willing heart and a call to serve.

What has God given you a heart to pray for? Nehemiah prayed for Israel and then was called. Similarly, Isaiah prayed for his nation, confessing their sins, and God called him to be part of the solution. The disciples prayed for the harvest and then were sent into the field.

Godly leaders are assertive. They want to get involved.

Application Question: In what ways have you experienced intimacy with God leading to a call or assertiveness as a leader?

31

Godly Leaders Learn to Wait on God

> These are the words of Nehemiah son of Hacaliah: It so happened that in the month of Kislev, in the twentieth year, I was in Susa the citadel … Then in the month of Nisan, in the twentieth year of King Artaxerxes, when wine was brought to me, I took the wine and gave it to the king. Previously I had not been depressed in the king's presence.
> Nehemiah 1:1; Nehemiah 2:1

Interpretation Question: What can we learn about godly leadership from the fact that Nehemiah started praying in December (Kislev; 1:1) but approached the king about Israel in April (Nisan; 2:1)?

Godly leaders are patient in waiting on God. It is clear from the text that Nehemiah heard about the problem around November-December (Kislev) and nothing happened until March-April (Nisan).[12] He waited and prayed for four months to be used before God provided an opportunity to talk to the king.

It is very possible to get in front of God. I almost wonder if that is what happened with Joseph as he shared his dream to his dad and brothers about them bowing down before him (Gen 37). It was not his time, and it only made his jealous brothers even angrier with him. Consequently, though the vision was true, he suffered for his unwise sharing.

Interpretation Question: What other godly leaders in the Scripture had to wait on God to be used?

- Abraham had to wait on God. It was twenty-five years before he received the son God promised. In addition, he had to wait hundreds of years before his people inherited the promised land (Gen 15:13). And it further took 2,000 years before the promised "seed" which blessed all nations came.

- Moses had to wait to be used by God. He acted hastily in the court of Egypt and killed an Egyptian who was fighting an Israelite (Acts 7:24-26). He then went into the wilderness for forty years as a shepherd before God called him to lead Israel (Acts 7:30).

- Joseph had to wait to be used. He had a vision, and then waited many years as a slave and a prisoner before God fulfilled the vision.

32

- David had to wait on God to become king. He went from being a shepherd to a general, but soon after, he was hunted by Saul the king of Israel. It took years before the promise was fulfilled.

- Paul had to wait. Many scholars believe it was around fourteen years after he received his initial call that he was sent to the Gentiles with Barnabas in Acts 13 (cf. Gal 2:1).

In the same way, godly leaders must learn to patiently wait on the Lord. In our societies leaders are known for initiative, but biblical leaders are also identified by waiting. There is a season to plow and a season to harvest.

Nehemiah waited some four months before God opened an opportunity. For many of us "A-type" personalities, the waiting seasons are the worst seasons. However, Psalm 46:10 (NIV 1984) says, "Be still and know that I am God." It is when we wait on God and stop our striving that he reveals himself.

Many of us have to learn to wait on God. Some of us may be waiting for a vision for what is next, waiting for a godly spouse, waiting to be delivered from a difficult trial. Yes, there is a time to be active, but there is also a time to wait, and we must discern the times. A flower dies if it blooms in winter.

Certainly, we can see that though Nehemiah waited, he was not inactive. He spent day and night in prayer for those four months (Neh 1:6).

This is the normal process for somebody who God is preparing to lead. He sends them into a waiting season, and in this waiting season, he prepares them for greater leadership. Even Christ waited for some thirty years and then forty days in the wilderness before he began his ministry. We should be prepared for this as well. We must learn to wait on God.

Application Question: In what ways has God been teaching you to wait on him? What makes this a difficult lesson to learn?

Conclusion

What are characteristics of a godly leader?

Here, we see Nehemiah who will confront a problem that has been going on for over 140 years. It, no doubt, seemed impossible, but nevertheless, he sought the Lord who would soon begin to open doors to serve Israel.

What impossible situation is God calling you to pray about and get involved in? What burdens has he given you?

1. Godly leaders are concerned and responsive to problems.
2. Godly leaders are constant in prayer.
3. Godly leaders can identify with the failures of others.
4. Godly leaders are strengthened by the promises of God.
5. Godly leaders are assertive.
6. Godly leaders learn to wait on God.

Characteristics of Godly Leaders
Part Two

Then in the month of Nisan, in the twentieth year of King Artaxerxes, when wine was brought to me, I took the wine and gave it to the king. Previously I had not been depressed in the king's presence. So the king said to me, "Why do you appear to be depressed when you aren't sick? What can this be other than sadness of heart?" This made me very fearful. I replied to the king, "O king, live forever! Why would I not appear dejected when the city with the graves of my ancestors lies desolate and its gates destroyed by fire?" The king responded, "What is it you are seeking?" Then I quickly prayed to the God of heaven and said to the king, "If the king is so inclined and if your servant has found favor in your sight, dispatch me to Judah, to the city with the graves of my ancestors, so that I can rebuild it." Then the king, with his consort sitting beside him, replied, "How long would your trip take, and when would you return?" Since the king was amenable to dispatching me, I gave him a time. I said to the king, "If the king is so inclined, let him give me letters for the governors of Trans-Euphrates that will enable me to travel safely until I reach Judah, and a letter for Asaph the keeper of the king's nature preserve, so that he will give me timber for beams for the gates of the fortress adjacent to the temple and for the city wall and for the house to which I go." So the king granted me these requests, for the good hand of my God was on me...
Nehemiah 2 (NET)

What are characteristics of godly leaders? As we look at Nehemiah, we see a man who had a burden for the people of God. He was over 800 miles away in the Kingdom of Persia serving as the king's cupbearer. It would have been very easy for him to feel like he couldn't do anything to help or that he could only pray; however, he not only prayed, he also volunteered to help.

The city of Jerusalem's walls were broken down and Israel wasn't practically a nation anymore, as they were scattered throughout the world.

Years earlier, there were two migrations back to the land of Israel led by Zerubbabel and then Ezra. They had rebuilt the temple and begun a renewal of worship. However, a great deal of work still needed to be done, as the walls of the capital city lay in ruins, leaving it an easy target for looters. Therefore, God calls Nehemiah to continue the work of restoration in Israel.

God is still looking to raise up leaders to rebuild walls around the world: to restore Christians, churches, and nations to himself. What are characteristics of godly leaders—leaders with character, who tackle God-sized tasks for the Lord? How can we become a leader that God uses? Commentator Donald Campbell found twenty-one principles of effective leadership.[13] However, in this study we will only consider ten.

Big Question: What characteristics of godly leadership do we see in Nehemiah throughout chapter 2?

Godly Leaders Are Patient and Respectful towards Authority

> Then in the month of Nisan, in the twentieth year of King Artaxerxes, when wine was brought to me, I took the wine and gave it to the king. Previously I had not been depressed in the king's presence. So the king said to me, "Why do you appear to be depressed when you aren't sick? What can this be other than sadness of heart?" This made me very fearful. I replied to the king, "O king, live forever! Why would I not appear dejected when the city with the graves of my ancestors lies desolate and its gates destroyed by fire?"
> Nehemiah 2:1-3

In chapter one, Nehemiah, the cupbearer of King Artaxerxes, heard about the problem in Israel and began to pray that God would give him favor with the king (v.11). However, it is clear from the text that God did not answer his prayer for four months. Nehemiah initially heard about the problem in November-December (Kislev, Neh 1:1) and nothing happened till March-April (Nisan, Neh 2:1). He waits on God for at least four months before God opened the door to talk to the king.

As we consider how Nehemiah responded to the king, we can learn a great deal about how to respond to leadership that may be difficult or hard to deal with.

Persian kings had a reputation of being extremely harsh and oppressive. Even though Nehemiah had been praying for four months, it is clear he was not only waiting on God but also the king. Up to this point, he had mentioned nothing to him. While Nehemiah was serving, the king just happened to notice the sorrow on Nehemiah's face. For a cupbearer to even appear sad in the presence of a monarch could have meant death. This is probably why verse 2 says Nehemiah became "very fearful."

To add to the difficulty of working for a harsh and oppressive king, many scholars believe this is the same King Artaxerxes who previously had ordered Israel to stop building the walls of Jerusalem in the book of Ezra (cf. 4:11-23). Listen to what commentator James Boice wrote about this scenario:

> Nehemiah's difficulties did not stop there. To be sad in King Artaxerxes' presence was dangerous enough. In addition to that, Nehemiah wanted to go to Jerusalem and rebuild its walls, and it was this king who earlier had been petitioned and had stopped work on the rebuilding of the walls as a result of that petition. Nehemiah's plan meant asking him to reverse his own policy.[14]

In fact, to show how difficult this would have been, "the law of the Medes and the Persians" was a proverbial saying referring to a law that was unalterable (cf. Dan 6:8).[15]

Nehemiah's waiting for four months showed his patience in dealing with a difficult superior. Have you ever had a difficult superior—a boss, a pastor, a father, a husband, etc.? This is not the first time we see this in Scripture. David worked for King Saul, an employer who was jealous of his popularity and wanted to kill him (1 Sam 18). This happens in business, in ministry, and also in the home.

How should we deal with superiors with whom we do not see eye to eye?

Application Question: What can we learn about working with a difficult authority from Nehemiah's interaction with the king? What does Scripture teach about this?

1. Patience can be effective in changing the heart of an authority.

Consider what Solomon said: "Through patience a ruler can be persuaded, and a soft tongue can break a bone" (Prov 25:15).

Nehemiah waits four months; he does not rush in, and he doesn't simply give up. He patiently prays to God, serves the king, and waits for God to open a door.

This is a great principle when working in a less than ideal situation; "through patience a ruler can be persuaded." Godly leaders must learn how to wait not only on God but also on the leaders that God has given them.

2.   God can change the hearts of those in authority.

Proverbs 21:1 says this: "The king's heart is in the hand of the Lord like channels of water; he turns it wherever he wants."
Like water in a person's hand, God changes the heart of the king in whatever direction he chooses. This is a good reminder to pray for even wicked authorities since God is ultimately in control. Look at what Paul told Timothy:

And the Lord's slave must not engage in heated disputes but be kind toward all, an apt teacher, patient, correcting opponents with gentleness. Perhaps God will grant them repentance and then knowledge of the truth. 2 Timothy 2:24-25

God is the one who grants repentance and changes hearts, not us. I have seen many Christians who actually made their situations worse by not waiting on God to change the heart of their leader. Instead they became a thorn in their leader's side and destroyed their opportunity to minister to their superior and others.

3.   We should show honor to those in authority.

Not only was Nehemiah patient with this king, but he continued to honor him as he served. Look at his response to the king's inquiry: "I replied to the king, 'O king, live forever!'" (Neh 2:3).
This is how we should respond to superiors who are difficult or hard to work with. We should respect them and honor them. David even did this with King Saul, a man who was trying to kill him. He constantly said, "I will not touch God's anointed." David realized that even a bad king is a representation of God's authority, and there is no authority other than God's.
Romans 13:1-2 says this:

Let every person be subject to the governing authorities. For there is no authority except by God's appointment, and the authorities that exist have been instituted by God. So the person who resists such authority resists the ordinance of God, and those who resist will incur judgment.

Scripture teaches that Christians are called to honor their superiors, including presidents, employers, parents, teachers, and even pastors. We should do this even when they are ungodly. This doesn't mean that we don't challenge them, admonish them, or pray for them, but we do these things in such a way that shows respect for their authority.

Paul said this to Timothy who was a young pastor serving in a church with people older than him: "Do not address an older man harshly but appeal to him as a father. Speak to younger men as brothers" (1Timothy 5:1).

Paul said that we should even express this honor in daily relationships with older people in the church. We should treat them with honor, even in correction.

Application Question: What makes it so difficult to honor and be patient with a bad authority figure? How can we practice patience and honor in those situations?

Godly Leaders Practice a Lifestyle of Prayer

The king responded, "What is it you are seeking?" Then I quickly prayed to the God of heaven and said to the king...
Nehemiah 2:4-5

Interpretation Question: What can we learn from Nehemiah's prayer while talking to the king?

In chapter 1, we saw Nehemiah praying night and day for four months. However, in this text, we see him pray a quick prayer in the midst of talking to the king. This showed that he not only had times of deep prolonged prayer, but he also tried to live a lifestyle of prayer.

Paul says this in 1 Thessalonians 5:17: "constantly pray." What does it mean to pray without ceasing? Does it mean to pray every moment of the day? Steven Cole, author of the Riches from the Word devotional series, said this about the phrase "constantly pray":

The Greek phrase translated "constantly pray" does not mean without any break, which would be impossible. It is used of a hacking cough and of repeated military assaults. It means that prayer should be something we return to again and again until we obtain an answer.[16]

We pray without ceasing by continually bringing our thoughts before God and talking to him throughout the day. Some have called what Nehemiah did an arrow prayer. It is similar to Peter sinking into the water and crying out, "Lord save me." It was not an extended prayer but a quick request.

This is what godly leaders do. They practice prayer without ceasing. They have long periods of prayer as seen in Nehemiah's praying for four months or Christ's fasting in the wilderness, but they also pray throughout the day, as they are living in God's presence.

I often practice this in the midst of counseling. As soon as somebody approaches me with a theological question, a request for help, or for my opinion on a situation, I often automatically shoot up an arrow prayer to the Lord for wisdom. We have a God who is all-wise and all-powerful, and therefore, we should petition for wisdom, strength, and grace throughout the day.

Application Question: How are you developing the character trait of praying without ceasing? What are some tips in order to help us pray more like Nehemiah?

Godly Leaders Are Valuable Followers

> Then the king, with his consort sitting beside him, replied, "How long would your trip take, and when would you return?" Since the king was amenable to dispatching me, I gave him a time.
> Nehemiah 2:6

Interpretation Question: What can we learn about Nehemiah from the fact that the king asked him, "How long would your trip take, and when would you return?" What does this say about Nehemiah's service?

After Nehemiah asked to be sent to his home country, the king responded by saying, "How long would your trip take, and when would you return?" The implication of the king's response was that he valued Nehemiah's service and wanted to have him back in the palace soon.

This should be normal for Christians serving in companies, businesses, schools, or churches. We should be a blessing to those we serve. We also see this reality with other men of God in the Scripture.

Interpretation Question: What other men or women of God in Scripture are portrayed as being a blessing to their employers?

- We saw this with Jacob as he was serving Laban. God prospered Laban because of Jacob's faithfulness.

- We saw this with Joseph when he was serving under Potiphar as his chief slave; he worked so hard that he was exalted to the head servant. The same thing happened while Joseph was in prison; he was exalted to the head prisoner. Finally, Joseph was exalted to second in command over Egypt, as he faithfully served Pharaoh.

- We also saw this with Daniel as he was working in Babylon. Though Babylon was a wicked and ungodly kingdom, King Darius sought to put Daniel over the majority of his kingdom because of his diligence (Dan 6:3).

Christians should be the most hardworking employees and have the most integrity. Many times, this will bring disdain from others as it did with Daniel. His co-workers, the Chaldeans, plotted behind his back and got him thrown into the lion's den (Dan 6). They were jealous of his favor with Darius, the King of Persia.

Colossians 3:23-24 says this:

Whatever you are doing, work at it with enthusiasm, as to the Lord and not for people, because you know that you will receive your inheritance from the Lord as the reward. Serve the Lord Christ.

The reason godly leaders should be diligent in their service is because we are working for the Lord and not for men. He is the one who will reward us, even if we are mistreated by our employers or others.

In fact, one of the things we know from ancient history is that when Christian slaves were sold in the market they went for a higher price. When they were bargaining, the slave trader would say, "But this man is a Christian. He will work hard for you." It was for this reason that they typically were more costly.

No doubt, Nehemiah's diligent labor and righteous conduct played a part in his request being granted by the king and, later, God using him to be a future leader of Israel.

It has often been said a great leader is also a great follower. In the military, there is a lot of writing about followership; one cannot be a great leader unless he has been a great follower. One cannot be a great employer unless he has been a great employee. We see this with Nehemiah. He was faithful with little, and God made him faithful over much (Matt 25:23).

Are you a great follower? Do you serve your superiors as though you are serving the Lord? Remember what Paul said to the slaves in Colosse: "Slaves, obey your earthly masters in every respect, not only when they are watching—like those who are strictly people-pleasers—but with a sincere heart, fearing the Lord" (Col 3:22).

We live in a culture where people, often times, only work hard when the boss is watching or is nearby. Paul essentially said, "Do not serve diligently for their favor or for a promotion, but do it for the Lord."

Are you being a good follower and a diligent worker? That is one of the characteristics of a great leader.

Application Question: Why are great followers often great leaders? In what ways is God calling you to grow in your followership?

Godly Leaders Are Planners

> Since the king was amenable to dispatching me, I gave him a time. I said to the king, "If the king is so inclined, let him give me letters for the governors of Trans-Euphrates that will enable me to travel safely until I reach Judah, and a letter for Asaph the keeper of the king's nature preserve, so that he will give me timber for beams for the gates of the fortress adjacent to the temple and for the city wall and for the house to which I go."
> Nehemiah 2:6-8

Interpretation Question: What can we learn from the fact that Nehemiah gave the king a set time and asked for letters for the trip? What does this say about godly leaders?

What is another characteristic of a godly leader? A godly leader is a planner. The king asked Nehemiah how long he would be gone, and he was able to quickly "give him a time." It seems from the narrative that he stayed at least twelve years in Jerusalem (cf. Nehemiah 5:14).

He also asked for letters to give the governors of the Trans-Euphrates to ensure safe travel to Judah (v.7). While traveling, he would have to go through other lands, and, if he did not have letters, they might have sent him back. Having a letter from the king would be the equivalent to having a passport today. He also received a letter for timber to build the gates, the city wall, and his residence while in Jerusalem (v.8).

While Nehemiah was waiting for four months, he was not just praying, he also was planning, and God used that planning to meet Nehemiah's needs.

Application Question: Have you ever met Christians who claimed to be walking by faith, which meant that they had no real plan? Are faith and planning at odds with one another? In what ways do we see God as a planner?

Often you will find Christians who neglect planning or preparing and claim that they are living by faith. However, when you look at Scripture, this seems to contradict the character of God. God is a God of order—he is a planner.

It is wonderful to look at the story of creation because you can see God's plan and order there. In the first three days, God created the spheres of the earth: water, land, and sky (Gen 1:1-10), and then, in the next days, he filled them (Gen 1:11-27). There is a clear order—create and then fill.

We also see the order of creation in science. When you look at human bodies, nature, and even the solar system, we see a God who meticulously planned and then created.

We also see God's order for church worship. In 1 Corinthians 14, people were speaking in tongues without an interpreter, giving prophesies with no one to judge, and the women were abusing their role in the church. God essentially said, "Hold up! I am not a God of disorder" and gave them instructions on how to have order in the church (1 Cor 14:28-32). First Corinthians 14:33 says, "For God is not characterized by disorder but by peace."

Some in the church think being led by the Spirit means to not plan and to just be free. That's what was happening in Corinth and, hence, why God gave them a very meticulous plan for how worship should be done including the use of tongues, prophecy, and even the teaching ministry of women in the church. He says, "I am not a God of disorder. I have a plan for worship."

I remember one time I was invited to give a prayer at a wedding, and I had written down my prayer. Another pastor there had also been asked to perform a ministry at the wedding. While I was reading over my prayer and praying over it, the pastor said, "Oh don't use that; just be led by the Holy Spirit." I wanted to say, "Have you ever read the Psalms. Many of them are written down prayers given by the Holy Spirit. In fact, the whole written Word is inspired by God." The fact that my prayer was written down did not mean it was not led by the Holy Spirit. God is a God of order.

We, also, see God's order in his instructions on how families should be run. He teaches wives to submit to their husbands, husbands to love their wives, and children to submit to their parents (Eph 5:22- 6:1). God is a God of order; he made plans for creation, worship, and the home. As godly leaders, we should make plans as well.

Now certainly, when all our planning fails, we can trust that our God will lead and provide by faith. But faith does not neglect planning. Planning is a proof of our faith; we plan because we trust that God is leading us (cf. Romans 8:14). Proverbs 21:5 says this: "The plans of the diligent lead only to plenty, but everyone who is hasty comes only to poverty."

The plans of the diligent lead to profit, and haste leads to poverty. Godly leaders are planners, and we see that in Nehemiah's response to the king. What is God calling you to plan for?

Application Question: What are some good principles to use in our planning?

1. In planning, it is good to have prolonged prayer and waiting. Nehemiah prayed and fasted for four months, and in that time, God gave him a plan.

2. In planning, it is good to seek wise counselors. Proverbs says, "But there is success in the abundance of counselors" (Prov 11:14). No doubt, Nehemiah probably had to talk to various people about the different regions that he would go through, what was needed, and where the best trees would be found. He probably figured out some of his needs by talking to his brother who had just come from Israel (Neh 1:2).

3. In planning, it is good to make long term and short term plans. Nehemiah was planning for at least four months into the future and, probably, years into the future. He had to tell the king how long he would be away. Again, he was probably away for at least twelve years. He had made a long term plan.

We should make short term and long term plans about how to cultivate our professional lives, our spiritual lives, and our health. We should make long term and short term plans about how to cultivate our marriage and family relationships. Plans lead to profit.

4. In planning, it is good to write out our plans. We can assume that Nehemiah wrote down his plans since he kept the memoirs that we are reading here in his book. Sometimes writing down our plans will help us solidify them.

This is true for long term planning but also daily planning. Some people waste lots of time on the Internet, the TV, or other endeavors. Writing down an hourly schedule and a weekly schedule can help us maximize our time and become more efficient. Godly leaders are planners.

44

Application Question: What are some other principles that one can use in order to become more effective in planning both long term and short term?

Godly Leaders Are Humble, and Therefore, Experience God's Abundant Grace

> So the king granted me these requests, for the good hand of my God was on me. Then I went to the governors of Trans-Euphrates, and I presented to them the letters from the king. The king had sent with me officers of the army and horsemen.
> Nehemiah 2:8-9

Interpretation Question: What can we learn from Nehemiah's interpretation in verse 8 of how all his requests were answered because of the gracious hand of God on his life?

In verses 8 and 9, we see that the king granted all of Nehemiah's requests and even blessed him with more than he asked. In addition, the king sent Nehemiah on his journey with officers and a cavalry for protection (v. 9). What should stand out to us in this text is Nehemiah's interpretation of the king's favor. He said, "so the king granted me these requests, for the good hand of my God was on me" (v. 8).

One cannot help but notice Nehemiah's humility. In the world today, leaders often boast about their degrees, their performance, their charitable work, their salary, their houses, their cars, and anything else they can find to boast about. They boast because they see their success as coming from themselves (that's essentially what a resume is). But, not Nehemiah! Nehemiah saw his success as something that came directly from God.

Nehemiah was humble, which is a scarce commodity in today's world; however, it is crucial for having favor with God. James 4:6 says, "God opposes the proud, but he gives grace to the humble."

In order to receive the blessing and favor of God, humility is necessary. When Nehemiah received not only his requests but also an army and a cavalry from the king, we cannot but attribute this to God's gracious favor poured out on Nehemiah's humble life.

This is common for a godly leader. We also saw this with Moses. God said this about Moses: that with all other prophets he spoke through visions and dreams but with Moses he spoke face to face (Numbers 12:6-8). Scripture declared that Moses was the humblest man on the earth (Numbers 12:3). The

45

great favor on Moses' life certainly was grace, but this grace was multiplied because of his humility.

In contrast with a world that is prideful and boastful (1 John 2:16), godly leaders are humble, and therefore, God graciously favors and blesses them.

Application Question: In what areas can we identify pride in our own lives that may be hindering God's blessing? How can we grow in humility?

Godly Leaders Practice Intentional Solitude

So I came to Jerusalem. When I had been there for three days, I got up during the night, along with a few men who were with me. But I did not tell anyone what my God was putting on my heart to do for Jerusalem. There were no animals with me, except for the one I was riding.
Nehemiah 2:11-12

Interpretation Question: After Nehemiah's travel to Jerusalem, why do you think Nehemiah chose not to work for the first three days? What do you think he was doing?

Many times people think of leadership as being equal to busyness. However, this is not necessarily true. It is not primarily what one does in the open that makes them a successful leader, but what they do in solitude. When Nehemiah got to Jerusalem after a two month journey,[17] he did not immediately go to work; he just stayed there for three days.

What does he do for three days? The text says, "I did not tell anyone what my God was putting on my heart to do" (v. 12). No doubt, while Nehemiah was waiting, he was abiding in God's presence and allowing God to put things in his heart so that he could lead the people effectively.

Application Question: Why is this intentional time before the Lord important for us as godly leaders?

It is not what the Sunday school teacher or pastor does on Sunday that is most significant. It is what they do in their closet before God, as they study and meditate on the Word. A leader is made by what he does in solitude, and a leader is broken down by what he does in solitude.

46

We see this happen all the time as leaders stumble with pornography, adultery, shady business practices, etc. Everything that has been built is destroyed by what a person does when nobody is watching.

Nehemiah spent time alone with God so the Lord could continue to put things into his heart and prepare him for this new ministry to Israel. Isaiah 40:30-31 says:

> Even youths get tired and weary; even strong young men clumsily stumble. But those who wait for the Lord's help find renewed strength; they rise up as if they had eagles' wings, they run without growing weary, they walk without getting tired.

We often have to wait and be still in order to hear God and let him strengthen us for the work he has called us to do. It is while waiting on God and being near him that he gives strength and direction.

Certainly, we see a good example of the need for solitude for a godly leader in the story of Joshua. When God called Joshua to lead Israel, he told him his success would be dependent upon his faithfulness to the Word of God. Joshua 1:8 (NIV 1984) says this:

> Do not let this Book of the Law depart from your mouth; meditate on it day and night, so that you may be careful to do everything written in it. Then you will be prosperous and successful.

Obviously, much of his meditation would have been done alone in the quiet place and that would affect whether he was successful or not.

Similarly, Jesus said this:

> Remain in me, and I will remain in you. Just as the branch cannot bear fruit by itself, unless it remains in the vine, so neither can you unless you remain in me "I am the vine; you are the branches. The one who remains in me—and I in him—bears much fruit, because apart from me you can accomplish nothing.
> John 15:4-5

Because intentional solitude is so important to the leader's success, leaders must learn time management skills to maximize their personal time with God. They also need to learn how to say, "No." Leaders are always in demand, and, if we don't learn how to say, "No," we will eventually burn out. Even Jesus went to the mountain to pray, though he knew the crowds were needy and looking for him (Mk 1:35-37). He needed to be alone with God, and so do we. It

47

is what the leader does in the quiet place that brings the blessing of God and ultimately success.

Application Question: How do you practice and guard your solitude with God? How important is it to develop time management skills and the ability to say, "No," in order to make solitude a priority?

Godly Leaders Practice Critical Examination in Order to Build

> I got up during the night, along with a few men who were with me. But I did not tell anyone what my God was putting on my heart to do for Jerusalem. There were no animals with me, except for the one I was riding. I proceeded through the Valley Gate by night, in the direction of the Well of the Dragons and the Dung Gate, inspecting the walls of Jerusalem that had been breached and its gates that had been destroyed by fire. I passed on to the Gate of the Well and the King's Pool, where there was not enough room for my animal to pass with me. I continued up the valley during the night, inspecting the wall. Then I turned back and came to the Valley Gate, and so returned.
> Nehemiah 2:12-15

Interpretation Question: What can we learn from Nehemiah's inspection of the walls late at night?

At night, Nehemiah inspected the walls. The Hebrew word for "inspecting" means "to inspect something carefully." "It's a medical word for probing a wound to see the extent of the damage."[18] Nehemiah was like a loving doctor inspecting the walls of Jerusalem. No doubt, this inspection included planning to see how it could be fixed, what types of skills and equipment would be needed. Nehemiah examined the wall for the purpose of rebuilding it.

In the same way, godly leaders practice critical examination for the purpose of building. Certainly, we see this critical examination in the life of Christ and other godly leaders in the Scripture. Christ critically examined Israel and corrected her in order to draw her back to God. When Christ came to Israel, he essentially inspected the walls in the same way Nehemiah did. Much of his ministry was pointing out the misuse of the law, the faulty character of the Pharisees, and the hard hearts of Israel (Matt 5:20, 13:10-16). He called the nation to repent.

48

In some way, this is still Christ's present ministry as seen in Revelation 2-3. John sees Christ walking among the seven lampstands—the churches—and for each church he gives a critique. He told them what they were doing right and what they were doing wrong so they could fix it. He inspects them for the purpose of edification.

Similarly, most of Paul's letters do the same. They were written to encourage churches and to correct them. He corrects both their teaching and their actions. He critically examined the churches so they could be built up.

Application Question: In what ways should godly leaders practice critical examination in order to better build God's kingdom?

1. Godly leaders should practice critical examination of the teachings they hear.

We see this with the Bereans who were called "noble" by God because they critically inspected Paul's teachings against the Word of God. Acts 17:11 (NIV 1984) says this:

> Now the Berean Jews were of more noble character than the Thessalonians, for they received the message with great eagerness and examined the Scriptures every day to see if what Paul said was true.

One of the problems with our churches these days is that there is a lack of critical examination of teaching. They don't critically examine the sermons and teachings they receive against the Word of God. We are not talking about criticizing the sermons and the pastors. There is plenty of that. There is a lack of critically examining the worship, the preaching, or even people's "experiences" in the church to see if they align with Scripture. For that reason, much of what is happening in our churches is not true worship (cf. John 4:23-24) and is not pleasing to God. Godly leaders critically examine, not in pride, but in accordance with the Word of God.

This is even more important because Scripture teaches that in the last days people will no longer be able to stand sound doctrine; instead, they will gather to themselves teachers that will teach what their itching ears want to hear (2 Tim 4:3-4). We are now in this period where much of the teaching happening in our churches does not align with Scripture, or it only teaches parts of Scripture that people want to hear and disregards the rest. How much more do we need Christians who critically examine the Word taught?

49

John taught us this very principle in his epistle. He said to test the spirits for they are not all of God. "Dear friends, do not believe every spirit, but test the spirits to determine if they are from God, because many false prophets have gone out into the world" (1 John 4:1).

2. Godly leaders should practice critical examination of the world culture.

Paul said this:

Do not be conformed to this present world, but be transformed by the renewing of your mind, so that you may test and approve what is the will of God—what is good and well-pleasing and perfect.
Romans 12:2

In order for us to not be conformed or pressed into the mold of this world, Christians must critically examine the world culture which includes the books, the music, the TV shows, the teachings, and the customs we encounter. If we do not examine these things, we will inevitably accept them and be conformed to them.

This is important as a protection for us but also as a protection for those we lead. We must point out the folly of the world culture: its sexual immorality, its values, its worldview, and its godlessness. We must examine and openly reveal these things, especially in our teachings, so that those we minister to can be alerted and protected.

3. Godly leaders should practice critical examination of their own lives.

Paul said this: "Put yourselves to the test to see if you are in the faith; examine yourselves! Or do you not recognize regarding yourselves that Jesus Christ is in you—unless, indeed, you fail the test!" (2 Corinthians 13:5).

Paul commands the individuals in the church of Corinth to essentially test if they are really saved. Were fruits evident in their lives that proved the genuineness of their faith? This is one of the most important things we can do in our lives. We must ask ourselves, "Are we truly saved and is there fruit to prove it?"

We must remember that Christ said that many Christian leaders in the last days will say to him, "Lord, Lord." They prophesied, cast out demons, and did many mighty works in his name; however, Christ will respond to them, "I never knew you. Go away from me, you lawbreakers!" (Matt 7:21-23). Maybe, he says this about leaders (those who were serving) because they are more prone to be self-deceived than others. As leaders, we must critically examine our lives. Is Christ living in us?

Another way that we examine our own lives is not necessarily in discerning our salvation but in discerning our sanctification. We need to constantly evaluate our spiritual lives before God. David, a godly leader, prayed this: "Examine me, and probe my thoughts! Test me, and know my concerns! See if there is any idolatrous tendency in me, and lead me in the reliable ancient path!" (Psalm 139:23-24). David knew that we have a tendency to be blind to our sins, especially sins of our hearts. Therefore, he prayed for God to reveal any offensive way in him. We should do the same.

Certainly, we must practice this in order to be pleasing to the Lord, but also to minister more effectively. Christ said that in order to properly remove the speck from someone's eye, we must first remove the plank from ours (Matt 7:1-5). An uninspected life cannot minister to others. We won't be able to see properly.

4. Godly leaders should practice critical examination of how they minister to others.

    Paul said this:

    According to the grace of God given to me, like a skilled master-builder I laid a foundation, but someone else builds on it. And each one must be careful how he builds. For no one can lay any foundation other than what is being laid, which is Jesus Christ.
    1 Corinthians 3:10-11

    Paul was an expert builder, building the foundations of the church and people's lives on Christ. He didn't build on psychology, business principles, or worldly philosophy but on Jesus and his words alone. He said a person should "be careful how he builds." We must critically examine how we teach, how we counsel, how we lead, etc., for one day God will judge us for how we built (cf. 1 Cor 3:10-14). Many churches and Christian ministries are being built on principles of the world and not the Word of God. Worldly principles can only produce natural results, but godly principles, which come from God's Word, produce supernatural results. Are we building in such a way that reflects our full dependence upon God?

5. Godly leaders should practice critical examination of the people they minister to.

In the same way that Nehemiah examined the wall so he could build it, we must examine those we minister to, so that we can discern how to better serve them. We do this by asking them questions, watching their behavior, and testing their lives against the Word of God. Then, we can speak the Word of God to them in order to build them up (2 Tim 3:16-17). Paul said that we must speak the truth in love so others may be built up (Eph 4:15). Godly leaders critically examine in order to bring edification.

Application Question: In what ways is God challenging you to practice critical examination so that you can be a more effective leader?

Godly Leaders Work Hard

> I got up during the night, along with a few men who were with me. But I did not tell anyone what my God was putting on my heart to do for Jerusalem. There were no animals with me, except for the one I was riding. I proceeded through the Valley Gate by night, in the direction of the Well of the Dragons and the Dung Gate, inspecting the walls of Jerusalem that had been breached and its gates that had been destroyed by fire. I passed on to the Gate of the Well and the King's Pool, where there was not enough room for my animal to pass with me. I continued up the valley during the night, inspecting the wall. Then I turned back and came to the Valley Gate, and so returned.
> Nehemiah 2:12-15

Another characteristic we discern about Nehemiah, and therefore a godly leader, is his strong work ethic. Godly leaders work hard. We can discern this about Nehemiah by the fact that he worked late into the night examining the walls and making a plan. He mentions the phrase "during the night" twice in this passage in verses 12 and 15. Obviously, he did this for emphasis as he worked late into the night inspecting the various parts of the wall. Nehemiah, obviously, had a tireless work ethic.

We see this with many other leaders in Scripture as well. Paul said this in Colossians 1:29 in describing his apostolic work ethic: "Toward this goal I also labor, struggling according to his power that powerfully works in me."

The word "labor" in the Greek means "to work to exhaustion." Paul worked till exhaustion in serving churches and seeking to help them conform to the image of Christ. Consider what he said to the Thessalonians: "For you recall, brothers and sisters, our toil and drudgery: By working night and day so as not to impose a burden on any of you, we preached to you the gospel of God" (1 Thessalonians 2:9).

Paul said they worked night and day so they would not be a burden to the Thessalonians. No doubt, this referred to his common practice of tent making so people would not have to support him financially. Paul did this not only for himself but to set an example for the Thessalonians of how to work hard for God (cf. Acts 20:35).

In fact, Paul declared that he worked harder than all the apostles in his service for the Lord.

> But by the grace of God I am what I am, and his grace to me has not been in vain. In fact, I worked harder than all of them—yet not I, but the grace of God with me.
> 1 Corinthians 15:10

Paul declared that the grace of God in his life enabled him to work hard, and this must be true of us as well if we are going to be godly leaders. Godly leaders set the example for others by working hard. It is very common for leadership to be a veil for laziness (cf. 1 Peter 5:2, 3). Leaders often have very little accountability because everybody works under them, making it easier to be lazy. However, this privilege should instead encourage them to work harder than everybody else in order to set an example. Godly leaders work hard.

Application Question: In what ways have you seen leadership as a veil for laziness? In what ways has God been challenging you to work hard in order to honor him and set an example for others?

Godly Leaders Motivate Others

> Then I said to them, "You see the problem that we have: Jerusalem is desolate and its gates are burned. Come on! Let's rebuild the wall of Jerusalem so that this reproach will not continue." Then I related to them how the good hand of my God was on me and what the king had said to me. Then they replied, "Let's begin rebuilding right away!" So they readied themselves for this good project... I responded to them by saying, "The God of heaven will prosper us...
> Nehemiah 2:17-18, 20

The next thing Nehemiah did was motivate the Jews. He did this in several ways.

Observation Question: How does Nehemiah motivate the people in this passage and what can we learn from this?

1. Nehemiah motivates them by identifying with them.

Look at the "we" and "us" pronouns/contractions in this passage. He says, "You see the problem that we have: Jerusalem is desolate and its gates are burned. Come on! Let's rebuild the wall of Jerusalem so that this reproach will not continue." Poor leaders often separate themselves from those they are leading, especially when it comes to failure or disappointment. They separate from the group and blame them for shortcomings. However, they typically associate with the group when it comes to successes. This further alienates the leader from the group. In sports or business, it often creates a team vs. coach situation or employees vs. the employer situation.

Nehemiah does not do that; he becomes one of them. Their problem was his problem. This is probably even more important when one works with "volunteers," as they are not serving for money or external motivation. Godly leaders lead by identifying with their people instead of isolating them.

2. Nehemiah motivates them through sharing his own personal experience with God.

Godly leaders are often transparent with those they serve which creates intimacy. They are strategically open with both their successes and their failures. Look again at what Nehemiah said: "Then I related to them how the good hand of my God was on me and what the king had said to me. Then they replied, 'Let's begin rebuilding right away!' So they readied themselves for this good project" (Nehemiah 2:18).

Do we not see this throughout Scripture?

Paul was tremendously open and vulnerable with those he served. In Romans 7, he said, "The things I do, I would not do, and the things I would not do, I do. Who can save me from this body of death?" In 2 Corinthians 1:8, he talks about how he "despaired even of living." He was depressed and down, and he shared that with those who he ministered to. In 1 Timothy 1:15, he called himself the chief of sinners (NIV 1984). In 2 Corinthians 12, he shares with the congregation the thorn in the flesh that was given him, and he also shares God's magnificent grace in his weakness (v. 7-10). He was a transparent leader, which made it easy to follow him.

Some leaders are taught to show no vulnerability. The pastor acts as if he does not struggle with pride, lust, or anger, which keeps the congregation

54

from seeing his vulnerability and building intimacy with him. Churches need to hear something about both their leader's struggles and successes. Knowing he is human helps them to pray for him, to practice both humility and transparency, and to follow him. Godly leaders are transparent.

3. Nehemiah motivated others by pointing to God.

Finally, he encouraged the Jews by pointing to God's faithfulness. In verse 18, he shared with them all that God's gracious hand had provided for completing the great work. Then again in verse 20, he says this to those who mocked and doubted: "The God of heaven will prosper us" (Nehemiah 2:20).

Nehemiah did not point to his leadership, their natural resources, or the strength of the people. He pointed to God as the source of their power and their future success. This is something that separates a godly leader from a secular leader. While the worldly trust in their strength, wisdom, money, etc., the godly trust in God. Psalm 20:7 says, "Some trust in chariots and others in horses, but we depend on the Lord our God."

Remember what David said to Israel before defeating Goliath, "Who is this uncircumcised Philistine, that he defies the armies of the living God?" (1 Samuel 17:26). He also declared his reliance on God before Goliath and the Philistines. He said, "You are coming against me with sword and spear and javelin. But I am coming against you in the name of the Lord of hosts" (1 Samuel 17:45). David's confidence was fully in God and this was evident to everyone he spoke with.

What are you putting your confidence in? Is it in the economy? Is it your job? Is it in your degree or your grades? The only place worthy of putting our faith and pointing the faith of others is in God.

Application Question: What are some other effective principles for motivating people, especially volunteers? Have you experienced the difference between leadership that identifies with people and leadership that does not? Which is more effective and why? In what ways can we practice being vulnerable with those we lead?

Godly Leaders Should Expect Opposition

When Sanballat the Horonite and Tobiah the Ammonite official heard all this, they were very displeased that someone had come to seek benefit for the Israelites... But when Sanballat the Horonite, Tobiah the Ammonite official, and Geshem the Arab heard all this, they derided

55

us and expressed contempt toward us. They said, "What is this you are doing? Are you rebelling against the king?" I responded to them by saying, "The God of heaven will prosper us. We his servants will start the rebuilding. But you have no just or ancient right in Jerusalem." Nehemiah 2:10, 19-20

Interpretation Question: What can we learn about godly leadership from the appearance of the characters Sanballat, Geshem, and Tobiah in chapter 2?

After Nehemiah spoke to Israel, he found that three people were very upset about his plan and ministry to the Israelites. Their names were Sanballat, Tobiah, and Geshem. "A document of 407 BC (38 years after the events of this chapter) refers to Sanballat as 'governor of Samaria.'"[19] Horonaim was a town in Moab, meaning that he was probably from Moabite descent (v. 10).[20] Tobiah was an Ammonite official with a Jewish name that meant "God is good." Like other Samaritans, he was part Jewish. Finally, the text tells us that Geshem was Arab. These three became major antagonists to the work of God throughout Nehemiah's memoirs.

Application Question: What can we learn from this opposition?

1. Godly leaders will experience opposition. This opposition sometimes comes through people, but even more so, it comes from our enemy the devil (Eph 6:10-19).

Look at what Paul said: "For we wanted to come to you (I, Paul, in fact tried again and again) but Satan thwarted us" (1 Thess 2:18).
Paul said how much he missed the Thessalonians and desired to minister to them; however, it was clear that a force hindered them from coming and that force was Satan. Satan "thwarted" or hindered them again and again.
We should expect opposition as we serve the Lord. In fact, the greater the work or ministry we are planning, the more we should expect a great attack. It is not uncommon that when going out on the mission field, new missionaries start having demonic dreams, sickness, discouragement, etc. The wise leader should discern this as the necessary attacks that always come with doing the will of God, as Paul did (1 Thess 2:18, 2 Cor 2:11).

2. Godly leaders must respond to attacks with faith in God.

Sanballat, Tobiah, and Geshem mocked the work of building the wall. But Nehemiah responded with rebuking them and putting his trust in God. He declared, "The God of heaven will prosper us" (v.20). We must trust God in the face of attacks as well. God is sovereign and in control; we must believe that he is guiding his work and that he is ultimately in control of all things, including Satan (Eph 1:11, Job 1, 1 Cor. 10:13). Let us trust God with our work and also with the attacks of the enemy trying to stop it.

Application Question: In what ways have you experienced opposition in doing the Lord's will? How did you handle it?

Conclusion

What characteristics of a godly leader do we see in this narrative?

1. Godly leaders are patient and respectful towards authorities.
2. Godly leaders practice a lifestyle of prayer.
3. Godly leaders are valuable followers.
4. Godly leaders are planners.
5. Godly leaders are humble, and therefore, experience God's abundant grace.
6. Godly leaders practice intentional solitude.
7. Godly leaders practice critical examination in order to build.
8. Godly leaders work hard.
9. Godly leaders must motivate others.
10. Godly leaders should expect opposition.

Application Question: Which characteristics of a godly leader do you feel God is calling you specifically to work on and why? How do you plan to pursue these characteristics?

When Revival Happens

Then Eliashib the high priest and his priestly colleagues arose and built the Sheep Gate. They dedicated it and erected its doors, working as far as the Tower of the Hundred and the Tower of Hananel. The men of Jericho built adjacent to it, and Zaccur son of Imri built adjacent to them. The sons of Hassenaah rebuilt the Fish Gate. They laid its beams and positioned its doors, its bolts, and its bars. Meremoth son of Uriah, the son of Hakoz, worked on the section adjacent to them. Meshullam son of Berechiah the son of Meshezabel worked on the section next to them. And Zadok son of Baana worked on the section adjacent to them. The men of Tekoa worked on the section adjacent to them, but their town leaders would not assist with the work of their master...
Nehemiah 3 (NET)

When does revival happen? What characteristics are necessary in order to have revival? How do we bring radical change in our work place, ministry, or the family God has placed us in? We can learn principles about this from Israel's response to Nehemiah's leadership in Nehemiah 3.

As we read this text, we will be tempted to think there is nothing in this chapter for us. It is just a bunch of hard names to pronounce and details about the building of the walls of Jerusalem. Though we do not have a diagram, it is detailing the rebuilding of the circular walls around Jerusalem in a counter clockwise motion from the Sheep gate mentioned in verse 1 to the other side of the sheep gate at the end of the chapter.[21]

However, what is written here is actually very practical to our lives. Let us remember the context; Israel was in rebellion towards God and, therefore, was sent into exile into Babylon. Israel was called to be a light to the world. As a nation of priests, they were to bring the Gentile world to Yahweh. However, instead of being a light to the world, they became like the world and worshiped the gods of this world. Therefore, they forfeited the blessing of God and received his curses instead. For this reason, they were exiled in Babylon. Israel was no longer fulfilling God's will; they were a derision, a reproach, and a shame (2:17).

Those who had returned from exile were constantly open to attack because the city had no walls. This left the nation open for continual derision, mocking, and even raids from those who would steal their crops.

In fact, in chapters 2 and 4 specifically, we see the anger of the neighboring nations, even at the possibility of Israel rebuilding their walls. This would mean less profit for them, and therefore, they worked hard to sabotage the building project.

How does this apply to the church? This applies in many ways. When Nehemiah started rebuilding the wall, he was essentially helping to restore the call of God on the nation. He was turning them back from their depression, their scorn, and restoring their call to be a light to the world.

The church has also been called to be salt and light to the world (Matt 5:13-14). Where Israel failed and received the judgment of God, the church today is called to be a "holy nation," a nation full of priests to bring the world to himself (1 Peter 2:9).

However, as we look at the church today, it is similarly in much disarray. It is far from being the light that it has been called to be and reaching the world for Christ. I have no doubt that many churches have encountered the curse that Jesus promised the church of Ephesus in Revelation 2:5. Listen to what he said: "Therefore, remember from what high state you have fallen and repent! Do the deeds you did at the first; if not, I will come to you and remove your lampstand from its place—that is, if you do not repent."

Jesus told this church that if they did not repent, he would blow out the lights of the church. It would no longer be a light to the world; it would no longer be effective in reaching people for Christ. It would be alive but dead. Ephesus was the church that had the apostle Paul as pastor, then his disciple Timothy, and finally John the apostle, as seen in 1 John. It had a tremendous history, but sadly, it is no longer here today. The lights were eventually blown out.

When we look at many churches and ministries today, they are a shell of what they used to be. It is very possible for our lights to be blown out as well, for lack of putting God first. The history of Christianity is full of Christian churches, institutions, and nations who once were on fire for God but now are just an edifice of what they once were for God. All they have now is a history of how God used them. The walls were broken down that initially kept the enemy out, allowing him to bring compromise and then destruction.

Yes, what happened to Israel happens to Christian churches, Christian institutions, and even individual Christians every day. They get put on a shelf and the grace of God is removed from them. In the book of Ezekiel, the prophet Ezekiel, through a vision, actually saw the glory of God leave the temple and leave Israel before Babylon destroyed her. Yes, it is possible to have the lights turned out on us, becoming ineffective and unprofitable for the kingdom of God—lamps with no oil that are good for nothing (cf. Matt 25:3).

This makes Nehemiah's work in motivating Israel very real to us. How do we rebuild the walls of our church to keep out the attacks of liberalism, false teaching, and apathy that are running rampant among the people of God? How do we begin to have the revival God wants in our churches so that we again can return to the high calling God has for us?

As we look at this text of Nehemiah reviving the hearts of the Israelites, we see aspects that were necessary for every revival from the beginning of time. In this chapter, we will see six principles that leaders must know about reviving the hearts of people to do the work that God has called them to do.

Big Question: When does revival happen? What characteristics of revival do we see in this text, and how can we apply these principles as leaders?

Revival Happens When Leaders Set the Example

> Then Eliashib the high priest and his priestly colleagues arose and built the Sheep Gate. They dedicated it and erected its doors, working as far as the Tower of the Hundred and the Tower of Hananel.
> Nehemiah 3:1

Interpretation Question: What was the Sheep Gate and what is significant about the priests' activity in rebuilding it?

As we start to study the rebuilding of the walls, what must jump out to us first is that the spiritual leaders led the way. Eliashib, the high priest, and the fellow priests began to rebuild the Sheep Gate. There was only one high priest, and therefore, Nehemiah means to show us that when the rebuilding started, the spiritual leaders began the work.

No doubt, the priests would be highly interested in the Sheep Gate for this was the gate animals would go through in order to be sacrificed.[22] The priests were willing to use their hands to do manual labor. This set the tone for reviving the hearts of the people.

This was not the priest's job; the Levites were the ones who did the manual labor, especially in the temple. The priest, typically, offered the sacrifices and taught the people, but, nevertheless, they were willing to get their hands dirty and set the example.

But, even more than them being mentioned first, we also see that they were doing more work than most people. They are mentioned again in verses

22 and 28: "After him the priests worked, men of the nearby district… Above the Horse Gate the priests worked, each in front of his house." They were leading by example.

Listen to what Peter said about elders in 1 Peter 5:1-3:

So as your fellow elder and a witness of Christ's sufferings and as one who shares in the glory that will be revealed, I urge the elders among you: Give a shepherd's care to God's flock among you, exercising oversight not merely as a duty but willingly under God's direction, not for shameful profit but eagerly. And do not lord it over those entrusted to you, but be examples to the flock.

Peter gives three vices that are common to those in leadership. Sometimes they serve out of laziness (as a duty), greed for money, or for power. Peter was appealing to them to serve properly. In a sense, he is trying to revive the leaders so that they can revive the flock.

Let this then challenge us as leaders: small group leaders, deacons, elders, leaders of our families and communities. If there is going to be a stirring of people's hearts from apathy, it must start with us. Much of the teaching in the church is void of power simply because the leaders' lives don't demonstrate it.

No doubt, when Nehemiah came to Israel, one of the primary jobs he focused on was motivating the leaders to get on fire and to lead the way. Peter did the same in his epistle to scattered and discouraged Christians living throughout the Roman Empire. Peter said to the leaders, "be examples to the flock."

Therefore as leaders, if we are going to preach evangelism, let us be evangelists. If we are going to preach on prayer, let us be zealous on our knees. If we are going to preach on zeal, let us burn with the fire of God. If we are going to preach on the importance of Scripture, let us be zealous in study.

Paul told Timothy this:

Take pains with these things; be absorbed in them, so that everyone will see your progress. Be conscientious about how you live and what you teach. Persevere in this, because by doing so you will save both yourself and those who listen to you.
1 Timothy 4:15-16

The saving of the hearers only happens when one's life and doctrine are both being protected from sin or blemish. Revival and transformation only happen when the leaders set the example, when they not only teach on humility, perseverance, diligence, and honesty, but also embody it with their lifestyles. It is only then that our hearers and those who watch us can be transformed.

Decay through Leadership

In fact, because of their crucial role in bringing revival to churches, institutions, and communities, leaders are constantly assaulted by the enemy. In chapter 5, Nehemiah will share about the corruption of the previous governors who overtaxed the people and abused their power (v.15). We also saw this with the kings of Israel. Saul fell away from God, and it negatively affected Israel. Solomon fell away as well, leading Israel into a cycle of disobedience and idolatry.

Biblical history is full of corrupt leaders who helped bring decay amongst the people of God, and for this reason, we can be sure that leadership is the focus of many of Satan's attacks. In fact, when you look at some of the battles the church is fighting, much of it is over leadership. There is a battle about whether homosexuals can be in leadership; there is a battle over gender in leadership.

Why is that? It is because the enemy is always attacking the leadership of the church. He knows that when the leadership falls, the people fall. He knows that David's pride in taking a census of Israel brought the judgment of God upon the people (1 Chronicles 21). He knows that when Solomon fell away from God, it led the people away from God as well.

Therefore, the enemy works overtime in coming against the leaders of the church in order to bring spiritual decay. However, when there is revival it similarly starts with the leadership.

Application Question: How should we respond to this strategic call on the lives of leaders in helping bring revival?

1.   We must remember to pray for our leaders.

   First Timothy 2:1-3 says,

   First of all, then, I urge that requests, prayers, intercessions, and thanks be offered on behalf of all people, even for kings and all who are in authority, that we may lead a peaceful and quiet life in all godliness and dignity. Such prayer for all is good and welcomed before God our Savior.

Leading from the front is never easy. It makes our leaders special targets of the enemy. Let us remember them in prayer daily. Let us lift them up, and let us serve them at all times for they watch over our souls. If we do not pray for them, it will affect our ability to live a "peaceful and quiet life in all godliness and dignity" (1 Tim 2:2).

2. We must submit to our leaders.

Nehemiah 3:5 says this: "The men of Tekoa worked on the section adjacent to them, but their town leaders would not assist with the work of their master."

Here, it seems that these town leaders were marked not only for not getting involved but also for not submitting to their "master." Romans 13:1-2 says this:

> Let every person be subject to the governing authorities. For there is no authority except by God's appointment, and the authorities that exist have been instituted by God. So the person who resists such authority resists the ordinance of God, and those who resist will incur judgment

By not submitting to our leaders, we actually rebel against God (v. 2).

In this text, God honored those who submitted to the leadership by sharing their work and names in the book of Nehemiah; however, God also dishonored those who did not. The town leaders were dishonored in the reading of the book then, and they are dishonored now before us. We must obey and submit to our leaders, and by doing this, we obey and submit to God. If the hearts of the people are going to be revived in serving the Lord, it must first begin with the leadership.

Application Question: Why is leadership so important? In what ways is God challenging you to better serve your leaders or to become a more effective leader to help bring revival?

Revival Happens When Everyone Is Unified

Observation Question: What are some of the various types of people seen in this text rebuilding the wall?

One of the things that must stand out as we study this text is the great number of different people God used in rebuilding the wall. Look at some of the people who were used. There were builders from diverse regions of Judah: the men of Tekoa in verse 5 and the residents of Zanoah in verse 13. They came from diverse professions: the goldsmiths and the perfumers in verse 8. There were both sexes working on the wall: Shallum and his daughters in verse 12. Even the spiritual leaders served including the high priest and his fellow priests (v. 1), the Levites (v. 17), and many district leaders (verse 9, 12, etc.). In fact, Malkijah, the "head of the district of Beth Hakkerem, worked on the Dung Gate" in verse 14.

Revival happens when there is unity. We see in this text that people from various backgrounds came together to serve. Men, women, sons, daughters, goldsmiths, perfumers, priests, Levites, and district leaders worked together in order to accomplish this great task.

Similarly, unity always precedes revival amongst the people of God. Listen to what Christ said in John 17:20-23:

> "I am not praying only on their behalf, but also on behalf of those who believe in me through their testimony, that they will all be one, just as you, Father, are in me and I am in you. I pray that they will be in us, so that the world will believe that you sent me. The glory you gave to me I have given to them, that they may be one just as we are one—I in them and you in me—that they may be completely one, so that the world will know that you sent me, and you have loved them just as you have loved me.

Jesus said when the church is unified, we will see many souls come to Christ; the world will know that Jesus came from God. In fact, when we consider Billy Graham crusades or revivals, where thousands of people got saved, unity was always one of the characteristics that marked those revivals.

With Billy Graham's crusades specifically, he would call together Christians from Methodist, Baptist, Presbyterian, Brethren, Catholic backgrounds, etc., in order to reach the city for Christ. He often was criticized for this, and in some cases the criticism may have been valid. Sometimes, these crusades did not discriminate, even amongst those who professed a different gospel.

Sadly, most ministries swing to the other extreme. Most churches and ministries work very independently. In fact, they are often so worried about losing members that they never work with other churches at all. However, when you look at the early church, which also experienced revival, they were very unified. When there was a doctrinal question about Gentiles practicing the Law,

65

the church got together in Jerusalem to discuss it (Acts 15). When the Jerusalem church was suffering, the churches in Macedonia and Corinth sent finances (2 Cor 8). These churches were interacting over hundreds of miles. It is no wonder that the church multiplied at such a fast rate. It is also no wonder why evangelism has slowed to a crawl in most churches and denominations. Often churches, even in the same denomination and the same city, rarely work together.

When we are unified, Jesus said the world will know. Now this works on a macro level and on a micro level. Listen to what David said:

> Look! How good and how pleasant it is when brothers live together! It is like fine oil poured on the head which flows down the beard— Aaron's beard, and then flows down his garments. It is like the dew of Hermon, which flows down upon the hills of Zion. Indeed, that is where the Lord has decreed a blessing will be available—eternal life.
> Psalm 133

David said that when brothers are in unity, this is where God's blessing is. If we are going to have revival even on a micro-level in our individual church homes, we must start to reconcile relationships and we must start to work together.

We can be sure that because of this reality, Satan works over time to bring division. He knows that when there is disunity, there is no blessing from God. In fact, it only opens the door for Satan to bring destruction. Listen to what Paul said in Ephesians 4:26-27 (NIV 1984): "In your anger do not sin: Do not let the sun go down while you are still angry, and do not give the devil a foothold."

Paul used war terminology. To allow division in the church or in our families is to break down the walls and allow the enemy to attack. It gives the devil an "foothold," a base to attack us and God's church from all different angles. If we are going to have revival, we must have unity.

Application Question: What can we do to help bring unity, and therefore, the blessing of God upon the church?

1. To bring unity, we must labor to reconcile any relationships that the enemy has divided.

If there are any relationships out of order, we must seek reconciliation. This means forgiving anybody who has hurt us and trying to restore those relationships. It includes laboring to restore relationships between others in the church. Paul said this in Philippians 4:2-3:

66

> I appeal to Euodia and to Syntyche to agree in the Lord. Yes, I say also to you, true companion, help them. They have struggled together in the gospel ministry along with me and Clement and my other coworkers, whose names are in the book of life.

Paul called for a person in the church to help these two women agree in the Lord. Many times there is a need for a mediator—a peacemaker to help bring reconciliation. It is not okay for us to say that it is not our problem and we don't need to get involved. It is our problem because division removes the blessing of God on the church (Psalm 133). We must labor to be peacemakers in our churches.

Ephesians 4:3 says, "making every effort to keep the unity of the Spirit in the bond of peace."

2. To bring unity, we must labor to reconcile churches so that the world may know that God sent the Son (cf. John 17:23).

The early church worked together as they served the Lord (Acts 15, 2 Cor 8). We also must work together to spread the gospel and bring revival in our nations and communities. Certainly, there is a place for separation from those who are in error. However, if we are unified on the gospel, then I believe we can partner together in select ways such as: prayer, service, evangelism, fighting for righteous laws in society, etc.

Paul handled those who had wrong doctrine and a false gospel totally differently. Those with a false doctrine such as the church of Corinth, he lovingly corrected. To anyone with a false gospel he cursed saying, "let him be condemned to hell!" (cf. Gal 1:8-9). Sadly, the church often curses both those with different doctrine and a false gospel as though they were the same. One is a part of God's family who is in error, and the other is at enmity with God. There is a great difference, and therefore, they shouldn't be treated the same. God calls for us to labor to keep the unity of the Spirit, and we must do that if we are going to experience revival.

Application Question: In what ways have you seen or experienced God's blessing through unity? In what ways have you seen Satan make churches or ministries ineffective through division? How can we help be agents of unity?

Revival Happens When Everyone Does His or Her Part

This stems from the last point on unity. Not only must there be unity for revival but also each person must do his part. When we look at the rebuilding of the wall, it is clear that almost everybody was involved. It is no different in the church when there is revival. Everybody begins to do his part. Listen to what Paul said: "From him the whole body grows, fitted and held together through every supporting ligament. As each one does its part, the body grows in love" (Ephesians 4:16).

Paul says the church grows "as each one does its part." The counselor counsels, the person with the gift of service serves, and the person with the gift of helps, helps people. This is how the church grows. In fact, I love the analogy of the ligament that Paul uses. See, ligaments connect things together; they connect the joints. This means if we have ligaments in the church that are not functioning properly, the rest of the body can't grow or operate correctly. The body begins to limp; it can't run, jump, or do many of the things it is supposed to. In fact, other parts of the body start to overcompensate, which eventually wears them down. When each person doesn't do his part, the church essentially handicaps itself and ceases to grow.

In the same way, most churches, ministries, or organizations are handicapped because their ligaments, muscles, vital organs, etc., are not doing their part.

Application Question: What can we learn about each person serving and doing his part in the church from Israel's rebuilding of the wall? What applications can be made?

1. Sometimes serving means doing what you do not want to do or what you are not equipped to do.

When you look at this story, you see priests, perfumers, and women rebuilding the wall who probably did not have training in this area. Often the church has focused on spiritual gifts and how we need to make sure that we are serving in our gifting. However, God often calls us to do things that we are not equipped for and maybe don't want to do.

In fact, there is one person who served in the building of the Dung Gate who should be noted. Listen to this: "Malkijah son of Recab, head of the district of Beth Hakkerem, worked on the Dung Gate. He rebuilt it and positioned its doors, its bolts, and its bars" (Nehemiah 3:14).

The Dung Gate was the place where the excrements were taken to be discarded. No doubt, Malkijah probably had a "wonderful perfume" he could smell while serving. Now, I have no doubt that the Jews who read this would be shocked. "A district leader did this? Certainly, he would have used his power to get a better job, a better ministry."

I can imagine Nehemiah asking for volunteers for different locations. He says, "Dung Gate? Dung Gate? Anybody want the Dung Gate?" The people are quiet and start looking in other directions, and then Malkijah steps up and says, "I will do it."

I think sometimes we overemphasize spiritual gifts and what we like to do. God does not always call us to do something we like. Many times he just says, "Who would like to serve?" "Who will go for me?" "Who would like to get involved with what I am doing?" The believer says, "I'll do it," and then, God equips them to do the work.

Sometimes God's work will not be in your preferred area; it may not even be your gifting. But, will you do it to honor God and to bring pleasure to him? I cannot but think that this type of service is many times a sweeter offering to him.

2. Sometimes serving means doing more than others.

We see this with the men of Tekoa and the priests mentioned several times in the text.

> The men of Tekoa worked on the section adjacent to them... After them the men of Tekoa worked on another section, from opposite the great protruding tower to the wall of Ophel.
> Nehemiah 3:5, 27

> Then Eliashib the high priest and his priestly colleagues arose and built the Sheep Gate... Above the Horse Gate the priests worked, each in front of his house.
> Nehemiah 3:1, 28

Sometimes, it is hard to keep a good attitude when you are doing more work than others, when you are doing something you do not feel competent to do, or that you just do not like. I believe that is when God's words to Paul come into play. "But he said to me, 'My grace is enough for you, for my power is made perfect in weakness.'" (2 Cor 12:9).

God delights to put us in circumstances that are sometimes hard, that may not be part of our gifting, and may feel like too much work, in order to give us more grace (James 4:6). Sometimes his grace is seen in him providing people with those giftings to help us out; other times he may supernaturally empower us to complete the job. God always gives grace as we do our part.

69

In what ways is God calling you to serve?

Application Question: In what ways do you feel God has equipped you to serve him? Has God ever put you in areas of service where you did not feel equipped or did not like the job? What was the result of that scenario?

Revival Happens when We Take Responsibility for Home

What other things do we notice in the building of the wall? We cannot but notice the places that God called many people to serve. Look at Nehemiah 3:10, 23, 28 and 29:

> Jedaiah son of Harumaph worked on the section adjacent to them opposite his house... After them Benjamin and Hasshub worked opposite their house. After them Azariah son of Maaseiah, the son of Ananiah, worked near his house.... Above the Horse Gate the priests worked, each in front of his house. After them Zadok son of Immer worked opposite his house

As people were discerning how they could best serve the Lord, many of the places that God called them to serve were right next to them. They served and rebuilt the walls right next to their houses. This teaches a great deal about serving the Lord and being part of revival. Many times the Lord calls for us to serve in areas right in front of us and with people who are often closest to us.

We have many people who want to serve the world in missions, go here and there, and that is great. But most times, God will first call us to serve right where we are, where ever home is. Revival often begins at home. How do we see this in the rest of Scripture?

Application Question: What applications can we take from the fact that in the revival many were called to rebuild right beside their house?

1.   Revival starts with ministering to our family.

   Look at what Malachi prophesied about the coming of Elijah:

   See, I will send you the prophet Elijah before that great and dreadful day of the LORD comes. He will turn the hearts of the fathers to their children, and the hearts of the children to their fathers; or else I will come and strike the land with a curse.

70

Malachi 4:5-6 (NIV 1984)

Malachi 4:6 prophesied that Elijah would come to turn the hearts of the fathers back to the children. This prophecy was fulfilled in part at Christ's first coming with John the Baptist. I believe this prophecy will also be fulfilled at his second coming by another Elijah figure (cf. Rev 11:6). When God called John to rebuild the walls and start a revival in Israel, he started with the family. He turned the hearts of the fathers back to the children and the children back to the fathers. Revival starts at home.

Since that prophecy was only partially fulfilled and awaits another Elijah figure, it means that before Christ's second coming the nations of the world will be characterized by broken families. There will be a need for God to restore these families before Christ comes again.

Is this not true of families today? Divorce is all but the norm. How many families have been neglected for career, education, church ministry, or work? Many children, even among our pastor kids and missionary kids, harbor great anger towards their parents for this very reason. There is a need to restore the family.

Certainly, we see this call to prioritize family in the New Testament as well. Listen to what Paul told Timothy about how to run the church in Ephesus. He said:

> But if a widow has children or grandchildren, they should first learn to fulfill their duty toward their own household and so repay their parents what is owed them. For this is what pleases God... But if someone does not provide for his own, especially his own family, he has denied the faith and is worse than an unbeliever.
> 1 Timothy 5:4, 8

Paul said believers should first put their religion into practice by serving their family, and if anybody does not care for their family, they are worse than an unbeliever—they probably are not saved. It is no wonder that those who truly get on fire for the Lord often are agents of change first with their families. It is only natural for one's heart to burn for their brother, their sister, their mom and their dad. In fact, in order for one to be a pastor they must already show this special care for their family, "He must manage his own household well" (1 Tim 3:4).

This priority of serving at home first has often been neglected for other pursuits, and therefore, the walls of our families are in disarray and again need to be rebuilt.

71

Application Question: How can we be faithful in seeking revival with our families first? How can we apply this?

Maybe this renewal starts with forgiving a mom, a dad, or a sibling. Maybe it starts with beginning a Bible study with relatives or inviting them to church. I had a close friend who would Skype with her mom weekly for Bible study. This was her way of putting family first. As husbands, we must prioritize being the spiritual leader of our families, leading our wife and children in seeking God daily, and serving in a Bible preaching church. Certainly, one of the ways we put our family first is by constantly praying for them.

In what ways is God calling you to serve your family? Revival starts with our own family.

2. Revival starts in the areas where God has placed us, such as our church, our workplace, our community, and our city.

Look at what Christ taught his own disciples before they began the mission of winning the world, right before he ascended into heaven. He said, "But you will receive power when the Holy Spirit has come upon you, and you will be my witnesses in Jerusalem, and in all Judea and Samaria, and to the farthest parts of the earth" (Acts 1:8).

It is no surprise that they had to start their ministry in Jerusalem, then Judea, then Samaria, and then to the ends of the earth. This is where revival had to start; it had to start in the city where they were before it went to the world.

As people are considering missions and serving the kingdom abroad, they should ask themselves, "Am I serving in my Jerusalem? How am I building up the community or city that God has placed me in?"

To be placed here (wherever that may be) means to have a responsibility here. It was only after serving Jerusalem that the apostles were to go to Judea, Samaria, and the rest of the earth.

Are there homeless people near you? Serve them. Are there youth near you? Mentor them. Are there unbelievers near you? Evangelize them. Let us first consider how we can best serve those closest to us before we go elsewhere.

Application Question: How is God calling you to help rebuild right by your house? How can we make sure that we don't neglect our family for ministry?

Revival Happens When a Few Souls Get on Fire

After him Baruch son of Zabbai *worked* on another section, from the buttress to the door of the house of Eliashib the high priest.
Nehemiah 3:20

Interpretation Question: What is significant about Baruch son of Zabbai? Why does Nehemiah give special attention to his work?

What else can we learn about revival from the description of the rebuilding of the wall? Certainly, one of the verses that must stand out is verse 20 and the description of Baruch. As we look at Baruch, we see a man to whom Nehemiah gives special attention. The NET says Baruch "worked" but the NIV 1984 translates it "zealously repaired." The word "zealously" means "to burn or glow."[23]

Each of the people listed as serving were on the honor roll. They would have been exalted as the list was read before the families of Israel. However, Baruch gets special honor; he is basically the valedictorian.

In some way or another, this man worked more zealously than others. As we look at times when God brought revival or renewal throughout history, a few men or women glowed more brightly than others. Consider what Christ said about John the Baptist: "He was a lamp that was burning and shining, and you wanted to rejoice greatly for a short time in his light" (John 5:35).

Matthew 11:12 (NIV 1984) says this: "From the days of John the Baptist until now, the kingdom of heaven has been forcefully advancing, and forceful men lay hold of it." Forceful men, those who really get on fire for God, are especially used as agents of revival. They get on fire for evangelism. They get on fire for the youth. They get on fire for the nations, and it is these forceful people who have always been greatly used to advance the kingdom of God. No doubt, Baruch's zeal in serving the Lord inspired and challenged all those around him, and it is for this reason that God exalted his name in the Holy Scriptures.

I once had a pastor who often said, "One soul on fire for the Lord can do innumerably more than a million souls who have simply been enlightened by the Spirit." Another person said, "Get on fire for the Lord and people will come and watch you burn." Every revival needs souls like this, souls who get on fire and inspire us all. Their witness challenges every Christian to be what he should be and do what he is called to do.

Let the fact that typically only a few get on fire and inspire others not relinquish our responsibility to get on fire for God. For they represent what we should be. Listen to what Paul says:

Do not lag in zeal, be enthusiastic in spirit, serve the Lord.

Romans 12:11

So then, dear brothers and sisters, be firm. Do not be moved! Always be outstanding in the work of the Lord, knowing that your labor is not in vain in the Lord.
1 Corinthians 15:58

God is calling each one of us to be filled with zeal; he is calling each one of us to glow. Jesus said, "let your light shine before people, so that they can see your good deeds and give honor to your Father in heaven" (Matt 5:16).

Are you glowing? Do you glow at work while you serve the Lord? Do you glow while studying at school? Do you burn with zeal for God? Have you lost your fire? Your fire or lack of fire affects the corporate flame of your church and it fulfilling God's will.

How is God calling you to get that fire back? We need people who are willing to get on fire for God and keep that fire burning.

Application Question: In what ways have you been inspired by people who were on fire for God? Recall the time when you were most on fire for God. What was it like; how can you get it back and keep that fire burning?

Revival Happens When Everyone Practices the Humility of a Servant

Interpretation Question: Why is Nehemiah never mentioned in the honor roll of those who built the wall? What can we learn from this?

What cannot but stand out in this narrative about the rebuilding of the wall is the fact that Nehemiah never mentions his own name. He is the governor, the mastermind around the rebuilding. He brings many of the resources such as the logs from the forest of the king (cf. 2:8), but he does not mention himself in the passage at all when honoring those who served.

What can we learn from this?

Nehemiah practiced servant leadership. See, a servant serves, many times behind the scenes, but often never gets the glory for his service. The glory goes to the master. Well, Nehemiah not only served God, but he also served Israel and gave honor to them instead of himself. This is how Jesus taught us to serve:

So you too, when you have done everything you were commanded to do, should say, 'We are slaves undeserving of special praise; we have only done what was our duty.'"
Luke 17:10

But when you do your giving, do not let your left hand know what your right hand is doing, so that your gift may be in secret. And your Father, who sees in secret, will reward you.
Matthew 6:3-4

It is great to have a pat on the back, but Jesus says a servant should not expect one. He serves because it is his duty to serve the master. He also practices secrecy in his service, as he is not seeking honor from man but from God. Nehemiah demonstrates this as he takes no glory for himself in this honor roll of those who rebuilt the walls of Jerusalem.

Listen to this: one of the greatest hindrances to revival is pride. Pride says, "I do not want to get involved." "I do not want to commit." "I do not like the leadership's plan or what they are doing." When pride does work, it seeks glory and brings division. We saw this amongst the young disciples who argued about who would be greatest and lobbied to sit at Christ's right hand in heaven. Pride is a poisonous root that can spoil revival. James said this:

But if you have bitter jealousy and selfishness in your hearts, do not boast and tell lies against the truth. Such wisdom does not come from above but is earthly, natural, demonic. For where there is jealousy and selfishness, there is disorder and every evil practice.
James 3:14-16

How many of our churches and ministries have been destroyed because people want glory—they want to be seen? They want to serve as elders and deacons so people can look up to them and give glory to them. I have seen this at work in many churches. Leadership brings power and honor, and therefore, many seek to be in these positions in order to be served instead of serving.

If we are going to rebuild the walls of our communities, churches, families, and our lives, we must let go of our pride. We must let go of our selfish ambition and become servants of God and others. That cannot but standout as we look at Nehemiah who does not even mention his name in the honor roll of those who built. Humility does not care who gets the glory as long as God is glorified and others edified.

75

Let this be our passion as well. Let us bring glory to God and honor to others.

Application Question: In what ways have you seen a desire to be recognized and honored hinder fruitfulness in a church, organization, or simply somebody's life? How can we better practice the humility of a servant?

Conclusion

When does revival happen? What are its characteristics? How can leaders start to be agents of change in their communities? Leaders must understand that:

1. Revival happens when leaders set the example.
2. Revival happens when everyone is unified.
3. Revival happens when everyone does his or her part.
4. Revival happens when people take care of home.
5. Revival happens when a few souls get on fire.
6. Revival happens when we practice the humility of a servant.

Application Question: How is God calling you to help bring revival in your own life? How is God calling you to take steps toward being an agent of revival in your family, church, or organization?

How Godly Leaders Battle Discouragement

Now when Sanballat heard that we were rebuilding the wall he became angry and was quite upset. He derided the Jews, and in the presence of his colleagues and the army of Samaria he said, "What are these feeble Jews doing? Will they be left to themselves? Will they again offer sacrifice? Will they finish this in a day? Can they bring these burnt stones to life again from piles of dust?" Then Tobiah the Ammonite, who was close by, said, "If even a fox were to climb up on what they are building, it would break down their wall of stones!" Hear, O our God, for we are despised! Return their reproach on their own head! Reduce them to plunder in a land of exile! Do not cover their iniquity, and do not wipe out their sin from before them. For they have bitterly offended the builders! So we rebuilt the wall, and the entire wall was joined together up to half its height. The people were enthusiastic in their work....
Nehemiah 4 (NET)

How do godly leaders battle discouragement? Jesus was weary unto death (Matt 26:38). Elijah prayed that he would die (1 Kings 19:4). Even Moses asked that God would take him (Num 11:15).

It is impossible to live life and not encounter discouragements. Chapter 4 could be called the discouragement chapter. Nehemiah encounters many discouragements while leading the rebuilding project of the Jerusalem wall.

In fact, after the wall was half way done, all the discouragements and attacks got worse (v. 6-8). Sanballat and Tobiah corralled an army to attack the Jews while they were working, but by God's grace, Nehemiah inspired the Israelites to defend themselves and to continue working on the wall. In this chapter, we will see thirteen principles about how a godly leader battles discouragement.

Big Question: What discouragements did Nehemiah experience in chapter 4? Also, what can we learn about battling discouragement from his responses?

Godly Leaders Battle Discouragement by Knowing Their Enemy and His Tactics

> Now when Sanballat heard that we were rebuilding the wall he became angry and was quite upset. He derided the Jews, and in the presence of his colleagues and the army of Samaria he said, "What are these feeble Jews doing? Will they be left to themselves? Will they again offer sacrifice? Will they finish this in a day? Can they bring these burnt stones to life again from piles of dust?" Then Tobiah the Ammonite, who was close by, said, "If even a fox were to climb up on what they are building, it would break down their wall of stones!"
> Nehemiah 4:1-3

What is the first thing we notice about the enemy's attacks in this chapter? We see that Sanballat became "angry" and "quite upset" when he heard about the rebuilding project (v.1). While the Jews were dormant, content to have their walls broken down and open for attack, Sanballat was not agitated. However, when they started rebuilding the walls, the attacks began. It started with criticism, and later Sanballat and the Samaritans tried to start a war to make Israel stop building.

Yes, we can be sure that it is no different with our spiritual lives. We also have an enemy of our souls, who becomes very angry when we are doing the will of God, and he will stop at nothing to make us quit. Paul said this in 2 Corinthians 2:11: "so that we may not be exploited by Satan (for we are not ignorant of his schemes)." Certainly, we must know our enemy's tactics as well. As long as we are content to be on the sidelines, content to sit in the pews, the enemy is often content to leave us alone.

I have talked to many Christians who said that when they started to read their Bible more, it was then that everything started going wrong in their lives, which actually made them not want to read their Bible. In fact, I heard the story of one seminary student who was studying to be a missionary, and while in school, his children started to have demonic nightmares. After these dreams persisted for a while, he set an appointment with the dean of the school. During the meeting, he shared that he knew this was an attack of Satan, and he realized that it would probably get worse when he went on the mission field. The dean replied, "Yes, you are possibly right." Then the student proceeded to tell the dean that he had decided to drop out of school because he wanted to protect his family.

Yes, Nehemiah and the Israelites could have quit when their enemy became angry, and the coming attacks probably would have stopped. However, quitting wouldn't have made them safer. It is the person who is unfaithful who is in the most danger. Satan's desire is to steal, kill, and destroy (cf. John 10:10). The safest place is always in the will of God.

Similarly, we should expect attacks to increase while faithfully doing God's will. Did we not see this in the life of Christ? While he was preparing for ministry in the wilderness, Satan came and tempted him to make him stop. After beginning his ministry, he received constant attacks from the Pharisees who he called children of their father, the devil (John 8:41). Eventually, the Pharisees, with the help of the Sadducees, murdered Christ. Christ's attacks increased as he progressed in his ministry.

We should not be unaware of Satan's tactics as well. When he hears that you are rebuilding the image of God in your life and others, there will be attacks. As we seek to serve the Lord and do his will, they will increase. We should not be surprised when this happens because our serving makes the enemy angry.

Application Question: In what ways have you seen or experienced the increase of spiritual attacks while doing the will of God?

Godly Leaders Battle Discouragement by Bringing It to the Lord in Prayer

> Hear, O our God, for we are despised! Return their reproach on their own head! Reduce them to plunder in a land of exile! Do not cover their iniquity, and do not wipe out their sin from before them. For they have bitterly offended the builders!
> Nehemiah 4:4-5

In Nehemiah 4:2-3, we saw that not only did Sanballat criticize the Jews but so did Tobiah. Tobiah mocked their effort and said that even if "a fox were to climb up on what they are building, it would break down their wall of stones!" They mocked and ridiculed the Jews.

How does Nehemiah respond in verse 4? He didn't stop building the wall, nor did he wallow in the criticism. It is very easy to let criticism affect us in such a way that we get discouraged, stop, or slowdown in completing the work that God has called us to. However, Nehemiah did not do any of that, he responded by bringing the criticism to God in prayer. Look at what he said:

> Hear, O our God, for we are despised! Return their reproach on their own head! Reduce them to plunder in a land of exile! Do not cover

their iniquity, and do not wipe out their sin from before them. For they
have bitterly offended the builders!
Nehemiah 4:4-5

Application Question: Why is it important to bring criticism and discouragements
to God first in prayer?

1. It is important so that we can discern if the criticism is of God or not.

Sometimes, criticism may actually reflect the opinion of God even if
given in the wrong manner. We, in fact, may need to reevaluate. Other times,
we may need to disregard the criticism. Therefore, before we react, we should
pray about it and submit it to God, so we can better discern.

2. It is important because it will help deliver us from the common
response of returning the criticism or getting angry.

Fights can only happen if two sides are involved. Many times, we'll
receive a harsh comment and instead of bringing it to God, we'll bring it right
back to the person who gave it. And the next thing you know, we are in a fight.
Prayer brings God into our perspective and helps keep us from responding
negatively.

In fact, Nehemiah didn't initially respond to Sanballat at all; he just
asked God to fight their battles for them. Listen to what Paul says in Romans
12:19: "Do not avenge yourselves, dear friends, but give place to God's wrath,
for it is written, '*Vengeance is mine, I will repay,*' says the Lord."

Nehemiah prayed that God would defend Israel and do what is just.
But, there is more that we can learn from this prayer.

Application Question: What are some negative ways that people often respond
to criticism? How do you normally respond to it?

Godly Leaders Battle Discouragement through Corporate Prayer

Hear, O our God, for we are despised! Return their reproach on their
own head! Reduce them to plunder in a land of exile! Do not cover
their iniquity, and do not wipe out their sin from before them. For they
have bitterly offended the builders!
Nehemiah 4:4-5

80

It is clear from the fact that Nehemiah uses the pronouns "our" and "we" in verse 4, that when he heard the criticism, he probably gathered the leaders of Israel and began to pray corporately. When Christ was weary unto death, he called his disciples to pray (Matt 26:38). Similarly, when the apostles were commanded by the leaders of Israel to no longer speak in the name of Christ, they called a prayer meeting. Acts 4:23-24 describes this:

> When they were released, Peter and John went to their fellow believers and reported everything the high priests and the elders had said to them. When they heard this, they raised their voices to God with one mind

> Many times instead of finding people to pray with, we just find people to complain to and instead of removing the discouragement, it actually increases it. The friends we talk to often encourage the negativity, instead of encouraging corporate prayer and faith.
> Who do you go to for prayer when you are discouraged?

Application Question: Who do you share your discouragements with? How often do you use corporate prayer as a remedy for discouragement? How effective is it?

Godly Leaders Battle Discouragement by Praying the Will of God

> Hear, O our God, for we are despised! Return their reproach on their own head! Reduce them to plunder in a land of exile! Do not cover their iniquity, and do not wipe out their sin from before them. For they have bitterly offended the builders!
> Nehemiah 4:4-5

Certainly, we must notice how Nehemiah prayed. He prayed essentially that God would fight against the Samaritans; he prayed a curse. This is very different from what Christ taught in Matthew 5:44. We are called to love our enemies, to bless, and to not curse them. This doesn't sound like a blessing prayer to me. How should we reconcile this with Christ's teachings? Was Nehemiah wrong in praying this prayer?

Interpretation Question: How should we explain the fact that Nehemiah prayed a curse upon the Samaritans? How should we reconcile this with the teachings of the New Testament?

I don't think Nehemiah was wrong because he was praying in conjunction with the Scripture revealed to Israel. In Deuteronomy, God made a covenant with Israel that they were to follow him, and as they followed him, God would give them the land of Canaan and defeat their enemies. Consider Deuteronomy 28:7: "The Lord will cause your enemies who attack you to be struck down before you; they will attack you from one direction but flee from you in seven different directions."

When the Israelites were disobedient, they would be defeated by their enemies, and when they were obedient, God would fight for them.

This is exactly what happened with Joshua when he led Israel to conquer the Canaanites. The Jews, at this time, were under the Mosaic Covenant, and therefore, Nehemiah was praying in accordance with that covenant.

With that said, we are no longer under the Old Covenant, but the New Covenant in Christ. Moses is not our mediator; Christ is (cf. Rom 7:4, 1 Cor 9:20-21) and he taught us to pray blessing over our enemies and not curses (Matt 5:44). We should pray for their salvation, for them to be led into repentance and righteousness. However, there is a place for trusting a holy and just God to do what is right in his time. Vengeance is the Lord's, and he will repay (Romans 12:19).

I have met Christians who actually pray curses over those who oppose them, which only adds to their discouragement and frustration and never allows them to have peace. Christ prayed "Father, forgive them, for they don't know what they are doing" (Lk 23:34). Christ knew that they were ignorant and blinded by the enemy (2 Cor 4:4), and therefore, he prayed for their forgiveness.

One of the things we can take from Nehemiah's prayer is that he prayed according to the will of God as revealed in Scripture. We should do the same in order to overcome discouragement. This will give us peace and remove discouragement.

Jesus when confronting the cross and persecution prayed, "Yet not my will but yours be done" (Lk 22:42), and while on the cross, he prayed for the forgiveness of his persecutors. Similarly, Paul taught that we should pray for the salvation of everyone including unjust leaders (cf. 1 Tim 2:1-4). Certainly, we should pray for the salvation of those who persecute us or that they may know Christ more. We should pray in accordance with God's will as revealed in Scripture, even as Nehemiah did, in order to battle discouragement.

Application Question: Why is it important to pray for our enemies? How does it affect us?

Godly Leaders Battle Discouragement by Continuing to Work with All Their Heart

> So we rebuilt the wall, and the entire wall was joined together up to half its height. The people were enthusiastic in their work.
> Nehemiah 4:6

We must notice the other way that Nehemiah and the Israelites responded to the criticism. First, he prayed to God, but secondly, he and the Israelites continued to work with "enthusiasm." This is a very important way for believers to respond as well.

Satan often uses criticism, problems, or difficulties to discourage believers and to make them quit. However, instead of quitting, the Israelites responded by being "enthusiastic in their work." They were fully devoted to doing God's will and worked with all their energy to complete the wall. In fact, in the face of criticism, they worked until it was half way done (v. 6).

Consider what Paul told Timothy in 1 Timothy 4:12-15. Timothy may have been in similar circumstances. The implication from the context is that he was receiving criticism because of his youth. He was young for Greek standards, and this may have made it harder for him to minister to those who were older. Paul said this:

> Let no one look down on you because you are young, but set an example for the believers in your speech, conduct, love, faithfulness, and purity. Until I come, give attention to the public reading of scripture, to exhortation, to teaching. Do not neglect the spiritual gift you have, given to you and confirmed by prophetic words when the elders laid hands on you. Take pains with these things; be absorbed in them, so that everyone will see your progress.
> 1 Timothy 4:12-15

Even in the face of criticism, Paul told Timothy to be an "example," to "give attention," to "take pains," and to be "absorbed" in the work of God, so that everyone would see his progress. Timothy was essentially called to work with all his heart, even in the face of criticism. In the same way, the Israelites worked heartily until it was half way done. We must do the same. Instead of quitting or slowing down in God's work, which is the enemy's desire, we must work with all our hearts in order to glorify God.

Application Question: In what ways does the enemy try to make you stop or slow down in doing God's work by bringing discouragement? How can we practice being more devoted to the ministry God has given us even when facing discouragement?

- Remember that we are ultimately seeking to please God (cf. Col 3:23).
- Remember the grace of God that is available to us (cf. 2 Cor 12:9).
- Remember the people we are serving (cf. Phil 2:3-4).

Godly Leaders Battle Discouragement by Being on Guard against Attack

> When Sanballat, Tobiah, the Arabs, the Ammonites, and the people of Ashdod heard that the restoration of the walls of Jerusalem had moved ahead and that the breaches had begun to be closed, they were very angry. All of them conspired together to move with armed forces against Jerusalem and to create a disturbance in it. So we prayed to our God and stationed a guard to protect against them both day and night.
> Nehemiah 4:7-9

We see here that, because the completion of the wall was advancing, the enemies of the Jews decided to take the next step and bring an army against them. How did the Jews respond?

The Jews prayed again, but they also posted guards to watch for any attacks. Nehemiah heard the rumor and responded by protecting the Israelites and their work through posting guards day and night.

Similarly, as believers in a spiritual battle, we also must be on guard and protect ourselves from constant attacks. In the Old Testament, Israel battled against the Hittites, the Philistines, the Assyrians, the Babylonians, the Samaritans, etc. However, our battle is not against flesh and blood, but it is a spiritual battle against powers, principalities, and rulers of the darkness (cf. Eph 6:10-12). How do we guard ourselves?

We do this primarily by guarding our hearts and minds since we know that our enemy is always attacking as well. Listen to what Solomon said: "Guard your heart with all vigilance, for from it are the sources of life" (Proverbs 4:23).

84

Solomon said that our heart, which is our mind, will, and emotions, affects everything. It affects our worship, our service, our relationships, our leisure, etc. Therefore, it is the place that the enemy focuses his attacks, and therefore, it must be guarded, especially against discouragement.

Application Question: How should we practice guarding our hearts so we do not succumb to discouragement and attacks from the devil? What types of attacks on our heart should we be aware of?

1. We must guard our hearts against anxiety or fear.

Proverbs 12:25 says, "Anxiety in a person's heart weighs him down." Our enemy is constantly trying to bring worries about the future, worries about relationships, worries about deadlines, etc., because he realizes where there is anxiety, soon comes depression. When depression comes, the work stops, or it is not done well. Scripture also says that worry chokes the Word of God and makes it unfruitful (cf. Matt 13:22). Anxiety or fear will keep us from being fruitful in our understanding of the Lord and ministry to him.

Similarly, in Proverbs 29:25, Solomon said, "The fear of people becomes a snare" or it can be translated "a trap." Many people are ensnared by what people say or think about them; their family's opinion or the opinion of friends or employers ensnare them and discourage them from moving forward in God's plan. Nehemiah discerned that the initial criticism was not of God, and we must do that as well. Many Christians are ensnared by the fear of man.

2. We must guard our hearts against sexual temptation.

Paul said, "Flee sexual immorality" (1 Cor 6:18). It is interesting that in 1 Peter 5:9, we are called to resist the devil, but when it comes to lust, Paul said, "Run away." It is a very potent attack that Satan uses to ensnare Christians and keep them from progressing spiritually. Sexual immorality is extremely dangerous. It destroys people's minds, bodies, and relationships. It traps Christians and keeps them from progressing in the Lord. Scripture says that it is the "pure in heart that will see God" and the pure in heart alone (Matt 5:8). It is for this reason that it is a common snare of the devil. We must at all cost guard against sexual immorality.

3. We must guard our hearts against idolatry.

We were made to worship, and therefore, idolatry is a common sin of our hearts. Some have called the human heart an "idol factory." If we don't

85

worship God, we will worship something else. First Corinthians 10:14 says, "So then, my dear friends, flee from idolatry."

Satan will try to bring an idol to take our focus off God and his work. It can be a relationship; it can be a job; it can be a hobby; it can be school; it can be entertainment; etc. He will even use good things like family or ministry to come between us and our worship of God.

Listen again to what Solomon said: "Guard your heart with all vigilance, for from it are the sources of life" (Prov 4:23).

This must be our priority if we are going to battle discouragement. We must guard our hearts so that we can complete whatever God has called us to do. We certainly see this with Nehemiah and the Israelites as they later had a weapon in one hand and a brick in the other while building (v. 17). We must build and guard at the same time because Satan is always trying to stop the work. Defense is one of the best protections from discouragement.

Application Question: In what ways is God calling you to guard your heart from Satan's attacks? In what ways does he commonly attack your heart and bring discouragement?

Godly Leaders Battle Discouragement by Being Balanced with Faith and Works

When Sanballat, Tobiah, the Arabs, the Ammonites, and the people of Ashdod heard that the restoration of the walls of Jerusalem had moved ahead and that the breaches had begun to be closed, they were very angry. All of them conspired together to move with armed forces against Jerusalem and to create a disturbance in it. So we prayed to our God and stationed a guard to protect against them both day and night.
Nehemiah 4:7-9

Application Question: Are there any other practical truths we can learn from Nehemiah's praying and then posting a guard to protect his people (v. 9)?

I think this reminds us of our responsibility to be balanced. Sometimes, people only pray in a difficult situation but never do their part to remedy it themselves. Sometimes, they will even claim to be walking in faith by doing this. However, faith always has corresponding works (cf. James 2:17). If we are praying for a spouse, we must put ourselves in a position to meet a potential spouse. If we are praying for future steps, we must be active in looking at doors. Certainly, there are times of waiting on the Lord, but many times, even then, God has called us to be active in our waiting.

Nehemiah trusted God to protect them, but he also knew they had to do their part. This will help remove many discouragements as we both trust God and, at the same time, do our part. Put it in God's hands through prayer, but actively work to solve the problem. Listen to what Paul said:

> Therefore, my dear friends, as you have always obeyed—not only in my presence, but now much more in my absence—continue to work out your salvation with fear and trembling, for it is God who works in you to will and to act according to his good purpose.
> Philippians 2:12-13 (NIV 1984)

Paul said to work out our salvation, our process of becoming like Jesus, because God is working in us to will and do of his good purpose.

Our responsibility and God's sovereignty is a mystery that somehow works together in perfect harmony; however, we have a tendency to tip to one side or another. One person works but doesn't rely on God. Another relies on God but doesn't work. I think we see a proper balance with Nehemiah; he called the people to pray, but he also called them to guard themselves. They trusted God but at the same time did their part.

It has been said, "Pray as though it all depends on God but work as though it all depends on you." There is a lot of truth in this. We must seek proper balance.

Keeping a proper balance will help us battle discouragement. How is God calling you to trust him and, at the same time, do your part? This could apply to situations such as finding a spouse, getting a job, reconciling some conflict, or discerning what's next in the future. We must trust God and actively do our part. This will help keep us from discouragement.

Application Question: In what ways have you seen people who say they are walking by "faith" but are not willing to do their part? How do we keep a balance between faith and works?

Godly Leaders Battle Discouragement by Being Aware of Weeds amongst the Good Seeds

> Then those in Judah said, "The strength of the laborers has failed! The debris is so great that we are unable to rebuild the wall." Our adversaries also boasted, "Before they are aware or anticipate

anything, we will come in among them and kill them, and we will bring this work to a halt!" So it happened that the Jews who were living near them came and warned us repeatedly about all the schemes they were plotting against us.

Nehemiah 4:10-12

In verses 10-12, we see several different discouragements that happen back to back. The tribe of Judah came to Nehemiah with a discouragement saying that the laborers were giving out and there was too much rubble. This would have been especially discouraging since the tribe of Judah was the noble tribe from which David came and the prophesied messiah would eventually come.

One of the things we know about the tribe of Judah, as seen later in the book, is that they were compromised. They were working with Tobiah, the enemy. Nehemiah 6:17-19 says this:

In those days the aristocrats of Judah repeatedly sent letters to Tobiah, and responses from Tobiah were repeatedly coming to them. For many in Judah had sworn allegiance to him, because he was the son-in-law of Shecaniah son of Arah. His son Jonathan had married the daughter of Meshullam son of Berechiah. They were telling me about his good deeds and then taking back to him the things I said. Tobiah, on the other hand, sent letters in order to scare me.

We see that the wealthy in Judah had actually partnered with Tobiah. They were loyal to him through marriage. We will also see in chapter 13:15-17 that the nobles in Judah were more worried about making money than doing the will of God. They will eventually start desecrating the Sabbath in order to make a profit.

Application Question: How can we apply Judah's compromise with the enemy to the church and to our lives?

Similarly, one of the greatest tactics of the enemy is attacking from within the body of Christ instead of from without. Attacks from the enemy often come through those who claim to follow the same Lord. The enemy will even raise up leaders from within the church to hinder the work of God.

The man or woman of God must be aware of this or he or she will become very discouraged while doing God's work. It could be a pastor, a Sunday school teacher, a friend, or a family member who unknowingly is not speaking the will of God. It is for this reason that the man or woman of God must clearly discern the voice of God among the many voices.

How do we see this in Scripture?

We see this reality in the Parable of the Weeds (Matt 13:37-40) where Jesus described how Satan has planted weeds amongst the good seeds. The false will always be among the true. Jesus taught his disciples this so that they would be prepared and kept from discouragement, and we must understand this as well. Listen to Christ's interpretation of this parable in Matthew 13:37-40:

> He answered, "The one who sowed the good seed is the Son of Man. The field is the world and the good seed are the people of the kingdom. The weeds are the people of the evil one, and the enemy who sows them is the devil. The harvest is the end of the age, and the reapers are angels. As the weeds are collected and burned with fire, so it will be at the end of the age.

In the context of teaching about the kingdom of heaven, Christ thought it would be very important for the disciples to be aware of this. Christians often think the church should be "heaven on earth," but no, the current state of the kingdom of God is "weeds" amongst the "good seeds." This is true because we have an enemy who is trying to stop the harvest.

No doubt, this knowledge would be important for Nehemiah to understand as well, especially as the leaders of Judah kept giving him discouraging messages. We must know the enemy's tactic of placing weeds amongst the good seeds. It will help keep us from being surprised and subsequently defeated.

Application Question: Why is it important to understand the state of the kingdom as weeds and good seeds in order to protect us from discouragement? How have you experienced this or seen others become discouraged in the church because of it?

Godly Leaders Battle Discouragement by Understanding the Tactic of the Evil Day

> Then those in Judah said, "The strength of the laborers has failed! The debris is so great that we are unable to rebuild the wall." Our adversaries also boasted, "Before they are aware or anticipate anything, we will come in among them and kill them, and we will bring this work to a halt!" So it happened that the Jews who were living near

89

them came and warned us repeatedly about all the schemes they were
plotting against us.
Nehemiah 4:10-12

Observation Question: What were the different discouragements against
Nehemiah and the Jews in Nehemiah 4:1-12, and especially verses 10-12?

When we look at all the different discouragements from v. 1-12, we will
see that the enemy was attacking the Jews with a great assault. First, we saw
the criticism from the Samaritans (v. 1-3), then we saw them gathering for war
(v. 8). Now, we see the nobles of Judah probably intentionally trying to
discourage Israel, the Samaritans' threats, and also the discouragement of the
Jews who lived near them (v. 10-12).

Is there anything we can learn from this barrage of discouragements
in verses 10-12?

Yes, I believe so. Our enemy commonly brings an "all-out assault" with
the intention of discouraging and making believers give up. I think Paul refers
to this when talking about spiritual warfare in Ephesians 6. Look at what he
says: "For this reason, take up the full armor of God so that you may be able to
stand your ground on the evil day, and having done everything, to stand"
(Ephesians 6:13).

Paul says that we need to be ready because at times the enemy will
bring an "evil day," a season of evil. There will be seasons when the enemy
brings an "all-out" attack on us. It may show up in problems at work or school,
family issues, a sickness, or all of the above. In these seasons, it is very easy
to have the same feelings shared by the Jews as they were anxious and ready
to give up. The enemy's tactic made them anxious.

These are common words and feelings in the "evil day." We, no doubt,
see this tactic and response with Job. In the season that God allowed the enemy
to attack him, he lost his children, his wealth, his health, and even his friends
turned against him. All he had left was a critical wife. This was an all-out assault
and even Job cried out, "I curse the day I was born" (Job 3:1). He didn't want to
live anymore.

Have you ever gotten to the point where you just wanted to give up,
you just wanted to throw in the towel? Moses felt that way and so did Elijah.
This is a common response to the day of evil, and Nehemiah 4 is a good picture
of this.

This is an important tactic to understand; otherwise, you will be more
inclined towards frustration and giving up. You could become angry with God
and with others if you do not understand the nature of Satan's tactics. He brings
the day of evil for the purpose of discouraging you and making you quit.

It is good to remember that God only calls for us "to stand" in the day of evil. Ephesians 6:13 says, "For this reason, take up the full armor of God so that you may be able to stand your ground on the evil day, and having done everything, to stand."

Essentially, God says, "Stand! Don't quit and don't give up! Persevere!" It is in this season that the words of James should be a great comfort to us, "But let patience [perseverance] have her perfect work, that ye may be perfect and entire, wanting nothing" (1:4, KJV). In this season God will build us up and mature us through perseverance. As with Job, sometimes God's primary purpose in the season is for us to faithfully persevere while trusting in him. Romans 5:3-4 says this: "Not only this, but we also rejoice in sufferings, knowing that suffering produces endurance, and endurance, character, and character, hope."

In battling discouragement, I think it is important to recognize the season of all-out assault, the day of evil. We are in a literal war, and we must be aware of this tactic of the enemy meant to discourage us and make us quit. Like Nehemiah, we must stand our ground and trust God in the day of evil (cf. Neh 4:14).

Application Question: Have you ever experienced this type of spiritual warfare where attack after attack tried to discourage you? How did you respond?

Godly Leaders Battle Discouragement by Focusing on the Lord

When I had made an inspection, I stood up and said to the nobles, the officials, and the rest of the people, "Don't be afraid of them. Remember the great and awesome Lord, and fight on behalf of your brothers, your sons, your daughters, your wives, and your families!"
Nehemiah 4:14

Observation Question: How did Nehemiah encourage the people in the face of war, threats from the enemy, and the worries of his people (v. 10-11)?

Nehemiah responded to all-out assault by helping Israel refocus on God. He stood up and called them to "Remember the Lord." Remember the promises in his Word; remember his great and awesome exploits in the past.

If we are going to stand in the day of evil, we also must renew our focus on God. Is this not what David did when fighting Goliath? Listen to what he said:

But David replied to the Philistine, "You are coming against me with sword and spear and javelin. But I am coming against you in the name of the Lord of hosts, the God of Israel's armies, whom you have defied! This very day the Lord will deliver you into my hand! I will strike you down and cut off your head. This day I will give the corpses of the Philistine army to the birds of the sky and the wild animals of the land. Then all the land will realize that Israel has a God
1 Samuel 17:45-46

When the armies of Israel were cringing at the site of this giant, David saw God and said, "This very day the Lord will deliver you into my hand." David focused on God and, therefore, was not discouraged like the rest of Israel.

Don't we also see this with Israel entering the land of Canaan? Eight of the ten spies only saw the giants in the land and, therefore, discouraged Israel from entering. However, Joshua and Caleb said this: "It is a great land and the Lord will hand it over to us" (Numbers 14:7-8, paraphrase). The fundamental difference between the two spies and the eight is their view point. The two saw God, and the rest saw only the giants.

In Nehemiah's scenario, the tribe of Judah was discouraged and felt it was impossible to finish because they only saw the rubble (v. 10). It was too much of a task. The Jews in the surrounding areas only saw the Samaritan's plots. However, Nehemiah saw God. "Remember the Lord," he said. One cannot but think of the story of Peter's wife being crucified as we consider Nehemiah's response to the army. When Peter's wife was going to be crucified, tradition says that Peter cried out to his wife, "Remember the Lord." He called her to focus on Christ in the midst of their trial.

The author of Hebrews taught the same thing as he spoke to the Jewish Christians who were being persecuted for their faith (cf. Heb 10:32-33). In chapter 12, he encouraged them to fix their eyes on Jesus. Look at what he said:

Keeping our eyes fixed on Jesus, the pioneer and perfecter of our faith. For the joy set out for him he endured the cross, disregarding its shame, and has taken his seat at the right hand of the throne of God. Think of him who endured such opposition against himself by sinners, so that you may not grow weary in your souls and give up.
Hebrews 12:2-3

The author of Hebrews told them to consider Christ so that they would not grow weary and lose heart. Like Nehemiah, Peter and his wife, and the Hebrew Christians, we must focus on God in the face of discouragements.

What are you focusing on in the midst of your trials? If you find yourself angry, frustrated, and worried then you are probably focusing on the size of the task and the detractors instead of focusing on God. Isaiah 26:3 said, "You keep him at perfect peace, whose mind is stayed on you" (ESV).

Nehemiah called the Israelites to "Remember the Lord." We must do the same thing for ourselves, and we must also remind those who we are leading to do the same. As leaders, we must call them to regain their focus on God through his Word, prayer, and fellowship with the saints, so that they may stand and not faint.

Application Question: How can we refocus on God in the midst of difficulties?

1. We must have godly accountability who constantly calls us to refocus.

We each need a Nehemiah, somebody who continually calls us to refocus on God. This could come by being in a Bible-preaching church where the messages constantly challenge us to get right with God. Sometimes it comes through personal relationships with mature Christians who are willing to invest in our lives. We need accountability to help us refocus.

2. We must have consistent spiritual disciplines.

Being in the Word of God, prayer, worship, and fellowship will always refocus us on God. Those who are undisciplined will find the giants in their lives too big, and this will discourage them and make them want to give up.

Application Question: How do you refocus on God in the midst of your trials? Who is your Nehemiah?

Godly Leaders Battle Discouragements by Taking Times of Rest and Retreat

So I stationed people at the lower places behind the wall in the exposed places. I stationed the people by families, with their swords, spears, and bows... It so happened that when our adversaries heard that we were aware of these matters, God frustrated their intentions. Then all of us returned to the wall, each to his own work.

93

Nehemiah 4:13, 15

After hearing about the Samaritan plot, it is clear from verse 15 that some of the Jews stopped working for a short time in order to focus on the oncoming attack. We may have seasons like that in serving the Lord where we need to solely "focus" on our spiritual battle as well. There is a Greek proverb that says, "You will break the bow if you keep it always bent."

In the same way, many of us stay "bent" all the time, which eventually wears us out and causes us to succumb to discouragement. We are always serving, always building, and always studying, but at times, we need to rest so that we can later build more effectively. For some, this may come through a time of fasting, further training in ministry, extended time studying the Bible and in prayer, or simply just resting and spending time with family so they can one day go back and build more effectively.

Many essentially lead themselves into discouragement because they don't practice proper rest and retreat. It is good to remember that when Elijah was depressed and ready to die in 1 Kings 19, God brought him food and allowed him to rest. The Lord led him to a cave where he spoke to him in a small voice, and then the Lord gave him Elisha to wash his feet—to help with the burden. Elijah needed a time of physical restoration and spiritual restoration. In what ways is God calling you to find rest and retreat so you can later build more effectively?

"You will break the bow if you keep it always bent."

Application Question: In what ways have you found yourself prone to depression and discouragement for lack of proper eating, sleeping, and rest? In what ways do you find rest and retreat in order to protect yourself from discouragement?

Godly Leaders Battle Discouragement by Developing Supportive Relationships

> I said to the nobles, the officials, and the rest of the people, "The work is demanding and extensive, and we are spread out on the wall, far removed from one another. Wherever you hear the sound of the trumpet, gather there with us. Our God will fight for us!"
> Nehemiah 4:19-20

In verses 19 and 20, we see that everybody was spread out while working, making them more vulnerable to attack. However, Nehemiah realized that if they were attacked, they would need each other's support. Therefore, in the event of an attack, the trumpet would be blown, and everybody would gather to the area of the battle to fight together.

It should be the same way in our lives. We were never meant to carry the burden of ministry, fighting in spiritual warfare, or serving our families and the Lord alone. When there is an attack, we need to sound the alarm and seek help.

Application Question: How should we practice this principle of developing supportive relationships in our lives, in order to battle discouragement?

1. We must be willing to be vulnerable with others.

One of the problems with many in the church is that they keep everything hidden. If families have financial problems, they tell their children, "Shhh… Let's keep this to ourselves." If the husband and wife are struggling in their relationship, they come to church and put on a smile like there is nothing wrong. People would rather act as if everything is okay instead of sounding the alarm and getting help. By allowing pride to keep them from being vulnerable, they ultimately allow the enemy to attack them and wound them severely, if not destroy them.

If we are going to develop supportive relationships in order to fight discouragement, we must be willing to share our problems with others. We must learn to be vulnerable. James 5:16 says, "So confess your sins to one another and pray for one another so that you may be healed. The prayer of a righteous person has great effectiveness."

2. We must be willing to support others.

Many Christians are just concerned about themselves. In the event of an attack on Israel, those who were doing their job and not under attack would flee their seemingly secure positions to help others. They carried the burdens of others. Many Christians are too consumed with their own work to carry the burdens of others. However, this is exactly what Scripture calls us to do. Galatians 6:2 says, "Carry one another's burdens, and in this way you will fulfill the law of Christ."

Carry one another's burden and so fulfill the law of Christ means to pick up somebody else's pain. It means to touch their dirty feet as Christ did (John 13). We all must be willing to do this if we are going to have supportive relationships where we not only receive but also help others when they are in trouble.

Are you willing to support others when they succumb to depression, lust, sickness or family discord?

David had Jonathan when he was down. God brought Elisha to Elijah when he struggled with depression in 1 Kings 19. Christ had the three apostles: James, John, and Peter, and then the nine. Who do you have? Who do you support and who supports you?

Application Question: Who do you support and who supports you when down or under attack?

Godly Leaders Battle Discouragement by Sacrificially Serving Others

> So we worked on, with half holding spears, from dawn till dusk. At that time I instructed the people, "Let every man and his coworker spend the night in Jerusalem and let them be guards for us by night and workers by day." We did not change clothes—not I, nor my relatives, nor my workers, nor the watchmen who were with me. Each had his weapon, even when getting a drink of water.
> Nehemiah 4:21-23

We must also notice that Nehemiah confronted the potential attack by making every man guard the base at night and work during the day. These men served the community by working "double duty." Listen again to what he said:

> At that time I instructed the people, "Let every man and his coworker spend the night in Jerusalem and let them be guards for us by night and workers by day." We did not change clothes—not I, nor my relatives, nor my workers, nor the watchmen who were with me. Each had his weapon, even when getting a drink of water.
> Nehemiah 4:22-23

He confronted the potential attack by finding a few good men, including himself, to serve the community as guards. They worked so hard that they never even took off their clothes (v. 23). These men refreshed and served the community.

I think there is a lesson in this about battling discouragement. We should often battle discouragement by serving others.

Those who are depressed often become the most selfish people in the world. There is a tendency to isolate oneself and separate from others.

96

However, Nehemiah and these men became selfless; they served the community as guards. They served so diligently they never even got to change their clothes. They sacrificed to serve others.

In the same way, serving others is one of the best ways to battle discouragement. Listen to what Solomon said: "those who refresh others will themselves be refreshed" (Proverbs 11:25 NIV 1984).

Jesus said something similar in John 13:17 to the disciples about washing one another's feet. He said, "If you understand these things, you will be blessed if you do them." This seems a little strange. You would think he would say "washing others' feet" blesses the people receiving it, but no, he focused on the fact that the givers would be blessed.

Yes, in the same way, there is tremendous value in battling discouragement through serving others. The men of Israel were ready to give up; there was too much rubble, too much work. They were frightened because they could be attacked at any moment, and they battled this by zealously serving the others in the community. Yes, they blessed others but the greatest blessing went to the people serving. Those who refresh others will be refreshed.

Who are you serving zealously? What community has God called you to serve so zealously and sacrificially that you lose sleep and some comforts in order to bless them? Yes, this does not only bless them, but it will bless you.

Listen to the blessings that God declares will go to those who serve others sacrificially in Isaiah 58:6-12 (NIV 1984):

> "Is not this the kind of fasting I have chosen: to loose the chains of injustice and untie the cords of the yoke, to set the oppressed free and break every yoke? Is it not to share your food with the hungry and to provide the poor wanderer with shelter— when you see the naked, to clothe him, and not to turn away from your own flesh and blood? Then your light will break forth like the dawn, and your healing will quickly appear; then your righteousness will go before you, and the glory of the LORD will be your rear guard. Then you will call, and the LORD will answer; you will cry for help, and he will say: Here am I. "If you do away with the yoke of oppression, with the pointing finger and malicious talk, and if you spend yourselves in behalf of the hungry and satisfy the needs of the oppressed, then your light will rise in the darkness, and your night will become like the noonday. The LORD will guide you always; he will satisfy your needs in a sun scorched land and will strengthen your frame. You will be like a well watered garden, like a spring whose waters never fail. Your people will rebuild the ancient ruins and will raise up the age-old foundations; you will be called Repairer of Broken Walls, Restorer of Streets with Dwellings.

97

Isaiah says that those who loose the chains of injustice, untie the cords of the yoke, set the oppressed free, share their food with others, provide the poor with shelter, and care for their own family will have tremendous blessings (v. 6-7). Their light will break forth, which no doubt refers to righteousness. They will be healed (v. 8). Doors will open for them as their righteousness goes before them (v. 8). God will protect them as their "rear guard." God will answer their prayers (v. 9). God will guide them and satisfy their needs even in desperate situations (v.11). They will be refreshed like a well-watered garden, and they will be given the opportunity to help more people (v. 12).

The blessings that come to those who serve are tremendous, and it is one of the ways we should battle discouragement. Yes, there is a tendency to pull away and isolate ourselves, but that goes against biblical and practical wisdom. Divine refreshment comes to those who sacrificially serve others. Yes, there is a need for balance in having times of service and times of rest. But when our service necessitates great labor, we can trust God will provide and give more grace (James 4:6).

Application Question: In what ways have you experienced blessing, refreshment, strength, etc., while serving others? How can we tell when it is time for us to rest or when we should extend ourselves in service to others?

Conclusion

How do godly leaders battle discouragement?

1. Godly leaders battle discouragement by knowing their enemy and his tactics.
2. Godly leaders battle discouragement by bringing it first to the Lord in prayer.
3. Godly leaders battle discouragement by corporate prayer.
4. Godly leaders battle discouragement by praying the Lord's will, as revealed in Scripture.
5. Godly leaders battle discouragement by continuing to serve with all their hearts.
6. Godly leaders battle discouragement by guarding their hearts from the enemy.
7. Godly leaders battle discouragement by being balanced with faith and works.

8. Godly leaders battle discouragement by being aware that there are weeds amongst the good seeds.
9. Godly leaders battle discouragement by understanding the tactic of the evil day.
10. Godly leaders battle discouragement by focusing on the Lord.
11. Godly leaders battle discouragement by at times taking rest and retreat.
12. Godly leaders battle discouragement by finding supportive relationships.
13. Godly leaders battle discouragement by sacrificially serving others.

How Godly Leaders Resolve Conflict

Then there was a great outcry from the people and their wives against their fellow Jews. There were those who said, "With our sons and daughters, we are many. We must obtain grain in order to eat and stay alive." There were others who said, "We are putting up our fields, our vineyards, and our houses as collateral in order to obtain grain during the famine." Then there were those who said, "We have borrowed money to pay our taxes to the king on our fields and our vineyards. And now, though we share the same flesh and blood as our fellow countrymen, and our children are just like their children, still we have found it necessary to subject our sons and daughters to slavery. Some of our daughters have been subjected to slavery, while we are powerless to help, since our fields and vineyards now belong to other people. I was very angry when I heard their outcry and these complaints. I considered these things carefully and then registered a complaint with the wealthy and the officials. I said to them, "Each one of you is seizing the collateral from your own countrymen!" Because of them I called for a great public assembly…
Nehemiah 5:1-13 (NET)

How do godly leaders resolve conflict?

Conflict is a result of the fall. After Adam sinned, he blamed God and his wife. He said, "The woman whom you gave me, she gave me some fruit from the tree and I ate it" (Gen 3:12). The woman then blamed the serpent. The blame game began when sin entered into the world. But also God prophesied that sin would have a terrible effect on the relationship of the man and the woman. In Genesis 3:16, God said this to the woman, "You will want to control your husband, but he will dominate you." Sin led to the battle of the sexes, and from that first relationship, we now have conflict in our homes, in our friendships, and in our work relationships. We have conflict between nations. The world has known no years without war. In fact, Paul taught that the acts of the flesh are hatred, discord, fits of rage, and factions (Gal 5:20). To be in discord is to be human.

However, in the midst of this world of discord, Christ said this: "Blessed are the peacemakers, for they will be called the children of God" (Matthew 5:9). In describing those who are part of the kingdom of heaven, he said that they would be known for working for peace and resolving discord.

How do godly leaders resolve conflict? How do we become the peacemakers that we have been called to be? Many people think being a peacemaker means never "ruffling feathers" or causing conflict; however, this is not true. Because there can be no true peace where there is sin, often the peacemaker will need to confront people in sin, so that there can be true peace. We see this with Nehemiah and how he responded to the conflict in Israel.

How can we best respond to conflict in order to bring true peace?

We can learn a lot from Nehemiah, as we consider how he resolved the conflict in Israel. In chapter 4, Nehemiah had conflict from without as the Samaritans persecuted him, but in chapter 5, he had conflict from within which threatened the completion of the wall. The nobles were mistreating the poor and instead of brushing it aside to focus on the wall, he addressed the issues and brought peace and righteousness. In this study, we will consider ten leadership principles on how to resolve conflict.

Big Question: What can we learn about conflict resolution from Nehemiah's response to the conflict in Israel and how can we apply these principles?

To Resolve Conflict, Godly Leaders Must Not Ignore Problems

> Then there was a great outcry from the people and their wives against their fellow Jews. There were those who said, "With our sons and daughters, we are many. We must obtain grain in order to eat and stay alive." There were others who said, "We are putting up our fields, our vineyards, and our houses as collateral in order to obtain grain during the famine." Then there were those who said, "We have borrowed money to pay our taxes to the king on our fields and our vineyards. And now, though we share the same flesh and blood as our fellow countrymen, and our children are just like their children, still we have found it necessary to subject our sons and daughters to slavery. Some of our daughters have been subjected to slavery, while we are powerless to help, since our fields and vineyards now belong to other people."
> Nehemiah 5:1-5

Observation Question: What were the internal problems threatening the completion of the wall?

First, they were running out of food because of a famine (v. 2). Secondly, because of this famine, people were selling their fields and vineyards (v.3). Third, people were borrowing money from Jewish nobles and going into tremendous debt as they sought to pay taxes to King Artaxerxes (v.4). As we will see later in the text, the Jewish lenders were charging exorbitant interest rates. Finally, the debt was becoming so high that many of Israel's children had to be sold into slavery to pay the debt (v.5). This is where the conflict was; it was between the poor and the nobles.

What can we learn from Nehemiah's response about resolving conflict?

In order to resolve conflicts, we must choose to not ignore problems. Now this principle seems simple enough, but the reality is that it's very easy to know about problems and, yet, give no attention to them. Nehemiah had many reasons for not getting involved. He had a great project going on. Why should he focus on the conflict when they hadn't built the wall yet? The conflict arose because of the nobles and officials. To challenge them would have brought tremendous pressure on him because they were the leaders of Israel. Many reasons can be found to not get involved. However, Nehemiah chose to not ignore the conflict but instead to address it.

It's the same for us. We are often tempted to ignore or to overlook conflict. However, good leadership understands the importance of not only getting involved but also resolving the conflict. Conflict has a tendency to spread. First, it is only two people fighting and then others begin taking sides. We can't ignore the conflict because it will spread like leaven and can eventually lead to destruction (cf. 1 Cor 5:6). Nehemiah doesn't ignore it, he immediately addresses it.

Similarly, we see a good example of not neglecting conflict in the early church. In Acts 6:1-6, the Greek widows were being neglected in the distribution of food, and when the apostles heard about it, even though they were busy, they responded by selecting the first seven deacons to care for the widows.

Sadly, many leaders simply choose to ignore conflict and focus on the bottom line. However, conflict always negatively affects the corporate climate and productivity. And from a spiritual standpoint, it removes the blessing of God (cf. Psalm 133). God is not a God of disorder but of peace (cf. 1 Cor 14:33)— he can't bless a community that's in discord. For that reason, godly leaders must not ignore or neglect conflict. They must get involved and seek to resolve it.

What problems or conflicts does God want you to pay attention to and get involved in?

Application Question: Why do people in leadership tend to ignore problems and conflict? What problems or conflicts is God calling you to get involved with in order to restore peace and righteousness?

To Resolve Conflict, Godly Leaders Must Develop a Righteous Anger

> I was very angry when I heard their outcry and these complaints.
> Nehemiah 5:6

Many leaders just bypass problems and never address them. They may do this, in part, because they are apathetic towards the situation. Therefore, they never develop a righteous anger which leads to fixing the problem.

Again, Nehemiah is not apathetic and does not brush the problems aside. He actually becomes passionate about the situation. It says that he became "very angry" (v. 6). Often, we, as the church, lack this righteous anger which keeps us from ever becoming part of God's solution.

Do you realize that anger is an aspect of being made in the "image of God"? Psalm 7:11 says, "God is a just judge; he is angry throughout the day."

Some people think it is always wrong to be angry; but this is not true. Sometimes, it is sinful to not be angry. The righteous anger of God should be within every believer.

Jesus was angry when he went into the temple. He made a whip and turned over the tables of the money changers (John 2:14-16). To some this might seem strange of Christ, even unChrist-like, but this was actually an example of righteous anger. He was angry at sin and therefore sought to bring righteousness.

We need a righteous anger in order to correct sin in our lives, our churches, and our nations. We need it to fight injustices like abortion, trafficking, and racism in society. We should have a righteous anger about sin, not to cause problems, but in order to help bring righteousness.

Interpretation Question: How do we discern if our anger is righteous like Nehemiah's?

1. Righteous anger should be motivated and confirmed by Scripture.

In this case, the charging of interest and treating their Israelite brothers as slaves was clearly against Scripture. We see this in Exodus and Leviticus.

If you lend money to any of my people who are needy among you, do not be like a moneylender to him; do not charge him interest.
Exodus 22:25

"'If your brother becomes impoverished and is indebted to you, you must support him; he must live with you like a foreign resident. Do not take interest or profit from him, but you must fear your God and your brother must live with you... "'If your brother becomes impoverished with regard to you so that he sells himself to you, you must not subject him to slave service. He must be with you as a hired worker, as a resident foreigner; he must serve with you until the year of jubilee,
Leviticus 25:35-36, 39-40

In this case, no doubt, Nehemiah's anger was spurred on by the knowledge of God's Word and the nobles disregard for it. Our anger should be something that is motivated and confirmed through Scripture as well.

2.   Righteous anger should be motivated by injustice towards God or others.

This is clearly seen in Jesus' example. When it caused offense towards God or others, he became like a lion (John 2:14-16). In the temple, he made a whip and turned over tables. He demonstrated a righteous anger. We should do the same. However, when considering personal offense, righteous anger should respond differently.

3.   Righteous anger should be gentle in response to personal offense.

Consider what Jesus taught in regards to personal offense:

"You have heard that it was said, '*An eye for an eye and a tooth for a tooth.*' But I say to you, do not resist the evildoer. But whoever strikes you on the right cheek, turn the other to him as well. And if someone wants to sue you and to take your tunic, give him your coat also.
Matthew 5:38-40

Most anger that men struggle with is selfish anger instead of righteous anger. It is not anger about offense towards God or others; it is anger because our pride has been hurt or we have been treated unjustly. It says, "I deserve better than this." Listen to what Peter said about Christ in describing his example for us as we go through suffering:

> He *committed no sin nor was deceit found in his mouth.* When he was maligned, he did not answer back; when he suffered, he threatened no retaliation, but committed himself to God who judges justly.
> 1 Peter 2:22-23

Application Question: How do we develop a righteous anger towards sin against God and others? How do we start to practice gentleness when personally offended?

To Resolve Conflict, Godly Leaders Must Be Patient and Self-controlled

> I was very angry when I heard their outcry and these complaints. I considered these things carefully and then registered a complaint with the wealthy and the officials.
> Nehemiah 5:6-7

One of the reasons that conflicts often do not get resolved in an amicable way is because people react too quickly. We see in this passage that Nehemiah took time to think about the situation. It says he "considered these things carefully." I have no doubt that he was considering whether his anger was right before God and what would be the best course of action.

Most people's anger and response are not this calculated. Instead of being patient and self-controlled, we tend to automatically respond with a harsh word or a witty comment. There is wisdom in being patient; there is wisdom in waiting. Sometimes, it may even be wise to wait because the situation might work itself out.

Listen to what Scripture says: "A fool lets fly with all his temper, but a wise person keeps it back" (Proverbs 29:11).

A wise person controls his anger and waits, and certainly, we see this with Nehemiah. What else do we see in Scripture?

Proverbs 17:27 says, "The truly wise person restrains his words, and the one who stays calm is discerning."

A wise person controls his tongue; he is always restraining it. Also, consider Proverbs 25:15 says, "Through patience a ruler can be persuaded, and a soft tongue can break a bone."

As mentioned previously in our study of chapter 2, sometimes we need patience in changing the hearts of others, especially leaders. Nehemiah demonstrates all these things. He is patient, self-controlled, and calculated in his response to injustice.

How do you respond when there is conflict? Are you quick to speak and quick to vent your anger? Are you impatient with God and others? Scripture says this is not wise. We must be patient and self-controlled

Application Question: Why is waiting and being patient before responding to a conflict important? Share a time when you practiced this while in a conflict or helping somebody in one.

To Resolve Conflict, Godly Leaders Must Get Counsel

I was very angry when I heard their outcry and these complaints. I considered these things carefully and then registered a complaint with the wealthy and the officials.
Nehemiah 5:6-7

I believe there is another principle we can take from this passage. The NET translates verse 7, "I considered these things carefully," but it can also be translated another way. The KJV says, "Then I consulted with myself," and the ESV translates it, "I took counsel with myself."

Not only was Nehemiah patient and self-controlled, but he also got counsel. He talked to himself and got counsel. Do you ever talk to yourself?

I think there is biblical wisdom in this practice. Nehemiah talked to himself and discerned how to respond. He probably thought about the Mosaic laws that the nobles were breaking and some of the Proverbs that Solomon wrote about on how to handle anger so that he could respond wisely. He considered the wisest course of action.

Certainly, we should do the same. We should not only be patient, but also we should get counsel. Now obviously, Nehemiah felt confirmation about how to respond to this situation because he didn't seek anybody else's opinion. However, I think that many times it will be wise to get counsel from others.

Listen to what Solomon says: "When there is no guidance a nation falls, but there is success in the abundance of counselors" (Proverbs 11:14). The KJV translates it this way: "Where no counsel is, the people fall: but in the multitude of counselors." Where there is no counsel people fall, people have more problems, more difficulties and this is certainly true with conflict resolution. People who don't get counsel often make their situation worse.

107

There is safety and victory in the multitude of counselors. This is a general principle; people make a lot of wrong decisions in life for a lack of good counsel.

Who do you have in your life to get wise counsel from? Do you have a mentor or mentors? Scripture says there is safety in the multitude of them.

Application Question: Who are your wise counselors that you communicate with, especially in a potential conflict? How have they helped guide you in the past?

To Resolve Conflict, Godly Leaders Must Practice a Biblical Method of Confrontation

> I considered these things carefully and then registered a complaint with the wealthy and the officials. I said to them, "Each one of you is seizing the collateral from your own countrymen!" Because of them I called for a great public assembly. I said to them, "To the extent possible we have bought back our fellow Jews who had been sold to the Gentiles. But now you yourselves want to sell your own countrymen, so that we can then buy them back!" They were utterly silent, and could find nothing to say. Then I said, "The thing that you are doing is wrong! Should you not conduct yourselves in the fear of our God in order to avoid the reproach of the Gentiles who are our enemies?
> Nehemiah 5:7-9

Observation Question: What was Nehemiah's process of confronting the nobles, as seen in Nehemiah 5:7-9?

Another way, we resolve conflict is by using a biblical method of confrontation. We see this clearly taught in Matthew 18:15-17. Even though this revelation had not yet been clearly spelled out in Scripture, Nehemiah followed these directives. Let's see what Christ taught about confrontation:

> "If your brother sins, go and show him his fault when the two of you are alone. If he listens to you, you have regained your brother. But if he does not listen, take one or two others with you, so that *at the testimony of two or three witnesses every matter may be established*. If he refuses to listen to them, tell it to the church. If he refuses to listen to the church, treat him like a Gentile or a tax collector.

Matthew 18:15-17

Here, Jesus said that we should approach people one on one. This is very important because this is where conflict often gets worse. Instead of speaking to the person in sin, people commonly tell everybody else about the sin without bringing it first before him or her. Then, we should take one or two others. If they still will not respond, we should bring it to the church. If they still won't respond, they should be disciplined by the church.

Observation Question: How does Nehemiah demonstrate these steps of biblical confrontation?

1. First, Nehemiah challenged the leaders privately.

Application Question: Why is first approaching the person(s) privately important?

- It is important because there could be a misunderstanding.

- It is important because sometimes the people are struggling with sin and really want help.

- It is important because if they hear about the rumors or the fact that you were talking behind their back, you could possibly lose a friend and an opportunity for ministry. Scripture says a "whisperer separates friends" (Prov 16:28).

2. Second, Nehemiah challenged the leaders publicly.

It is clear that the leaders did not respond to Nehemiah when he challenged them privately so he challenged them publicly. This is where one might say Nehemiah departed from the pattern given by Christ. Instead of bringing one or two people, he immediately calls an assembly. Christ taught that it should be taken to the assembly after bringing one or two people for a second confrontation. Matthew 18:16 says this: "But if he does not listen, take one or two others with you, so that *at the testimony of two or three witnesses every matter may be established*".

However, the principles applied by Nehemiah are still practically the same. Jesus taught that the second confrontation was to confirm the sin— essentially to gain more evidence that the sin was happening. Two or three witnesses was the minimum amount of witnesses needed to convict anyone of a crime according to Deuteronomy 19:15. It said, "A single witness may not testify against another person for any trespass or sin that he commits. A matter may be legally established only on the testimony of two or three witnesses."

But, in Nehemiah's situation the leaders' sin was public; everybody knew about it, and therefore, it did not need to be established by the testimony of two or three. Thus, Nehemiah was still following the heart of Christ's teaching. After confronting them one on one, he publicly challenged them to repent.

This is something that we rarely see happen in our churches. Someone is living in sin, getting drunk on the weekends and then leading worship on Sunday. However, nobody wants to rock the boat so they say nothing. But Paul said, "a little yeast affects the whole batch of dough" (1 Cor 5:6). Sin spreads rapidly, and that's why it must be confronted.

We must confront in love with wisdom and discernment, and if they don't respond, then it should be done again with one or two more witnesses to confirm. And if they still don't respond, then it becomes a matter for the church. If they still don't respond after it has been confronted publicly, they should be shunned and removed from the congregation until they repent. This public confrontation will help others to fear God and turn from their sin. Paul said something similar to Timothy about rebuking an elder in sin, "Do not accept an accusation against an elder unless it can be confirmed *by two or three witnesses*. Those guilty of sin must be rebuked before all, as a warning to the rest" (1 Tim 5:19-20).

Again, it is implied that this elder had not repented, and therefore, it would need to become public. The public rebuke is so that they will feel ashamed and be led to repentance, but it's also meant to warn the church. This is something that needs to be restored to the church so we can be holy and have the power and effectiveness God desires for us.

When we choose to not confront and rebuke, then not only are we hurting the person in sin, but we are hurting the church as well. Sin will start to spread in the church and slowly destroy it (cf. Gal 5:9).

Now, this particularly applies to the church and its members; however, the principles can be applied at a school, a work place, or simply with friends and family. Meet with the person privately, then with one or two others for further accountability, and then it may be wise to bring the parties in conflict together or to bring it before the community. If they still don't respond, there will be a need for separation or some type of discipline if possible (cf. 1 Cor 5:11-13). The purpose of this is to help the erring person become convicted of their sin, to protect them from further consequences of sin (cf. James 1:14-15, Heb 12:5-12), to turn them back to God, and it is also to protect the community.

Conflict in churches and communities often escalate because people don't follow a biblical method of confrontation. Instead of meeting privately, rumors develop, creating anger and separating friends. Instead of confronting publicly those who are unrepentant, it is swept under the carpet and because of that, sin spreads.

Another example of church discipline is seen in Acts 5. In this chapter, God disciplined Ananias and Sapphira for their public sin. In the story, God killed them for lying in front of the whole church about selling their land and how they used the profit. What's interesting is that after this account, we have two seemingly conflicting statements. Look at what the text says:

> None of the rest dared to join them, but the people held them in high honor. More and more believers in the Lord were added to their number, crowds of both men and women.
> Acts 5:13-14

No one wanted to join the church (v. 13). However, God kept saving and adding to their number (v. 14). This was church growth through church discipline. God adds people to a healthy church. Why add people to a church that is unhealthy? Why send people to a church where there is a cancer that is affecting everybody, and nobody is willing to cut it out?

God wants to send people to a healthy church. This is a wonderful truth that godly leaders must practice in order to protect and to restore their communities.

Application Question: In what ways have you seen disorder in a church, a community, or other relationships for lack of using a biblical method of confrontation? In what ways have you seen or experienced church discipline? If you have, what was the process and result?

To Resolve Conflict, Godly Leaders Must Encourage the Fear of the Lord

> Then I said, "The thing that you are doing is wrong! Should you not conduct yourselves in the fear of our God in order to avoid the reproach of the Gentiles who are our enemies?
> Nehemiah 5:9

One of the ways that Nehemiah challenged the nobles to repent was by the fear of the Lord. The nation of Israel had previously been punished and kicked out of the land of Israel. They had already become a laughing stock to the nations surrounding them in their humble return. These were all part of God's discipline

111

on the nation for their sin (cf. Deut 28:32, 37). Therefore, he warned them, "Don't you fear God? Do you want God's judgment to fall on us again?"

This also is a very effective tool for us to use in conflict resolution. In Matthew 18:23-35, Peter approached Jesus and asked how many times he should forgive someone. "Seven times?" he asked. Jesus replied, "No, seventy times seven" (KJV). Jesus then gives a story of a master who punished a servant for not forgiving another servant.

In the story, a master forgave his servant a great deal of money, but the servant imprisoned his own servant for a far less debt. When the master heard about this, he became angry and put this servant in prison and had him tortured. Look at what Christ says in Matthew 18:33-35:

> Should you not have shown mercy to your fellow slave, just as I showed it to you?' And in anger his lord turned him over to the prison guards to torture him until he repaid all he owed. So also my heavenly Father will do to you, if each of you does not forgive your brother from your heart."

Christ told his own disciples that they would be turned over to the torturers if they didn't forgive from the heart. Now, because we know these disciples were saved, we do not believe this discipline had anything to do with hell. Christ's sacrifice paid the eternal penalty for our times of unrighteous conflict, just as it did our other sins. But, if we don't forgive others, God will not forgive us (Matt 6:14). In fact, like Christ taught, he will often hand us over to torturers, in order to bring us to repentance.

These torturers seem to be the devil and his demons, sent to discipline a believer. We see Paul command the Corinthian church to hand an unrepentant man over to Satan (1 Cor 5:5). We also see God discipline King Saul through a tormenting demon (1 Sam 16:14). Christ motivated the disciples to forgive by the discipline of God, the fear of God. He promised to send them to the torturers if they would not repent.

Often in counseling others in conflict, I commonly challenge them, as Nehemiah and Christ did, with the "fear of God," and specifically the promise of discipline in Matthew 18 for lack of forgiving from the heart. He disciplines everyone he loves (Heb 12:6), and therefore, we should have a healthy fear of God's discipline, especially in the area of conflict. Proverbs 9:10 says, "The beginning of wisdom is to fear the Lord."

Application Question: How do we develop a healthy fear of the Lord? Have you ever tried to motivate someone through fear of God's discipline? If so, how did you do it, and how did the person respond?

To Resolve Conflict, Godly Leaders Must Consider Evangelism

> Then I said, "The thing that you are doing is wrong! Should you not conduct yourselves in the fear of our God in order to avoid the reproach of the Gentiles who are our enemies?
> Nehemiah 5:9

Interpretation Question: Why does Nehemiah mention avoiding "the reproach of the Gentiles who are our enemies"? In what way was this meant to motivate them towards repentance and reconciliation?

Now when Nehemiah motivated the nobles by fearing God, he also mentioned "the reproach of the Gentiles." This could mean that God would use the Gentiles to discipline Israel as he did through Babylon, Assyria and many other nations. I'm sure it did mean that, but it was probably so much more. God had called Israel to be a light to the Gentiles. They were to be conduits of God's grace, leading many to faith. However, when they were walking in sin and under God's discipline, they forfeited their witness to the world.

It has often been said the "greatest cause of atheism is Christians." A lifestyle that does not match up to Jesus will often push people away from God. In the same way, Nehemiah is probably motivating the nobles to reconcile and do right because of their witness to the nations around them.

Remember Christ's prayer in John 17:20-23:

> "I am not praying only on their behalf, but also on behalf of those who believe in me through their testimony, that they will all be one, just as you, Father, are in me and I am in you. I pray that they will be in us, so that the world will believe that you sent me. The glory you gave to me I have given to them, that they may be one just as we are one—I in them and you in me—that they may be completely one, so that the world will know that you sent me, and you have loved them just as you have loved me.

He said that the church needed to be unified to let the world know that God sent the Son. Unity affects evangelism! Therefore, when churches are splitting, when Christians are divorcing, fighting over doctrine, and separating, the world says, "No, I really have no reason to believe in Jesus or to want what you claim to have."

113

Therefore, we should also encourage people to reconcile not only out of the fear of God, but also because of our witness to the world around us. It is sobering to consider that many times the greatest hindrance to world evangelism is probably church unity. And also, from a personal basis, somebody's eternal salvation or condemnation could depend on my reconciliation of a relationship in conflict.

Have you ever considered that Christian unity is an important aspect of evangelism? The world is always watching believers and what they see may affect their lives eternally. Evangelism is a serious motivation for conflict resolution.

Application Question: In what ways have you seen Christian discord and division push people away from Christ?

To Resolve Conflict, Godly Leaders Must Set the Example

> Even I and my relatives and my associates are lending them money and grain. But let us abandon this practice of seizing collateral! Nehemiah 5:10

Interpretation Question: Why does Nehemiah share that he and his brothers are also lending the people grain (Neh 5:10)?

While challenging the leaders of Israel about their taxation and slavery of the poor, he told them about how he and his men were also lending money and grain. Why did he share this?

I think he shared this in order to show them how bad their sin was. Nehemiah and his brothers were also lending money, but they were not trying to get rich by taxing and enslaving the disadvantaged Jews.

Another practical principle can be seen in this section about resolving conflict. If we are going to resolve conflict we must practice what we preach. It is hard for a person to challenge someone in sin while, at the same time, walking in blatant rebellion in his own life.

In fact, when we have sin in our life, we will be less prone to challenge people at all. As a result, "prophetic preaching" is largely absent in the house of God today. It is hard to speak the oracles of God (cf. 1 Peter 4:11) when our own conscience condemns us. Not only will it dull a preacher's sword, but it will also remove the trust and respect of the people.

If we are going to be ones who make "every effort to keep the unity of the Spirit in the bond of peace" (Eph 4:3), we cannot do it without a holy life.

Listen to what Paul told Timothy: "Be conscientious about how you live and what you teach. Persevere in this, because by doing so you will save both yourself and those who listen to you" (1 Tim 4:16).

Paul said that it is not just what you say (orthodoxy), but it's also how you live (orthopraxy) that will save the hearers. If Nehemiah preached a good sermon but did not live it, he would have been ineffective.

Similarly, we must practice what we preach if we are going to resolve conflict. We cannot talk about others behind their backs and, yet, try to help them restore their relationships or get out of sin. In fact, we cannot have any willful sin in our lives, if we hope to be truly heard by others. We must have both a righteous life and right doctrine if we are going to save our hearers. Reconcilers must practice holiness.

Application Question: In what ways have you seen a compromised life take away from the effectiveness of a person's words or doctrine?

To Resolve Conflict, Godly Leaders Must Encourage Proper Restitution

> This very day return to them their fields, their vineyards, their olive trees, and their houses, along with the interest that you are exacting from them on the money, the grain, the new wine, and the olive oil."
> Nehemiah 5:11

Next, it is clear that when Nehemiah was helping bring reconciliation, he also established proper restitution. It would have been unjust for the nobles to only give back the land or let go of the slaves. They had to give everything back that was illegal including the "interest" that was against the Jewish law. They had to make full restitution.

In the Old Testament, God wrote many laws on restitution. Exodus 22:1 says, "If a man steals an ox or a sheep and kills it or sells it, he must pay back five head of cattle for the ox, and four sheep for the one sheep."

If a person had stolen an ox, he was to give a restitution of five oxen; if he had stolen one sheep, he was to give a restitution of four sheep. In the OT law, restitution was anywhere from 100% up to 500%.

Why would a person sometimes have to give back more than 100% restitution?

It seems to be based on equity or what was fair. If a person's ox was stolen, days of work and profit would be lost. If a person was cheated, not only

115

would there be a loss of money but also pain and suffering. Often, we see this type of restitution in our penal system.

Sometimes when we are reconciling or helping others reconcile, restitution may be needed as well. We see this in the story of Zacchaeus in the New Testament. When he started following Christ, he decided to make restitution for every time he had cheated someone. Look at what he says:

> But Zacchaeus stopped and said to the Lord, "Look, Lord, half of my possessions I now give to the poor, and if I have cheated anyone of anything, I am paying back four times as much!" Then Jesus said to him, "Today salvation has come to this household, because he too is a son of Abraham!
> Luke 19:8-9

We see that Zacchaeus promised to restore up to four times what he had cheated people. Therefore, Jesus responded by saying that salvation had come to Zacchaeus's house. His repentance was proof that he was born again.

In the same way, sometimes when we hurt somebody, simply saying "I'm sorry" will not be enough. It may be wise to make some sort of restitution, as the nobles in Israel were required to do. They restored everything that was unfair. This restitution would be proof that they were truly repentant and that they were sorry. When there is true repentance, there will always be the corresponding action which proves the repentance is genuine (cf. Matt 3:8).

We should keep this in mind as we minister to others in conflict. Sometimes in order to resolve conflict, we have to discern the proper restitution. In 1 Corinthians 6:1-5, the believers in the church were suing one another in courts before unbelievers. Paul said instead of suing one another, they should have set up wise men in the church to arbitrate between them. Listen to what he said:

> So if you have ordinary lawsuits, do you appoint as judges those who have no standing in the church? I say this to your shame! Is there no one among you wise enough to settle disputes between fellow Christians?
> 1 Corinthians 6:4-5

In cases like this, leaders may have to make wise decisions about restitution. Certainly, one would have to use principles from the Scripture, and they also may need to get wise counsel in order to make an equitable decision.

With that said, sometimes the loss is too great and cannot be fully restored, and when it is this way, surely God knows the hearts and gives his grace. Even in the event of this unfortunate situation, the wronged party must still practice forgiveness as Christ taught. They should remember that the Lord also forgave them a great debt that they could never provide a proper restitution for (cf. Matt 18:23-35).

Application Question: Have you ever seen, given, or received restitution from some injustice or conflict? Please share. What would be some good principles to use in discerning proper restitution?

To Resolve Conflicts, Godly Leaders Must Use Accountability

> They replied, "We will return these things, and we will no longer demand anything from them. We will do just as you say." Then I called the priests and made the wealthy and the officials swear to do what had been promised.
> Nehemiah 5:12

Interpretation Question: Why does Nehemiah summon the priests and make the nobles and officials take an oath?

After Nehemiah's public challenge and call for restitution, the nobles agreed to make their wrongs right. However, in response, Nehemiah called the priest and made the nobles swear to it. Why did he do that?

It is clear that Nehemiah understood a very practical management principle, "People will do a hundred percent of what you check." If a teacher never checks the students' homework after telling them to do it, the chances are that most times it won't get done.

Similarly, Nehemiah established an accountability system amongst the priests and ultimately before God as they took an oath. Setting up an accountability system when doing conflict resolution is one of the best ways to make sure things get truly resolved. This is especially important because conflict often has a strong emotional component. A person forgives, but later on, all the negative thoughts and emotions come back. As these thoughts and emotions come back, they need to forgive again in faith as an act of obedience to God. Often, accountability can help people work through this process.

How can we practice this?

We should seek godly accountability partners and invite them to speak into our lives or in the lives of those we are helping. Nehemiah didn't invite just anybody for accountability; he invited the priests, the most holy people in the nation. In the same way, we must find people who have integrity and wisdom to counsel and help hold others accountable. We can invite these people to ask intimate questions, for example: "How has your relationship with your wife been?," "How is your problem with your roommate going?," and "Are you responding in a Christ-like manner to this conflict?"

In fact, this is a wise principle for battling all sins: lust, idolatry, anger, etc. We should invite trustworthy, wise people to check on us periodically, giving them freedom to ask us hard questions, and also to challenge us. This is a tremendous way to grow spiritually as well as to resolve conflict.

James 5:16 says this: "So confess your sins to one another and pray for one another so that you may be healed. The prayer of a righteous person has great effectiveness."

James says that confession of sins and prayer is a powerful remedy in the life of a believer. God can bring healing to sickness, depression, or even strongholds. We must make great use of this in our battle against sin and also in the process of reconciliation.

Application Question: Have you ever seen accountability used in a conflict resolution situation? How did the accountability work? Who are your accountability partners, and how do they help you faithfully live for God and stay in right relationship with others?

Conclusion

How can godly leaders be more effective in resolving conflict in their own lives and with others?

1. To resolve conflict, godly leaders must not ignore problems.
2. To resolve conflict, godly leaders must develop a righteous anger.
3. To resolve conflict, godly leaders must be patient and self-controlled.
4. To resolve conflict, godly leaders must get counsel.
5. To resolve conflict, godly leaders must practice a biblical method of confrontation.
6. To resolve conflict, godly leaders must encourage the fear of the lord.
7. To resolve conflict, godly leaders must consider evangelism.
8. To resolve conflict, godly leaders must set the example.
9. To resolve conflict, godly leaders must seek proper restitution.
10. To resolve conflict, godly leaders must use accountability.

How Godly Leaders Handle Prosperity and Promotion

From the day that I was appointed governor in the land of Judah, that is, from the twentieth year until the thirty-second year of King Artaxerxes—twelve years in all—neither I nor my relatives ate the food allotted to the governor. But the former governors who preceded me had burdened the people and had taken food and wine from them, in addition to forty shekels of silver. Their associates were also domineering over the people. But I did not behave in this way, due to my fear of God. I gave myself to the work on this wall, without even purchasing a field. All my associates were gathered there for the work. There were 150 Jews and officials who dined with me routinely, in addition to those who came to us from the nations all around us. Every day one ox, six select sheep, and some birds were prepared for me, and every ten days all kinds of wine in abundance. Despite all this I did not require the food allotted to the governor, for the work was demanding on this people. Please remember me for good, O my God, for all that I have done for this people.
Nehemiah 5:14-19 (NET)

How should godly leaders handle prosperity and promotion?

When we look at Christendom, we often find two extremes on the issue of wealth. We have those who look at Christ's commands to leave all and follow him. They see a poor savior, disciples who gave up their jobs and careers to follow Christ, and they would advocate living on the bare necessities. In fact, in the middle ages, Christians were encouraged to take a vow of poverty and enter the monastery as they followed Christ.

Today, we also have the other extreme in the prosperity gospel. They would look at God's covenant with Israel in the Old Testament where God promised them wealth and health if they were obedient, and sickness, poverty, and curses if they sinned. They would say that because Christ took our curse, we all are called to be rich, wealthy, and healthy. Both of these views are wrong.

119

However, as we look at Nehemiah, we find a balanced model of how Christians should handle prosperity and promotion.

In the book of Nehemiah, Israel had previously been judged by God and was no longer really a nation. They had been taken as captives to Babylon and scattered to other nations. During the days of Nehemiah, only a small remnant who had returned from captivity was dwelling in the land, and they didn't even have walls around the capital city, leaving them open for constant attacks.

Nehemiah left his job as cupbearer to the king of Persia to rebuild the walls of Jerusalem and bring revival in Israel. He does this under distress and attack from both outside and inside. At this point in the narrative, the wall is not finished, but Nehemiah takes a moment in his diary to talk about his time as governor. At some point while serving Israel, he was promoted to governor for at least 12 years (cf. Neh 5:14), and he shares how he handled the promotion and the new prosperity.

This is very important to us, not only because of the doctrinal division amongst Christians on the believer's relationship to wealth, but also because of the dangers of wealth. Listen to these two quotes:

Thomas Carlyle, a Scottish historian, once wrote, "Adversity is hard on a man; but for one man who can stand prosperity, there are a hundred that will stand adversity."[24]

Charles Swindoll said something similar:

Few people can live in the lap of luxury and maintain their spiritual, emotional, and moral equilibrium. Sudden elevation often disturbs balance, which leads to pride and a sense of self-sufficiency—and then, a fall. It's ironic, but more of us can hang tough through a demotion than through a promotion. And it is at this level a godly leader shows himself or herself strong. The right kind of leaders, when promoted, know how to handle the honor.[25]

The question we must ask ourselves is, "Are we prepared to handle promotion and prosperity?" Prosperity has destroyed many in the church. Scripture demonstrates this truth very clearly. We saw this in the history of Israel. Before Israel entered the promised land, which was dripping with milk and honey, God said this through Moses:

Then when the Lord your God brings you to the land he promised your ancestors Abraham, Isaac, and Jacob to give you—a land with large, fine cities you did not build, houses filled with choice things you did not accumulate, hewn out cisterns you did not dig, and vineyards and olive

groves you did not plant—and you eat your fill, be careful not to forget the Lord who brought you out of Egypt, that place of slavery.
Deuteronomy 6:10-12

This is the very thing that happened to Israel. It was when they were not being persecuted, when they were not in war; in fact, it was at the height of their prosperity that they fell away from God the farthest. We saw this with Solomon. Solomon was the wisest king ever and probably one of the wealthiest; however, when there was prosperity and peace all around, he began to worship the gods of his wives and led Israel away from God. It was because of Solomon that the kingdom of Israel divided.

Solomon fell in prosperity and so did his father, David. When things were going well in Israel, David counted his army with pride and God judged him for it (2 Samuel 24, 1 Chronicles 21). He also used his power to take another man's wife. He misused his prosperity.

Well, how then should we handle prosperity? The wisest man on the earth failed the test of prosperity. The man after God's own heart failed it before that. How do we escape its dangers?

Often in churches, we teach a great deal on trials and God's redemptive purposes in them, but we don't hear much about how to properly handle success and wealth. Scripture talks often about the dangers of wealth and prosperity. With money specifically, Christ speaks about it more than heaven and hell.

What are Nehemiah's secrets to being right towards God, even in the midst of success and promotion? How can we protect ourselves from the dangers that come with wealth and prosperity? In this study, we will see eight leadership principles about handling prosperity and promotion.

Big Question: How did Nehemiah respond to his promotion as governor of Israel? What can we learn about how a godly leader handles prosperity and promotion?

Godly Leaders Must Consider Accepting Prosperity and Promotion as from the Lord

From the day that I was appointed governor in the land of Judah, that is, from the twentieth year until the thirty-second year of King Artaxerxes—twelve years in all
Nehemiah 5:14

Before we consider how to protect ourselves from the dangers, it must first be said that Christians must be willing to consider accepting prosperity and promotion as from the Lord. Again, we see that Nehemiah came to Israel with the best intentions to honor God by helping Israel rebuild the wall; however, when presented with the opportunity to become governor, he didn't turn it down. He accepted it.

Often in the church, Christians tend to not seek the Lord for success, promotion, or leadership positions, whether in school, work, or government. Sometimes, it's even looked at as "unspiritual" or "worldly" to pursue or accept such things.

However, it must be understood that Scripture teaches that promotion is a gift from God. Consider what Asaph said in Psalm 75:5-7:

> Do not be so certain you have won! Do not speak with your head held so high! For victory does not come from the east or west, or from the wilderness. For God is the judge! He brings one down and exalts another

Asaph said that exaltation comes from the Lord. The word "exalt" means to "increase." Increase comes from God; it is not a bad thing. Often times in conservative, Bible preaching churches, we hit hard on the "prosperity camps" and for good reason. However, there is some truth to the view, though it has been taken to an unbiblical extreme.

I believe Scripture would support the fact that it is OK and good for Christians to seek the Lord for promotion—to seek the Lord for success—for the purpose of spreading his kingdom and his fame. One person in Scripture prayed an extremely, dangerous prayer to be blessed and prospered by God and his name was Jabez. Does anybody remember Jabez? Let's listen to his prayer:

> Jabez called out to the God of Israel, "If only you would greatly bless me and expand my territory! May your hand be with me! Keep me from harm so I might not endure pain!" God answered his prayer.
> 1 Chronicles 4:10

Jabez prayed for God to expand his territory, for God to expand his influence. We even see something similar in the messiah's prayer as predicted in the Psalms. Look at what God said to Jesus: "'You are my son! This very day I have become your father! Ask me, and I will give you the nations as your inheritance, the ends of the earth as your personal property" (Psalm 2:7-8).

He said to the messiah, "Ask me, and I will give you the nations as your inheritance." I heard this about the founder of the Navigators which is a Christian organization that focuses on Bible memory: the founder prayed to God with his hand on the globe, asking to be used, and now that ministry spans the entire globe.

I would say that part of the reason so many churches and Christians are so ineffective is because their prayers, and therefore, their faith is so small. They are not willing to pray dangerous prayers for God to use and expand their territory. "God open the doors for this church." "Lord give me the youth. I want to be used in a special way to reach the youth of my nation." "Lord give me Korea; use me to expand your kingdom here in a special way." The book of James says this: "You do not have because you do not ask" (4:2).

Let us remember that in the same way God exalted Nehemiah, God exalted Joseph to second in command in Egypt so he could save many souls (Gen 50:20). He exalted Daniel to demonstrate the glory of God in the idolatrous kingdom of Babylon. Proverbs says, "When the righteous are in authority, the people rejoice: but when the wicked beareth rule, the people mourn" (Proverbs 29:2 KJV).

The world is looking for righteous people to reign, to be in authority, and to serve. The first thing we must learn from Nehemiah is our need to consider accepting promotion and prosperity, which also implies a challenge to broaden our prayers and our faith.

Now with this said, let me add a disclaimer. Satan can promote people as well. Satan showed up to Jesus in Matthew 4:8-9 and said, "I will give you the nations if you bow down to me" (paraphrase). The enemy often offers promotion in order to fulfill his ungodly agenda, and therefore, we must be careful. Promotion that causes us to neglect serving God, our family, and the church is not of God.

Listen, God made you a part of his body, and you have a very specific role as a part of it. We must consider the church and our role in it. I'm leery of jobs that will keep one out of worship or demand so much that one can't faithfully serve God.

Moreover, promotion that causes a person to neglect his family is also not of God. Many godly men have turned down promotion or exaltation because it would take them away from their children and their wives. Too many marriages and families are destroyed at the altar of promotion.

Nehemiah teaches us that godly leaders must consider the possibility of accepting a promotion. Nehemiah, Daniel, Joseph, and David were promoted so that they could have more impact for God's kingdom. And, therefore, we must consider it as well.

Next, we will consider how to handle it when God does bring us prosperity and promotion.

Application Question: In what ways are you seeking for the Lord to expand your territory and ministry so you can affect more people? Are you afraid to pray these types of prayers? Why or why not?

In Prosperity and Promotion, Godly Leaders Must Often Give Up Their Privileges to Not Hinder the Work of God

> From the day that I was appointed governor in the land of Judah, that is, from the twentieth year until the thirty-second year of King Artaxerxes—twelve years in all—neither I nor my relatives ate the food allotted to the governor.... I gave myself to the work on this wall, without even purchasing a field. All my associates were gathered there for the work.
> Nehemiah 5:14, 16

What do we learn next from Nehemiah?

Promotion often comes with many perks that could destroy a person. What types of perks? It often means allowances: greater money, benefits, and sometimes even more privacy. Often those in leadership have an amount of freedom that those not in management do not have. How did Nehemiah handle the privileges given to him?

We see that Nehemiah chose to not take advantage of some of his rights, such as the food allotment (v. 14) and the right to purchase land (v.16). The people were in poverty, and he could have easily purchased great amounts of land which wouldn't have been a sin. However, he gave up his rights to do this.

Interpretation Question: Why did Nehemiah choose to not take advantage of the rights of food and property when it was not wrong to do so?

It seems that he chose to relinquish his rights in order to not hinder his ministry. We see something similar in the life of Paul. In 1 Corinthians 9, he says that he chose to give up his right to receive pay from the church (v. 12). Why? Certainly, Jesus taught he who preaches the gospel should live by the gospel (1 Cor 9:14). And similarly, the rest of Scripture teaches that pastors have a right to be paid (1 Tim 5:17). Listen to the reason Paul gives:

If others receive this right from you, are we not more deserving? But we have not made use of this right. Instead we endure everything so that we may not be a hindrance to the gospel of Christ.
1 Corinthians 9:12

He gave up his right so that it would not hinder his ministry. In Greek culture, there were many paid "orators" and many of them were greedy, doing it just to get money and not caring about the people. He chose to not take any chances of being associated with the "hirelings" and potentially hinder the gospel of Christ.

No doubt, Nehemiah did not want to hinder his opportunity to serve through taking advantage of his privileges, which included the food allowance and the opportunity to purchase property. The previous governors had overburdened the people (v. 15), and he did not want to be associated with them. How could he feast off their taxes when everybody else was poor? How could he buy up their land while they were going bankrupt? Would not using his privileges cause people to question his motives and possibly bring dishonor to God? He would have been perceived as a hireling instead of a good shepherd.

In the same way, God might want you to give up some rights in order to not hinder your ministry in serving him. Romans 14:21 says this: "It is good not to eat meat or drink wine or to do anything that causes your brother to stumble."

See many, especially young Christians, only ask themselves, "Is this wrong?" "Is it wrong for me to drink alcohol?" "Is it OK for me to smoke?" "Is it wrong for me to kiss my girlfriend?" It may not necessarily be wrong, but one may need to ask more questions.

Application Question: What are some good questions to ask in considering our privileges and freedoms?

1. "Could this potentially harm others or my ministry?"

Many things are not bad in themselves, but we must weigh their value based on how they could potentially affect others. Again, "It is good not to eat meat or drink wine or to do anything that causes your brother to stumble" (Romans 14:21).

2. "Will this edify me and others?"

See some things that we do are not clearly sin, but they may not be good either. They don't help us or others. We need to choose what is "best" and

125

not simply what is "OK" or "good." Paul said, "'Everything is lawful,' but not everything is beneficial. 'Everything is lawful,' but not everything builds others up" (1 Corinthians 10:23). Is it constructive? Will it help me and others?

3. "Could this potentially master me or make me addicted?"

Consider what Paul says again: "'All things are lawful for me'—but not everything is beneficial. 'All things are lawful for me'—but I will not be controlled by anything" (1 Corinthians 6:12).

One of the many dangers that comes with prosperity is the possibility of being mastered or overcome by them. Many things that are not sin such as: riches, alcohol, cigarettes, Facebook, popularity, approval, video games, movies, Internet, etc., have the possibility of mastering us and making us sin against God.

We live in a wealthy society that has many privileges that others do not have. But, we also live in a society of addictions, in part because of these privileges. In the U.S., people are seeking insurance to cover addictions to video games. I had a student fail out of his freshman year of college because he was playing video games all day. The wealth we have is not sin; the privileges we have access to are not wrong. But we must ask ourselves, "Could this cause harm? Will this edify me or others? Could this privilege master me?" Most people don't ask themselves these questions.

Many Christians are unprofitable for the kingdom because they are addicted to their phones, addicted to the Internet, addicted to money, and for many the resulting consequences are neglecting God and even sometimes family. Yes, privileges have the ability of mastering us, and we must be careful of this possibility. Addiction is simply another form of idolatry—it is sin. It's a form of mastery, and only God should be our master.

When I was single, I wouldn't own the Internet, and I wouldn't own cable either because I was afraid of being mastered by them. I am compulsive. Whatever I do, I'm typically consumed with and passionate about. Because of that, as a young Christian, I had to choose to let go of some privileges that I wasn't prepared to be disciplined with.

No doubt, when Nehemiah looked at all the food that was allotted to him as governor, he felt like it would not be beneficial. It was not wrong. Certainly, he had earned it, but he probably realized that it was not beneficial. It could hinder his ministry.

Feasting and buying up property while everybody was poor would have probably hindered his leadership as well. I have seen many people who don't want to come to church because the pastor is "flaunting" the finest clothes and the nicest car, and, even though this pastor may not be in sin, it opened a door for the enemy to accuse him.

That is why Paul gave up his right to receive money while serving in Corinth and many other privileges. And that is why Nehemiah did as well.

In what ways has God called you to give up your privileges that may come with prosperity or promotion? Are you addicted to anything? Are there some things you are doing with your freedom that are causing or could cause others to stumble? If so, God may be calling you to give up those things.

This is an important discipline that must come with prosperity. We must give up our rights in some areas in order to not hinder our growth or ministry.

Application Question: What privileges or rights do you have to be careful of in order to be most effective in your ministry?

In Prosperity and Promotion, Godly Leaders Must Avoid Abusing Their Authority and also Be Willing to Bring Reform

> But the former governors who preceded me had burdened the people and had taken food and wine from them, in addition to forty shekels of silver. Their associates were also domineering over the people. But I did not behave in this way, due to my fear of God.
> Nehemiah 5:15

What do we see next? It seems clear that when Nehemiah took over as governor, he entered a big mess. The previous governors took advantage of the people for their own benefit. They overtaxed them so they could make more money. The assistants were "domineering"—meaning they were abusive to the people. This sounds a lot like the modern politics in many governments. The people in leadership are often corrupt and abusive.

This is not only common amongst the world, but it also happens to believers who are successful as well. We saw this with King Solomon. He abused his leadership by overtaxing the people (cf. 1 Kings 12:4), which contributed to his great wealth. He abused his authority by taking many wives; he had a thousand wives and concubines combined (cf. 1 Kings 11:3).

Often in leadership, there are many doors for promiscuity. We see this with our successful athletes, businessmen, and politicians. King Solomon, though a godly, wise man, abused his authority and success. Sadly, this even happens to those in the pulpit. One survey of pastors said that around 40% admitted to having had an affair.[26]

A person in leadership will always battle temptations to abuse their authority. To compound these temptations, a culture of abuse—a culture of corruption—often creates negative pressure to continue these compromises.

I remember working at a company where my boss would take vacation time and tell the employees to tell anyone who asked about him, that he was just out of the office. Therefore, he could have a day off without using his vacation. Each of our leaders would cover for one another so that they could enjoy extra vacation time. This became a corrupt culture, and, in order to set myself apart, I had to let them know I wouldn't be part of it.

As a godly leader, when God promotes you, don't be surprised if he calls you to take a stand and maybe even implement changes to the previous administration. Leadership does not always mean character. Often our leaders are people with major character flaws and many times God raises up new, godly leaders to bring change. We saw this with God raising up David when Saul became corrupt.

Nehemiah took the position and chose to not lead in the same way the previous leadership did. No doubt, this probably made him unpopular with the nobles and those serving in government beside him. All the assistants from the previous governors would have made less money, and then, probably, would have pressed Nehemiah to conform.

For many Christian students who enter the work force, they are often surprised to find a culture of sin including drunkenness and sexual immorality. Many work cultures not only tend to spend time in drunkenness but also in visiting with escorts. Many work cultures will frequent the bars and the brothels in the late hours. Sadly, in these cultures, cheating on one's spouse has become the norm and is considered acceptable.

As one who has worked on college campuses, I can say with confidence that academic cheating is an epidemic. There is very little integrity on our college campuses. What do you think happens when graduates, who commonly cheated in college, go to the work force? When one is unfaithful with little, he will be unfaithful with much.

Don't be surprised when God promotes you or you take a new job, only to find there is a need for reform. You will have to be willing to take a stand and say, "I'm not doing that" or "It won't be done that way anymore." This won't make you popular. In fact, it will cause persecution, and it may cost you your job. But this is what you will have to do in order to be faithful to God.

A common temptation that comes with success is the tendency to abuse one's authority. Nehemiah chose not to. Where others have failed, Nehemiah stood. He instead chose to clean up the government in Israel. God may choose to exalt you for the purpose of cleaning up the culture at a law firm, a business, a school, a church, or some other type of ministry. Oh yes, even churches commonly have an abusive culture as well, and it happens way too often. Some pastors seek to be the "King" of their church instead of its servant. It shouldn't be this way.

In prosperity and promotion, we must be disciplined with our privileges, even letting some go. We also must not abuse our authority.

Application Question: In what ways have you seen abuses of authority and privileges in the work place? How can Christians remain faithful in an ungodly work culture?

In Prosperity and Promotion, Godly Leaders Must Fear God

> But the former governors who preceded me had burdened the people and had taken food and wine from them, in addition to forty shekels of silver. Their associates were also domineering over the people. But I did not behave in this way, due to my fear of God.
> Nehemiah 5:15

Observation Question: Why did Nehemiah not misuse his privileges like the previous governors (v. 15)?

The text says that he didn't misuse his power because he feared God. The reason many will fall while in leadership is because they fear man more than God.

We saw this with Saul who was previously exalted from nothing to being the king of Israel. God told Saul to wipe out the Amalekites and to even kill their animals. However, when the prophet Samuel showed up, he said, "Why do I hear the noise of sheep?" (1 Samuel 15:14, paraphrase). Saul replied, "I have sinned, for I have disobeyed what the Lord commanded and what you said as well. For I was afraid of the army, and I followed their wishes" (1 Samuel 15:24).

Why did Saul fail as a leader? He failed because he feared people more than God. Scripture says the "fear of man is a snare" (Proverbs 29:25).

It was the same with the priest Aaron while in the wilderness with Israel. Moses was up on the mountain with God receiving the Ten Commandments, and in the valley, the people pressured Aaron to build a golden calf, and so he did (Ex 32). Aaron sinned because he feared man more than God.

129

Many, because of desire to be promoted or to have favor with a boss, peers, or friends, will sin because they fear man more than God. King Solomon probably experienced this as well, since he said it was a trap or a snare. Be careful of it.

A Christian leader will often be confronted with these temptations to fear man more than God and to love the world and the things of the world more than God. What made Nehemiah successful was his great fear and reverence of God. Listen to what Jesus told his disciples:

> "I tell you, my friends, do not be afraid of those who kill the body, and after that have nothing more they can do. But I will warn you whom you should fear: Fear the one who, after the killing, has authority to throw you into hell. Yes, I tell you, fear him!
> Luke 12:4-5

Interpretation Question: What does it mean to fear God?

To fear God means to reverence him, to stand in awe of God's greatness and power, but it also means much more than that. It means to fear his judgment. Scripture says our God is a consuming fire (cf. Heb 12:29). It says in Hebrews 12:6, "For the Lord disciplines the one he loves." He struck Ananias and Sapphira for lying in Acts 5. He brought sickness and death to those who were abusing the Lord's Supper in 1 Corinthians 11. First John 5:16 talks about the sin unto death. Oh yes, it is a dangerous thing for a child of God to live in rebellion.

Many people only have a conception of God's love, and they know nothing of fearing God's wrath. His wrath is an outpouring of his love; he loves us too much to allow us to live in outright rebellion.

Proverbs 9:10 says, "The beginning of wisdom is to fear the Lord." Many people don't live godly lives, especially when the temptation of prosperity comes because they don't fear him. I think sometimes our churches have handicapped our congregations by focusing only on God's love, his forgiveness, and missing his holiness and his wrath.

Do you fear God? It will keep you out of much sin.

Application Question: How does the fear of God affect you? How do we develop a healthy fear of God?

In Prosperity and Promotion, Godly Leaders Must Be Fully Devoted to the Work of God

But I did not behave in this way, due to my fear of God. I gave myself to the work on this wall, without even purchasing a field. All my associates were gathered there for the work.
Nehemiah 5:15b-16

What else did Nehemiah do to protect himself from the dangers that come with prosperity?

Nehemiah devoted himself to doing the work of God—he served God and the people. He focused his attention on what God had called him to do—building the wall. Often in prosperity, we are tempted to serve ourselves instead of God. People commonly become career or success focused, instead of God and others focused.

Ephesians 5:15-16 says, "Therefore be very careful how you live—not as unwise but as wise, taking advantage of every opportunity, because the days are evil."

Take advantage of every opportunity, why? Because the days are evil, there is a tendency to fall into sin and neglect God. Nehemiah practiced this. Instead of getting involved with the sins of the previous administration, he made the most of his opportunity. He got busy. Staying busy serving God will be a protection from the tendency to sin, whether in prosperity or in trial.

Prosperity, though it comes with many temptations, should be a time of great zeal for the Lord. God prospers us so that we can have more influence for his name. He gives us a job, a leadership position, an opportunity to increase our knowledge through schooling, all for the purpose of serving him more. Listen to what Paul said: "So then, dear brothers and sisters, be firm. Do not be moved! Always be outstanding in the work of the Lord, knowing that your labor is not in vain in the Lord" (1 Corinthians 15:58).

What has God called you to do in the current situation he has placed you? What is the work he wants you to be fully devoted to?

Nehemiah was building a wall to protect the people of Israel. Sometimes God places us at a school, a job, or a ministry to build a wall around others through constant prayer. Sometimes the work he has called us to is to build ourselves up. Sometimes he gives us extra time—extra freedom—so it can be used to study his Word, pray, and grow through serving. What is the work God is calling you to be fully devoted to?

Application Question: What opportunities for his kingdom has God placed before you? How can you make the most of it and be fully devoted in your service?

In Prosperity and Promotion, Godly Leaders Must Be Generous and Hospitable

> There were 150 Jews and officials who dined with me routinely, in addition to those who came to us from the nations all around us. Every day one ox, six select sheep, and some birds were prepared for me, and every ten days all kinds of wine in abundance. Despite all this I did not require the food allotted to the governor, for the work was demanding on this people.
> Nehemiah 5:17-18

What else should we practice in order to protect ourselves when God opens the door for prosperity or promotion? Consider what Nehemiah 5:17 says: "There were 150 Jews and officials who dined with me routinely, in addition to those who came to us from the nations all around us."

One thing that must stand out, along with this, is that Nehemiah said he didn't use the governor's food allowance (v. 18) and, yet, still fed 150 Jews and officials, plus those from the surrounding nations. How did he do this? He must have paid for it out of his own pocket. He generously served others.

This is another discipline we must practice while in prosperity. Nehemiah protected himself from abusing his prosperity by being extremely generous. He fed 150 plus people out of his own pocket every day. That gives us an idea of how much God prospered him as the governor of Israel. Instead of using his prosperity to serve himself, he served others. Nehemiah was a channel of God's blessing instead of a reservoir.

Similarly, we protect ourselves from the temptations that come with prosperity by sharing and being generous as well. In fact, Scripture commands those who have wealth to share. Look at what Paul says:

> Command those who are rich in this world's goods not to be haughty or to set their hope on riches, which are uncertain, but on God who richly provides us with all things for our enjoyment. Tell them to do good, to be rich in good deeds, to be generous givers, sharing with others. In this way they will save up a treasure for themselves as a firm foundation for the future and so lay hold of what is truly life.
> 1 Timothy 6:17-19

Being generous is one of the ways that we must deal with prosperity. Paul told Timothy to tell the rich to be generous and willing to share so that they may be rewarded in heaven. It should be noted that Paul says this right after telling Timothy how the love of money is the root of all kinds of evil and how many have fallen away from the faith because of it. First Timothy 6:9-10 says,

> Those who long to be rich, however, stumble into temptation and a trap and many senseless and harmful desires that plunge people into ruin and destruction. For the love of money is the root of all evils. Some people in reaching for it have strayed from the faith and stabbed themselves with many pains.

What's the remedy for this ever present temptation of loving money and wealth?

One of the remedies is to give it away—to be generous. When money and prosperity has its grip on you, sharing will help remedy it and do wonders for your spiritual life. Jesus similarly told the rich man to sell his possessions and give the money to the poor (Matt 19). Being generous will help protect us from the temptations and traps of prosperity.

It should also be noted that when Paul told Timothy the character of those selected for eldership in the church, he says that they must be "hospitable" in 1 Timothy 3:2. "Hospitable" means "a lover of strangers." Godly leaders should be characterized by loving people, not just family and friends, but even people they have just recently met.

He essentially says to Timothy, "You can tell if these potential elders can handle promotion by their practice of hospitality—if they are a lover of strangers."

Do you love strangers? Do you open your home and offer your resources to others? If you are faithful with little, you will be faithful with much. This will protect you from many temptations.

Most Christians live like the world when they experience increase. God gives them a raise, and what do they do? They say, "All for me! I'm going to get a new car, a bigger house, and buy the newest computer and the newest phone!" They don't realize that God gives to us so that we can be a channel of his blessings to others. We are already commanded in Matthew 6:19-20 to not store up riches on the earth. For that reason, our homes and possessions should look drastically different from the world since we have a command to not store up. Why store it up only to leave it behind? We should use our wealth to build God's kingdom.

Are you practicing generosity? It will prepare you for promotion, and it will also help to keep you holy when God does promote you.

Application Question: In what ways does being generous protect us from the temptations of loving money and abusing our prosperity? How has the practice of hospitality been a blessing to you? In what ways is God calling you to be more generous?

In Prosperity and Promotion, Godly Leaders Must Pray

> Please remember me for good, O my God, for all that I have done for this people.
> Nehemiah 5:19

Probably, the greatest protection one can have to stay faithful in prosperity and promotion is a vibrant prayer life. We see the cry of Nehemiah's heart while serving as governor. He, no doubt, lived in prayer in order to both be protected and to be successful in his ministry.

Again, prayer is a major theme of the book. Nehemiah prays eleven times throughout the book, and here, he prays again. Prayer is an act of dependence upon God. Wealth has a tendency to make us trust in our riches instead of God. Prayer is the opposite. To pray is to recognize our weakness and need for God.

In fact, it must be noted, that wealth and prosperity are often a deterrent to prayer. Most people pray when things are bad and forget to pray when things are good. Some even forget God all together. This is a natural, sinful, human tendency. However, we see this was not true of Nehemiah. Even while wealthy, he was living in dependence upon God, as he lived in prayer. It must be the same for us.

The practice of prayer will help keep us from pride, independence, and many of the temptations that come with promotion. We never see Nehemiah asking for prayer, but we can have no doubt that his spiritual brother, Ezra, and others were constantly lifting him up. We should ask for prayer while in leadership. As leaders, we will be the target of many attacks, and we need divine protection and strength during those attacks.

This was also a characteristic of Paul's life; he was constantly praying. At the beginning of most of his letters, he detailed how he prayed for the congregation (cf. Rom 1:9, Col 1:3, Phil 1:3-4). However, we also see him commonly ask for prayer as well (cf. Col 4:3-4, Eph 6:19-20). As godly leaders, we must similarly live in prayer and constantly ask for prayer.

Application Question: Why is prayer so important? How do you try to maintain a vibrant prayer life? How often do you ask for prayer?

In Prosperity and Promotion, Godly Leaders Must Pursue the Favor and Reward of God

> Please remember me for good, O my God, for all that I have done for this people.
> Nehemiah 5:19

Finally, one of the protections against the temptations of prosperity is seeking the reward of God. No doubt, Nehemiah was not primarily looking for earthly reward in Nehemiah 5:19, but he was probably looking for reward in heaven.

The Mosaic Law did promise that those who were obedient would receive great blessing on the earth (cf. Deut 28). They would receive either a blessing or a curse based on their faithfulness to God. Therefore, he probably did feel that God would bless him on the earth, but Jews also had an understanding of heaven and heavenly reward. Hebrews 11:8-10 says this:

> By faith Abraham obeyed when he was called to go out to a place he would later receive as an inheritance, and he went out without understanding where he was going. By faith he lived as a foreigner in the promised land as though it were a foreign country, living in tents with Isaac and Jacob, who were fellow heirs of the same promise. For he was looking forward to the city with firm foundations, whose architect and builder is God.

As the church, our promises are not primarily earthly but heavenly. Most of the New Testament promises are spiritual, including every spiritual blessing in heavenly places (Eph 1:3). Jesus said, "Don't store up riches on earth but riches in heaven" (Matt 6:19, paraphrase). He gave this as a motivation for holiness and service on the earth. He gave the motivation of treasures in heaven.

> "Do not accumulate for yourselves treasures on earth, where moth and rust destroy and where thieves break in and steal. But accumulate for yourselves treasures in heaven, where moth and rust do not destroy, and thieves do not break in and steal. For where your treasure is, there your heart will be also.
> Matthew 6:19-21

Christ said when we accumulate riches in heaven that is where our hearts will be. Nehemiah's heart was not on the earth. It wasn't about a new house, a

135

new chariot, a new farm, a new promotion, etc. His focus and primary concern was the reward in heaven and that enabled him to handle prosperity well. He cried out to God to "remember" him.

Many Christians can't handle promotion because their heart is secular and worldly. It is all about what they can have here; it is about their comfort here. It is about being recognized here and not in heaven. That's why they don't handle promotions well, and for that matter, they don't handle trials well either. When your heart is in heaven, it will allow for you to receive grace to live faithfully here on earth.

Nehemiah said, "Lord remember me." This is one of the things that protected Nehemiah. His focus was on the favor of God and not man or money. This will protect us as well from the dangers of prosperity.

Application Question: How can we live a life with an eye towards storing up reward in heaven? What does that mean and look like? Is it selfish to pursue heavenly rewards?

Conclusion

How should we deal with prosperity and promotion? We learn many things from looking at Nehemiah who was promoted to the position of governor while serving Israel.

1. Godly leaders must be willing to consider accepting opportunities for prosperity and promotion.
2. In prosperity and promotion, godly leaders must at times give up their rights in order to not hinder the work of God.
3. In prosperity and promotion, godly leaders must avoid abusing their authority and also be willing to bring reform.
4. In prosperity and promotion, godly leaders must fear God.
5. In prosperity and promotion, godly leaders must be fully devoted to the work of the Lord.
6. In prosperity and promotion, godly leaders must be generous and hospitable.
7. In prosperity and promotion, godly leaders must pray.
8. In prosperity and promotion, godly leaders must seek the favor and reward of God.

Recognizing the Tactics of the Enemy

When Sanballat, Tobiah, Geshem the Arab, and the rest of our enemies heard that I had rebuilt the wall and no breach remained in it (even though up to that time I had not positioned doors in the gates), Sanballat and Geshem sent word to me saying, "Come on! Let's set up a time to meet together at Kephirim in the plain of Ono." Now they intended to do me harm. So I sent messengers to them saying, "I am engaged in an important work, and I am unable to come down. Why should the work come to a halt when I leave it to come down to you?" They contacted me four times in this way, and I responded the same way each time. The fifth time that Sanballat sent his assistant to me in this way, he had an open letter in his hand...
Nehemiah 6 (NET)

What are common tactics that the enemy uses to hinder the work of God?

In this story, the Jews have been living in Israel without walls around the city of Jerusalem. Because they rebelled against God during the reign of the kings, the Lord judged them and sent them to exile in Babylon. After 70 years in exile, small remnants started to return to the land of Israel. In chapter 1, the Lord stirred Nehemiah, a man serving under the king of Persia, to come back to Jerusalem and inspire the remnant to rebuild the wall of the capital city and to help restore the worship of Israel.

In chapter 6, Nehemiah had completed the walls but had not added the gates. Because of the progress and the certainty of completion, the attacks of the enemy increased.

From the beginning of this restoration project, Nehemiah and the Israelites had enemies trying to stop the work. Sanballat and other Samaritans had been trying to discourage Israel. In chapter 2, they became angry and incensed that somebody had come to "seek benefit for the Israelites" (2:10). In chapter 4, when Israel began to build, they mocked them saying that even if a fox went on the wall it would fall (4:10). However, when they saw that the building of the wall was progressing, they decided to secretly form an army and come against Israel (Neh 4:8). When Nehemiah heard about this, he warned

Israel and set up guards to fight in case of invasion. The building continued as they worked with a brick in one hand and a weapon in the other (Neh 4:17), and now all that remained was adding the gates (6:1).

Because of this, the enemies of Israel make one last major assault, specifically targeting Nehemiah. If they can stop Nehemiah, they can discourage the people and finally stop this work. This is important for us to see and consider.

The contents of this chapter, I believe, apply specifically to the spiritual warfare of a believer and especially to leaders. In Ephesians 6, we are called to prepare for this warfare. Paul said, "For this reason, take up the full armor of God so that you may be able to stand your ground on the evil day, and having done everything, to stand" (Ephesians 6:13).

Some commentators have said we always live in "the evil day," the time between Christ's first and second coming in which we are always under the attack of Satan. However, Paul is clearly referring to times when the enemy increases assaults for the purpose of discouraging God's people and hindering his work. He said "when the day of evil comes." We mentioned this briefly in chapter 4.

I think we get a picture of the evil day when Satan attacks Job. He loses his family, his wealth, and his health, all in a very short time period. There is an all-out attack on Job that he must stand against. Similarly, here in chapter 6, we see many different types of attacks that the enemy brings against Nehemiah. Nehemiah is going through an "evil day," an evil season of assault on his life and ministry.

We also are called to do the work of the Lord. You may be a student, a teacher, a businessman, or a mom, but you should not be mistaken, you are doing the Lord's work. Nehemiah's building of the wall wasn't preaching the gospel, but it was something that everybody eventually realized was "accomplished with the help of our God" (Neh 6:16). It was a work of the Lord. In the same way, when we are doing the will of the Lord, wherever he has called us, we are working for him and, therefore, will incur the attacks of the enemy in various forms.

How do we prepare for the attacks, and how do we defeat these attacks?

Yes, we must put on the armor of God, which is primarily a righteous life. But along with that, we must be aware of the enemy's tactics. Satan wants to immobilize us and keep us from progressing in our spiritual lives, and therefore, he will come with many different attacks. He wants to keep us from building and completing the work that God has called us to. Because our enemy is both wise and relentless, we must be aware of his tricks and schemes.

Second Corinthians 2:11 says this: "so that we may not be exploited by Satan (for we are not ignorant of his schemes)."

One of the reasons many Christians become immobilized and ineffective in their callings is because they are unaware of the enemy's schemes or tactics. We will see many of these tactics as we study this text. This will be especially important for those in leadership roles just as Nehemiah was. If Satan had one bullet, he would take out the leader because it would affect more people.

Big Question: What were the attacks on Nehemiah in chapter 6? How does our enemy similarly attack our lives, those in leadership, and God's work through his people?

The Enemy's Tactic of Deception

> When Sanballat, Tobiah, Geshem the Arab, and the rest of our enemies heard that I had rebuilt the wall and no breach remained in it (even though up to that time I had not positioned doors in the gates), Sanballat and Geshem sent word to me saying, "Come on! Let's set up a time to meet together at Kephirim in the plain of Ono." Now they intended to do me harm. So I sent messengers to them saying, "I am engaged in an important work, and I am unable to come down. Why should the work come to a halt when I leave it to come down to you?"
> Nehemiah 6:1-3

In verse 2, Tobiah contacted Nehemiah to ask him to meet at a neutral site. The implication is that the enemies of Judah were seeking peace and wanted a meeting in order to accomplish this.

Nehemiah, the governor of Israel, realized it was probably politically wise for him to make peace. In fact, as we see at the end of the chapter, many Jewish nobles were putting pressure on him to make peace (v. 16-19). It would not be a good political move to ignore the pleas of the enemy to have a meeting.

However, the text says that Nehemiah discerned that they were trying to hurt him (v. 2), and Nehemiah, in response, said that he was engaged in an important work and could not go down (v. 3).

How did Nehemiah protect himself against the attacks of the enemy?

First, he did it by discerning the lies of the enemy. This is important for believers as well. Consider what Jesus said about Satan:

You people are from your father the devil, and you want to do what your father desires. He was a murderer from the beginning, and does not uphold the truth, because there is no truth in him. Whenever he lies, he speaks according to his own nature, because he is a liar and the father of lies.
John 8:44

Jesus spoke this to the Pharisees who were also trying to set him up so they could kill him. He told them that they were of their father the devil, who was a liar and the father of lies.

This is important for us to understand because Satan is always trying to deceive us as well. He lies to many Christians about their identity. He lies about their future. He lies about how they should think and what they should wear.

Many Christians struggle with great insecurities and fears because they have been listening to the lies of the devil. He makes them insecure about their body, their wealth, the car they drive, and the job they have. He says they must have this and that to be successful and accepted.

We have a whole society built on lies. We have lies about what is beautiful, lies about what it means to be successful, lies about God, lies about creation, etc. Scripture says the evil one is the prince of this world (John 14:30).

Why does he lie?

He lies because he ultimately wants to harm us and keep us from walking in the calling that God has for us. These lies sometimes come from people who love us, sometimes it may come from our family, sometimes it comes from our churches or friends. Certainly, it comes from the media that we entertain ourselves with.

This is important for us to understand as leaders, not only because the enemy will attack us with lies, but also, because we will be constantly ministering to people who have been lied to. They have accepted the lies of the enemy and are stuck in a spiritual trap (cf. 2 Tim 2:26). We will have to identify the lie and impart the truth of God's Word to minister to them. Like Nehemiah, we must be able to identify the lies of the devil.

Application Question: How can we develop discernment like Nehemiah so we won't be deceived by the enemy and also so we can better minister to others?

1. Discernment comes from knowing the Word of God.

Listen to what Hebrews says:

Anyone who lives on milk, being still an infant, is not acquainted with the teaching about righteousness. But solid food is for the mature, who by constant use have trained themselves to distinguish good from evil. Hebrews 5:13-14 (NIV 1984)

The writer of Hebrews is describing the church as spiritual infants because they lived on "milk" and not the solid food of the Word. He said that the believers had not matured because they did not constantly "use" Scripture and therefore struggled with distinguishing between good and evil, just like an infant.

In the context of Hebrews, they were being tempted to go back to the Jewish law, and he writes to show them that the New Covenant is so much better. Christ is better than Moses; Christ is better than angels; Christ is better than the High Priest. They couldn't discern this because of their lack of spiritual maturity and therefore were being drawn back into the Old Covenant.

With that said, numerous Christians are like this because they don't constantly use the Word of God. They use it on Sundays when somebody preaches it and maybe they read it on occasion, but they don't know how to apply it because they don't constantly use it. Therefore, they lack discernment and are prone to be deceived by Satan's lies.

They have no discernment in their dating relationships. They have no discernment about how to respond when mistreated. They can't discern what's best for their future or their career because they haven't developed a mature understanding of the Word of God. This opens the door for many deceptions from the enemy.

In the context of spiritual warfare, Paul calls for believers to put on the belt of truth, which is probably referring to the truths of Scripture. Ephesians 6:14 says, "Stand firm therefore, by fastening the belt of truth around your waist."

In ancient armor, it was the belt that held all the other pieces together. Therefore, in knowing the Word of God—God's truth—one will be protected from many of the enemy's attacks. This is true primarily because one wouldn't be fooled by many of the enemy's lies.

Are you keeping on the belt of truth? By constant use of it, you will be able to discern the lies of the devil.

What else will help us gain discernment?

2.   Discernment comes from understanding human nature.

Consider what was said about Christ in John 2:23-25:

141

Now while Jesus was in Jerusalem at the feast of the Passover, many people believed in his name because they saw the miraculous signs he was doing. But Jesus would not entrust himself to them, because he knew all people. He did not need anyone to testify about man, for he knew what was in man.

This text says many people believed in Christ but that he did not entrust himself to them because he knew all people. In verse 25, the apostle John is telling us why Christ did not entrust himself to them. The reason was not based on his "omniscience" but his "doctrine of man." He said it was because Christ knew what was in man.

Jesus understood that even though the crowds were following him, the heart of man is deceitfully wicked. He knew people were following him for food and for healing but not really for who he was. He knew that men were prone to run after a person who did something sensational, though they were not truly committed. Christ didn't entrust himself to these crowds because he understood the nature of man.

This is something that we need to understand as well to develop discernment. We need to understand the nature of man, the fickleness of man. Certainly, we learn this from looking at our own hearts and how we are tossed to and fro in our passions and our dreams. The person who seeks to understand himself will have a great understanding of man. But, it is also developed through studying the nature of man in Scripture. Men are like sheep that are constantly prone to go astray (cf. Isaiah 53:6). Man is prone to rebel against God and the things of God (cf. Rom 8:7).

This may seem cynical, but it is true. Christ didn't commit to the crowds because he knew the nature of man. We are prone to go astray. I have no doubt that Nehemiah's understanding of the Scriptural teachings about mankind, as well as his personal experience, gave him great discernment as he contemplated Tobiah and Sanballat's request. I think he understood the nature of man, like Jesus did, and as we should as well.

If we better understood the nature of man, it would keep us from disappointment when friends, family, or church members fail us. This understanding would also help us put our hope all the more in God.

While in seminary, I asked my professor how he kept from discouragement when people in his congregation fell away from God or when friends he served with in ministry stumbled into sin. I asked how he stayed strong. At that time, the church where I was youth pastoring was going through a split, and I was very discouraged. He responded with this, "I have a strong theology of sin." Essentially, he said, "I understand man's sin nature, and I also

142

understand Satan and temptation. This helps me minister to people and not become discouraged." He understood man.

If we are going to have discernment like Nehemiah, we need to start to develop a doctrine of man as well.

3.   Discernment comes from prayer.

This is what Paul prayed, for the church of Philippi:

And I pray this, that your love may abound even more and more in knowledge and every kind of insight so that you can decide what is best, and thus be sincere and blameless for the day of Christ.
Philippians 1:9-10

He prays for their love to abound in knowledge and insight, so that they could "decide," also translated "discern," what was best. The word "discern" is used of a metallurgist testing a metal to see if it was real. God wants us to have wisdom to test and see what is genuine and what is best. This comes through prayer.

Many Christians have an unwise, undiscerning love, which gets them in all kinds of trouble. They love lots of things which actually keep them from what is best. Paul is teaching that we need discernment with our love. "Following our heart" can actually get us in a lot of trouble. We often see people on TV say, "Just follow your heart." I want to say, "No! Don't follow your heart." Get wisdom for your heart, and one of the ways we do this is by praying for wisdom (cf. James 1:5, Phil 1:9-10).

Many Christians commonly fall to the lies of the devil because they lack discernment.

Are you a discerning Christian? Are you seeking to grow in discernment? We need it because we have an enemy who, from the beginning, has used the weapon of deception. We need it to protect ourselves and also to help minister to those who are trapped in some deception of the enemy.

Application Question: What are some common lies that trip up Christians in their spiritual life and keep them from progressing in the work God has called them to? What lies does Satan commonly use to trip you up?

The Enemy's Tactic of Persistence

So I sent messengers to them saying, "I am engaged in an important work, and I am unable to come down. Why should the work come to a halt when I leave it to come down to you?" They contacted me four times in this way, and I responded the same way each time.
Nehemiah 6:3-4

Next, Tobiah sent four requests to meet with Nehemiah and each time Nehemiah turned him down. The enemy in this narrative demonstrated tremendous persistence. It seems like he was trying to wear Nehemiah down so that he would eventually give in.

Interpretation Question: Can you think of other times the enemy used persistence in Scripture?

We see this all the time in the attacks of the enemy.

1.   The enemy used persistence in the story of Samson and Delilah.

Do you remember? It said that she constantly harassed him, seeking the secret of his strength, and he eventually gave in. Look at the text below:

She said to him, "How can you say, 'I love you,' when you will not share your secret with me? Three times you have deceived me and have not told me what makes you so strong." She nagged him every day and pressured him until he was sick to death of it. Finally he told her his secret. He said to her, "My hair has never been cut, for I have been dedicated to God from the time I was conceived. If my head were shaved, my strength would leave me; I would become weak, and be just like all other men."
Judges 16:15-17

She nagged and nagged and nagged until he relented and gave her the secret to his power. Satan is persistent in his attacks.

2.   The enemy used persistence in the story of Joseph and Potiphar's wife.

Genesis 39:10 says that "day after day" she kept asking him to lie with her. The enemy was persistent in seeking to draw Joseph into adultery.

144

3. The enemy used persistence in the story of Christ being tempted by Satan in the wilderness.

In Matthew 4, when Satan tempted Jesus, he came to him three times with three different temptations until he eventually left Jesus alone.

4. The enemy used persistence in Peter's temptation to deny Christ.

Several people approached Peter and said, "Weren't you following Christ?" and with each question there was a temptation to deny Christ. In response, Peter denied him three times.

We have all experienced this, whether it was with lust, depression, anxiety, foul language, or some conflict. Satan is persistent and the purpose of being persistent in warfare is to wear down the other side into compromise and eventually giving up.

This persistence is also used to create deeper strongholds of sin. The more we compromise with the world, the more we give into a particular sin, the greater and deeper its roots become and the harder it becomes to break it and follow Christ.

Satan uses persistence. We see this as Tobiah sends a letter four times to Nehemiah. The hope is that Nehemiah would be worn down, which would open the door to harm him.

How does Nehemiah reply to the four attacks?

He gave them the same answer each time. I am busy with a great work; I cannot come down. He made a stand and would not compromise. In the same way, when the enemy attacks us, God's desire for us is to stand and not give in.

Application Question: What can we learn from Nehemiah's reply about how to stand against persistent temptation?

We can stand against Satan's persistence by realizing the magnitude of the work God has given us. If you don't realize the magnitude of God's work and plan for your life, it will be easy to compromise.

Paul taught Timothy something with similar ramifications. Listen to what he said: "Take your share of suffering as a good soldier of Christ Jesus. No one in military service gets entangled in matters of everyday life; otherwise he will not please the one who recruited him" (2 Timothy 2:3-4).

Paul told Timothy that he should consider himself a soldier for Christ. Practically, when our soldiers go to battle, they are fighting not just to protect themselves, but to protect what is behind them. A soldier fights for something

145

greater than himself. He fights because the cause is more important than his life, his family, his country, and his home. And, ultimately, the attacker is not really after the soldier, he is trying to destroy or gain what the soldier protects.

Similarly, Satan's attacks on us aren't so much about us. The attacks are primarily about the kingdom of God and the things God is concerned about. It was the same with Nehemiah. Tobiah and Sanballat were not really after Nehemiah. They were after Nehemiah's work.

That's why Satan's attacks are so persistent. He attacks all day long through the TV, the Internet, music, through teachings in the classroom, family, friends, etc., and by these attacks many lose their God-given convictions and give up ground to the enemy. They give up ground on what a biblical marriage is, between a man and woman. They give up ground on the inerrancy and sufficiency of Scripture. Satan constantly says, "Did God really say?" "Is this really true?" He persistently attacks the inerrancy of Scripture, just as he has done from the beginning of time with Adam and Eve.

Like Nehemiah, we must know that what we are fighting for is too big to compromise. It's too great of a work. Compromise in sin will not only affect us, but it affects friends, family, our church, and even the lost. You must realize how important your battle is and what you are fighting for. If you don't, you will be prone to compromise. Scripture says, "When there is no prophetic vision the people cast off restraint" (Prov 29:18).

When a person doesn't realize God's purpose for his life, he will constantly accept the lies of the devil or give up when attacked. This is because he doesn't realize how important his battle is.

Nehemiah said, "I am engaged in an important work. I cannot come down." If we are going to stand against the tactics of the devil, we must not only have discernment but we must realize how important our battle is.

Application Question: What are some of the ways you have experienced the enemy's persistence? How can we better understand how great our work is so we will not be prone to compromise or be deceived?

The Enemy's Tactic of Slander and Gossip

The fifth time that Sanballat sent his assistant to me in this way, he had an open letter in his hand. Written in it were the following words: "Among the nations it is rumored (and Geshem has substantiated this) that you and the Jews have intentions of revolting, and for this reason you are building the wall. Furthermore, according to these rumors you are going to become their king. You have also established prophets to

announce in Jerusalem on your behalf, 'We have a king in Judah!' Now the king is going to hear about these rumors. So come on! Let's talk about this." I sent word back to him, "We are not engaged in these activities you are describing. All of this is a figment of your imagination." All of them were wanting to scare us, supposing, "Their hands will grow slack from the work, and it won't get done." So now, strengthen my hands!
Nehemiah 6:5-9

We see that the enemy also attacked Nehemiah through slander. Initially, he sent four personal messages to Nehemiah, but on the last one, he sent an open letter. Typically, when sending a letter to a government official, it would be a closed letter so that no one else could see the contents. However, Sanballat sought to pressure Nehemiah to respond to this meeting by slandering his name. Therefore, this open letter would not only have been read before Nehemiah but, probably, all along the way till it reached Nehemiah.

Sanballat lied about Nehemiah by saying he was trying to become king (v. 6-7). If this had gotten back to Artaxerxes, it could have potentially meant Nehemiah's life, as Persian kings were known for quickly getting rid of any resistance.

Similarly with believers, when Satan is trying to stop the work of God, slander and gossip are common tactics. The very name "devil" means "slanderer" or "accuser." That is what he does, he slanders God; he slanders people. He speaks slander to anyone who will listen. He will even slander us to our own ears—offering an array of condemnation. Consider the heavenly description of Satan in Revelation 12:10:

> Then I heard a loud voice in heaven saying, "The salvation and the power and the kingdom of our God, and the ruling authority of his Christ, have now come, because the accuser of our brothers and sisters, the one who accuses them day and night before our God, has been thrown down.

Interpretation Question: In what ways do we see Satan's slander throughout Scripture?

1.   Satan slandered Job before God.

In the book of Job, he told God that Job only followed him because God blessed him. He said, "Touch his family, his riches, his body and you'll see that he doesn't love you." He slandered Job before God.

147

2. Satan slandered God before Eve.

In the Garden of Eden, Satan said, "you will not die but you will become like God." Satan slandered God before Eve, implying that God was keeping the best from her and Adam.

3. Satan slandered Jesus through the Pharisees.

Christ was slandered and accused by the Pharisees. They trumped up many false witnesses against him to lie about him.

> The chief priests and the whole Sanhedrin were trying to find false testimony against Jesus so that they could put him to death. But they did not find anything, though many false witnesses came forward. Finally two came forward.
> Matthew 26:59-60

Satan commonly uses slander. He brings discord and problems to individual Christians and the church by bringing false accusations. That is the devil's character; he is a slanderer.

Application Question: Why does the enemy use slander?

1. Slander is meant to discourage the Christian.

Listen to what Nehemiah said: "All of them were wanting to scare us, supposing, 'Their hands will grow slack from the work, and it won't get done'" (Nehemiah 6:9).
A discouraged, depressed Christian isn't very productive in serving the kingdom of God. Often they become so focused on their problems that it weakens their hands in serving the Lord. Therefore, Satan works relentlessly to weaken and discourage the Christian, especially through slander.

2. Slander is meant to change the focus of the Christian.

Many times in seeking to defend our own reputation, we will find ourselves drawn away from focusing on God and the work of God. Satan slanders in order to distract the Christian.

3. Slander is meant to bring division.

148

Solomon said, "a gossip separates the closest friends" (Prov 16:28). The enemy will divide the church through slander, as he sends his whisperers around the church.

Observation Question: How does Nehemiah respond to the slander? How should we respond to gossip and slander?

1. Confront slander by telling the truth.

Nehemiah 6:8 says, "I sent word back to him, 'We are not engaged in these activities you are describing. All of this is a figment of your imagination.'"
Nehemiah resisted the devil with the truth. He simply told them it was not true. Many times we cannot do much more than that.

2. Confront slander by trusting in God.

We see this by the fact that Nehemiah prays and puts the situation in God's hands. Nehemiah 6:9 says, "All of them were wanting to scare us, supposing, 'Their hands will grow slack from the work, and it won't get done.' *So now, strengthen my hands!*"
It should be said that at times, in entrusting things to God, it might be best to just remain silent and not defend ourselves. Because rumors are false, many times the truth will become evident. There were times when Christ was accused falsely, but instead of defending himself, he chose to remain silent and entrusted the situation to God. Consider Matthew 26:61-63:

> "This man said, 'I am able to destroy the temple of God and rebuild it in three days.'" So the high priest stood up and said to him, "Have you no answer? What is this that they are testifying against you?" But Jesus was silent.

Certainly, we should confront lies with truth, but sometimes, in trusting God, we should allow him to be our defense (cf. Rom 12:19).

3. Confront slander by living a life that is above reproach.

The lies about Nehemiah seemed to have had very little traction. This was because Nehemiah was a man who was above reproach in the way he lived. As governor of Israel, he brought reform to the previous administration's corruptness; he never even used his food allotment but instead paid out of his

149

own pocket to meet his needs and others' (cf. Neh 5:14-18). He had a reputation for being upright.

It becomes hard for anyone to lie about you if you consistently live a life that is above reproach. We see nothing in this text about the Jews or the king of Persia responding to this gossip, and we can have no doubt that it was because of Nehemiah's chaste and holy behavior.

Listen to what Peter commanded of the Christians being persecuted in the Roman Empire: "maintain good conduct among the non-Christians, so that though they now malign you as wrongdoers, they may see your good deeds and glorify God when he appears" (1 Peter 2:12). Let this be true of us as well.

Application Question: Why does the enemy use slander in the lives of believers? Have you experienced slander or gossip? How did you handle the situation?

The Enemy's Tactic of Infiltration through False Teaching

> Then I went to the house of Shemaiah son of Delaiah, the son of Mehetabel. He was confined to his home. He said, "Let's set up a time to meet in the house of God, within the temple. Let's close the doors of the temple, for they are coming to kill you. It will surely be at night that they will come to kill you." But I replied, "Should a man like me run away? Would someone like me flee to the temple in order to save his life? I will not go!" I recognized the fact that God had not sent him, for he had spoken the prophecy against me as a hired agent of Tobiah and Sanballat. He had been hired to scare me so that I would do this and thereby sin. They would thus bring reproach on me and I would be discredited. Remember, O my God, Tobiah and Sanballat in light of these actions of theirs—also Noadiah the prophetess and the other prophets who were trying to scare me!
> Nehemiah 6:10-14

The next tactic of the enemy was to intimidate Nehemiah through false teaching. In this scenario, Tobiah and Sanballat hired a prophet named Shemaiah to deceive Nehemiah. His intent was to get Nehemiah to protect himself from the enemy by hiding in the temple (v. 10).

It seems that Shemaiah was trying to give the illusion of a "prophetic utterance." When we see the prophet "confined to his home," he probably was acting out the prophecy. This was common for prophets in the Old Testament. For example, we see Isaiah prophesy naked against Egypt and Cush to demonstrate how Assyria would conquer them, take them captive, and lead them naked in order to shame them (Isaiah 20). We also see that Hosea was called to marry a prostitute to represent how Israel was adulterous in her relationship with God (Hosea 1).

Shemaiah said, "Let's close the doors of the temple, for they are coming to kill you" (v. 10). This utterance seemed to be written in the form of a poetic couplet in order to trick Nehemiah into sin.[27] However, Nehemiah realized that this prophet had been sent by Sanballat to make him commit sin and to give him a bad name.

This is important because one of the common tactics Satan uses to try to lure people away from God and their callings is through false teaching and false prophets. Listen to what Christ said:

> "Watch out for false prophets, who come to you in sheep's clothing but inwardly are voracious wolves. You will recognize them by their fruit. Grapes are not gathered from thorns or figs from thistles, are they?
> Matthew 7:15-16

Jesus said to beware of false prophets. They are deceptive; they come to us in sheep's clothing. However, they are really wolves trying to destroy. We will be able to recognize them by their fruits.

The enemy has led many astray through his false teachers. In fact, Paul said this:

> For such people are false apostles, deceitful workers, disguising themselves as apostles of Christ. And no wonder, for even Satan disguises himself as an angel of light. Therefore it is not surprising his servants also disguise themselves as servants of righteousness, whose end will correspond to their actions.
> 2 Corinthians 11:13-15

Paul said that these people are in the church masquerading as servants of righteousness. This is still happening today, and we must be aware of it. Consider what Paul taught Timothy about the last days:

> Now the Spirit explicitly says that in the later times some will desert the faith and occupy themselves with deceiving spirits and demonic teachings, influenced by the hypocrisy of liars whose consciences are seared.
> 1 Timothy 4:1-2

Paul said that false teachers and false teachings will be common in the last days. Essentially a new cult of Christianity pops up every day, and many people from the church are often led into them. If this will continue to increase in these last days, how much do Christians need discernment more than previous generations?

Interpretation Question: How did Nehemiah know this was a false prophecy? How can we know?

1. He tested it by Scripture.

Nehemiah knew this was a false prophesy because he knew it would be sin for him to enter into the temple and close the doors. The fact that the prophet talked about closing the door indicates that the prophet was calling him to enter the Holy Place, which was only for priests (Num 18:7).[28] For him to enter would have been sin and possibly led to his death.

He, no doubt, tested this prophecy by knowing Scripture. God would never tell him to enter a forbidden area of the temple. A king in the Old Testament actually entered the Holy place to offer a sacrifice and God struck him with leprosy (cf. 2 Chr 26:19).

The best protection from false teachers and false doctrine is through diligent study of the Word of God. Listen to the story of the Bereans:

> Now the Bereans were of more noble character than the Thessalonians, for they received the message with great eagerness and examined the Scriptures every day to see if what Paul said was true.
> Acts 17:11 (NIV 1984)

We need Christians who are diligent in the study of the Bible and test everything that comes out of the teacher's mouth. God is calling all of us to be "noble" Christians.

2. He knew his identity.

Nehemiah said, "Should a man like me run away?" Nehemiah knew his identity as governor, but more than that, as a servant of God and the people of Israel. In serving God and man, he could not sin against them.

In the New Testament, this reality is also true of us. Part of the reason many of us fall to the deceptions of Satan is because we really don't know who

152

we are in Christ. When people don't know their identity, then they will run around trying to find it in everything.

You will find your identity in wealth, education, relationships, or even sin, if you don't know who you are in Christ.

For example, Christ taught his disciples about their identity as children of God in order that they would not struggle with fear and worry about future provisions. Listen to what he says:

> So then, don't worry saying, 'What will we eat?' or 'What will we drink?' or 'What will we wear?' For the unconverted pursue these things, and your heavenly Father knows that you need them. But above all pursue his kingdom and righteousness, and all these things will be given to you as well.
> Matthew 6:31-33

Jesus essentially said, "The world runs after what they will eat, drink or wear, but you have a Father who takes care of you. Stop living for food, drink and clothing. The world does that, but you don't have to because your Father will provide." Knowing your identity will help free us from the lies of the enemy.

One of the ways we will be kept from the myriads of false teachings that will continue to increase as we get closer to the end times is by knowing the Word of God. Nehemiah knew it would be sin to enter the holy place in the temple. It was only for priests. But Nehemiah also knew his identity as a leader of Israel and servant of God. Knowing who we are will protect us from much of Satan's tactics.

Application Question: In what ways has knowing your identity in Christ helped set you free from various sins and temptations?

The Enemy's Tactic of Psychological Warfare

> I recognized the fact that God had not sent him, for he had spoken the prophecy against me as a hired agent of Tobiah and Sanballat. He had been hired to scare me so that I would do this and thereby sin. They would thus bring reproach on me and I would be discredited. Remember, O my God, Tobiah and Sanballat in light of these actions of theirs—also Noadiah the prophetess and the other prophets who were trying to scare me!....They were telling me about his good deeds and then taking back to him the things I said. Tobiah, on the other hand, sent letters in order to scare me.

Nehemiah 6:12-14, 19

We have already dealt with this a little previously, but since it happens twice in this passage, I think it needs a separate point. One of the enemy's primary tactics against Nehemiah was psychological warfare, more specifically, fear. We just read it in Nehemiah 6:13-14 and again in verse 19. In bringing a false prophet, Tobiah and Sanballat were ultimately trying to make Nehemiah scared, which would have led him to sin. Tobiah also tried to scare him through the sending of letters (v. 19).

It's important to see the enemy's intent of bringing fear behind the tactic of false teaching and the letters because it was also the same intent behind the tactic of slander. Nehemiah 6:9 said, "All of them were wanting to scare us, supposing, 'Their hands will grow slack from the work, and it won't get done.'"

Behind the tactic of slander, false teaching, and the letters, the enemy was ultimately trying to make Nehemiah afraid. Satan also constantly tries to do that with us. He is always trying to promote fear, anxiety, and worry in those who follow God. In fact, Peter compares Satan to a roaring lion seeking whomever he may devour. First Peter 5:8 says, "Be sober and alert. Your enemy the devil, *like a roaring lion,* is on the prowl looking for someone to devour."

Why does a lion roar? The roar is strategic to paralyze his prey with fear, so he can attack and devour it. In the same way, Satan commonly uses fear to try to devour believers.

Tobiah and Sanballat were trying to use fear to immobilize and paralyze Nehemiah. They tried to frighten him with gossip, which could have led to the king of Persia's wrath. The enemy tried to attack him with the threat of killing him. The enemy was trying to use fear to hinder the work of God. Our enemy, Satan, uses fear for similar purposes with us.

Interpretation Question: Why does Satan use fear as a tactic with believers and leaders specifically?

1. Satan uses fear to stop believers from doing God's work.

    We see this in the Parable of the Talents. Matthew 25:24-25 says,

    "Then the one who had received the one talent came and said, 'Sir, I knew that you were a hard man, harvesting where you did not sow, and gathering where you did not scatter seed, so I was afraid, and I went and hid your talent in the ground. See, you have what is yours.'"

154

In Matthew 25, the person with one talent never used his talent. His reason was fear; he was afraid. We see this same excuse all the time with believers. They are afraid of failure; they are afraid of success; they are insecure about their abilities. Many are paralyzed and kept from doing God's work because of fear. They won't serve in the leadership of a ministry; they won't evangelize; they won't pray. Fear keeps them from doing the work of God.

In fact, we commonly see this tendency with many God called for service. We saw this with Moses and Gideon. Both struggled with fear when God called them to serve. Similarly, many Christians are paralyzed by some type of fear which limits their usefulness. The enemy uses psychological warfare.

2.   Satan uses fear to hinder the work of God in believers.

We see this in the Parable of the Sowers. Matthew 13:22 (NIV 1984) says, "The one who received the seed that fell among the thorns is the man who hears the word, but the worries of this life and the deceitfulness of wealth choke it, making it unfruitful."

The worries of this life kept the Word from ever producing fruit in the thorny ground. The Word of God is ineffective in many Christians because of the thorn of worry. Maybe they hear the Word and agree with it, but their fears keep the Word of God from producing fruit. They are worried about the future, about the past, about family, about career, etc. These worries hinder the work of God in them. It chokes the power of the Word of God.

3.   Satan uses fear to lead believers into sin.

That was the enemy's plan with Nehemiah. He was tempting Nehemiah to fear with the hope that he would run into the temple and sin against God, weakening the people and causing them to doubt his leadership.

It's the same thing in our daily lives. A person's fear and insecurities will often lead them to sin. Abraham was afraid of losing his life because of his beautiful wife, so he lied to Pharaoh and said she was his sister. Abraham was afraid to not have a child, so he married a second wife, Hagar, and sinned against God. Fear led him into sin, and it is the same for us.

4.   Satan uses fear to lead a believer into discouragement.

Nehemiah 6:9 says, "All of them were wanting to scare us, supposing, 'Their hands will grow slack from the work, and it won't get done.'"

155

Tobiah's and Sanballat's desire was to make Nehemiah too weak to complete the work. Similarly, as mentioned before, a discouraged, depressed Christian won't be very productive in serving the kingdom of God. Their fear weakens their hands in the work. Proverbs 12:25 says, "Anxiety in a person's heart weighs him down." Because of this, Satan works hard in sowing seeds of fear to weaken and discourage the Christian.

Application Question: How do we combat the tactic of fear?

1.   In order to defeat fear, we must recognize that fear is not of God.

Listen to what Paul told Timothy: "For God did not give us a Spirit of fear but of power and love and self-control" (2 Timothy 1:7).

Paul tells Timothy, God has not given you that spirit of fear. He is calling Timothy to recognize that his insecurities, probably in ministry, were not from God. Paul said to the Philippians, "Do not be anxious about anything" (4:6). We should not accept fear as from God. Certainly, there are healthy fears, such as the fear of the Lord, but fear that keeps us from serving God or trusting him is not from the Lord. In fact, Paul commands us to let the peace of Christ rule in our hearts (Col 3:15).

2.   In order to defeat fear, we must recognize our resources in God.

Paul did not simply tell Timothy to reject fear, he also gave him reasons. Look again at what he said: "For God did not give us a Spirit of fear but of power and love and self-control" (2 Timothy 1:7).

Paul said, "Timothy you don't need to be afraid because God has given you power for whatever task he has called you to. He has given you love for people who are difficult. He has given you discipline to get the task done. Timothy, there is no reason to be afraid. Look at the resources God has given you." God has given us these resources as well: power, love, and self-discipline.

3.   In order to defeat fear, we must pray.

In two of the times that Nehemiah was tempted to be afraid, both the open letter and the false prophet, how did he respond? He prayed.

All of them were wanting to scare us, supposing, "Their hands will grow slack from the work, and it won't get done." *So now, strengthen my hands!*
Nehemiah 6:9

156

Remember, O my God, Tobiah and Sanballat in light of these actions of theirs—also Noadiah the prophetess and the other prophets who were trying to scare me!
Nehemiah 6:14

Aren't we encouraged to battle fear similarly in the New Testament? Remember what Paul told the Philippians:

Do not be anxious about anything. Instead, in every situation, through prayer and petition with thanksgiving, tell your requests to God. And the peace of God that surpasses all understanding will guard your hearts and minds in Christ Jesus.
Philippians 4:6-7

We combat it by: (a) choosing not to fear, (b) choosing to pray about everything, and by (c) giving thanks in everything.

This is the reason so many are crippled by fear and kept from doing the work God has called them to do. They have chosen to be anxious, chosen to be afraid. They have chosen to not pray about everything. And finally, most Christians don't give thanks in everything. They complain, they get mad, they get angry, and therefore, the enemy still wins the victory. The promise of peace only comes to those who practice all these disciplines. Nehemiah battled fear through prayer and we must as well.

Do you realize you have an enemy just like Nehemiah?

There are events that are happening to you and your family through which the enemy wants to immobilize you with fear; he wants to cripple you with worries. However, God wants you to have peace so that you can continue serving him. Do you recognize the enemy's tactics?

Application Question: What are common fears that the enemy attacks you with? How do these fears immobilize or affect you? How is God calling you to get free from these fears in order to better serve him?

The Enemy's Tactic of Attacking Immediately after Victory

So the wall was completed on the twenty-fifth day of Elul, in just fifty-two days. When all our enemies heard and all the nations who were around us saw this, they were greatly disheartened. They knew that this work had been accomplished with the help of our God. In those

days the aristocrats of Judah repeatedly sent letters to Tobiah, and responses from Tobiah were repeatedly coming to them. For many in Judah had sworn allegiance to him, because he was the son-in-law of Shecaniah son of Arah. His son Jonathan had married the daughter of Meshullam son of Berechiah. They were telling me about his good deeds and then taking back to him the things I said. Tobiah, on the other hand, sent letters in order to scare me.
Nehemiah 6:15-19

It says in verse 15 that the wall was completed in fifty-two days and all the surrounding nations were afraid because they realized God had helped. You might expect an end to the memoirs of Nehemiah or a "They lived happily ever after" because the wall was completed, but that doesn't happen. The enemy attacked again immediately.

The next attack came through the nobles of Judah, who would have been very influential, as Judah was the royal line. They were bound to Tobiah through marriage and were sharing everything Nehemiah said with him. At the same time, they continually spoke good words about Tobiah. However, these good words were ingenuous, as Tobiah kept sending intimidating letters to Nehemiah (v. 19).

Attacking immediately after a victory is a common tactic of Satan. We get a picture of Satan's opportunistic nature in Luke 4:13, right after Satan's temptation of Jesus. Look at what it says: "So when the devil had completed every temptation, he departed from him until a more opportune time" (Luke 4:13).

The devil is always looking for an opportune time. Though Jesus had won the victory, Satan was still looking and ready to attack. I think a good picture of attacking after victory is seen with Jesus and Peter in Matthew 16:15-23. Jesus said, "But who do you say that I am?" and Peter responded, "You are the Christ, the Son of the living God." Christ blessed him and said, "You are blessed, Simon son of Jonah, because flesh and blood did not reveal this to you, but my Father in heaven!" and he also said, "on this rock I will build my church."

Peter had been blessed by God; this was a great victory. Maybe, Peter felt really special after Christ's blessing. However, only minutes later, he would stumble greatly. Christ told the disciples that he would be crucified and raised from the dead. Peter immediately rebuked Jesus saying that he would not die. Christ responded by saying, "Get behind me, Satan! You are a stumbling block to me." Right after Peter's victory, the enemy found a door to speak through him.

Similarly, in 1 Kings 18, Elijah had a tremendous victory over the priests of Baal, as God sent fire down on the altar, and Elijah had all the priests

158

killed. However, in 1 Kings 19, Queen Jezebel promised to, likewise, kill Elijah, and he ran for his life. He became depressed and even asked for God to take his life. Right after his greatest victory came his greatest defeat.

Satan is always looking for an opportune time and typically that comes very shortly after a victory. Many Christians go to the mountain top only to stumble quickly down to the valley. This is a common tactic of the enemy.

As one who worked with youth over seven years, I saw this many times. The students would go to a retreat and get on fire for God, and it was right after the high that they would come stumbling down. It was right after the mountain top experience that they had a valley experience. They would have a major fight with a friend or family member, stumble on the Internet, start dealing with depression, etc. It was common.

Satan likes to attack right after a victory. Many couples stumble into an argument right after leaving a Spirit-filled service. Many are tempted right after getting out of their devotions and going to work. Satan attacks right after a victory. I think part of the reason this is common is because it is right after a victory that we have a tendency to let down our guard and relax.

Scottish minister Andrew A. Bonar said this, "Let us be as watchful after the victory as before the battle."[29] We must be as watchful after the victory as before the battle, especially because we know our enemy's tactics.

Application Question: In what ways have you experienced the enemy's tactic of attacking right after a victory or spiritual high? How can we more wisely protect ourselves from this tactic?

The Enemy's Tactic of Infiltration through Compromise

> So the wall was completed on the twenty-fifth day of Elul, in just fifty-two days. When all our enemies heard and all the nations who were around us saw this, they were greatly disheartened. They knew that this work had been accomplished with the help of our God. In those days the aristocrats of Judah repeatedly sent letters to Tobiah, and responses from Tobiah were repeatedly coming to them. For many in Judah had sworn allegiance to him, because he was the son-in-law of Shecaniah son of Arah. His son Jonathan had married the daughter of Meshullam son of Berechiah. They were telling me about his good deeds and then taking back to him the things I said. Tobiah, on the other hand, sent letters in order to scare me.
> Nehemiah 6:15-19

The last tactic the enemy used against Nehemiah was infiltration through compromise. As mentioned, the nobles of Judah were under oath to Tobiah through marriage. Like other Samaritans, Tobiah was ethnically mixed. He was part Jewish and part Ammonite (cf. Neh 2:9). His name in Hebrew meant "God is good." He had married a daughter of Judah, and the tribe of Judah had great influence in Israel.

It is obvious that the nobles were compromising. This is not only seen in the fact that they gave their daughter to someone from the surrounding nations, which was forbidden by God, but also in that they were praising Tobiah who had been antagonistic to Israel from the beginning. Proverbs 28:4 says this: "Those who forsake the law praise the wicked, but those who keep the law contend with them."

I think we see this in the church all the time, especially amongst our youth. It's common to find them pumping certain music stars that teach anti-God messages. They will be watching shows that dishonor God's design for man and woman or teach other forms of corrupt living. But not only do they watch and listen, they praise it. They boast about it. They honor those who dishonor God. Those who forsake the law praise the wicked.

Of all the attacks Nehemiah shared, compromise was probably the most dangerous because he doesn't share a resolution. It just says that the nobles kept reporting the good Tobiah had done and sharing what Nehemiah said. In fact, Nehemiah later shares that this compromise was still happening many years after the completion of the wall, even after all the reform in chapters 8-12. When we get to Nehemiah 13:7, we see that Tobiah had moved into the temple. Israel had given a room in the temple to a person who was not a priest which was clearly forbidden.

In addition, in chapter 13, the Israelites again started to marry foreign women, which was also forbidden by God. It was the same compromise Solomon committed, which eventually led Israel away from God and into judgment.

Compromise is one of the enemy's most dangerous tactics; it commonly destroys individual Christians, churches, and Christian organizations. It's like a weed that is hard to pluck out. It can stay rooted for years, causing havoc amongst an otherwise healthy harvest.

Interpretation Question: Why does the enemy work so hard to bring compromise amongst believers?

1. Compromise spreads very fast like yeast.

Look at what Paul says: "Your boasting is not good. Don't you know that a little yeast affects the whole batch of dough?" (1 Corinthians 5:6).

Compromise and sin quickly spread throughout a congregation or ministry. It will open the door for more sin and deeper strongholds in a person's life and a community's life. Paul said that it must be removed because it will spread.

2.   Compromise removes the blessing of God.

David said this: "How blessed is the one who does not follow the advice of the wicked, or stand in the pathway with sinners, or sit in the assembly of scoffers!" (Psalm 1:1). David said that those who compromise lose the blessing of God on their lives. Only the one who does not walk in the counsel of the wicked is blessed.

What is the advice of the wicked? It is anything that proclaims the opposite of God's revelation. This includes things we read, watch, listen to, or meditate on. James says that friendship with the world is enmity with God (4:4).

Many Christians miss the blessing of God on their lives because of compromise.

3.   Compromise hinders intimacy of God.

Consider what Paul said about being partnered with unbelievers:

Do not become partners with those who do not believe, for what partnership is there between righteousness and lawlessness, or what fellowship does light have with darkness? ... Therefore "*come out from their midst, and be separate,*" says the Lord, "*and touch no unclean thing, and I will welcome you, and I will be a father to you, and you will be my sons and daughters,*" says the All-Powerful Lord.
2 Corinthians 6:14, 17-18

Now this Scripture is often used for not marrying unbelievers, but its applications are much broader than that. Paul gives a promise to those who separate from the world, "I will be a Father to you, you will be my sons and daughters" (v.18).

This seems like a weird promise since he is writing to Christians. Paul is writing to the Corinthian church. What does he mean by the promise, "I will be a Father to you"? It is a promise of intimacy with God. Many Christians lack the intimacy God wants to give them because of compromise. They say, "God where are you; I can't hear your voice?" They find their time in the Word and

161

worship as dull. The problem may be that they are compromised and, therefore, can't hear the voice of the Father or truly experience his love. Paul says that we must separate from the world in order to have this promise.

Compromise spreads quickly. It removes the blessing of God and hinders intimacy with him. One of Satan's greatest tactics is infiltration through compromise. Many Christians' lives have been destroyed by a little compromise. Churches have been destroyed by compromise. They compromise their teaching because the doctrine is unpopular in the culture. Christian universities have been destroyed when they have allowed liberalism to creep in; they compromised the gospel by focusing on grants, money from the government, and the approval of the world.

Even today, there are many Tobiahs in the house of God, and we often have welcomed them in to our demise. Nehemiah clearly ends the chapter saying, "The problems are not yet over. The enemy is still attacking."

In what ways are we compromising? A little leaven leavens the whole lump (1 Cor 5:6). Sin will keep spreading. Satan only needs a little room to destroy a harvest—to make a Christian or a Christian community ineffective.

Application Question: In what ways have you seen compromise harm Christians and Christian communities? What temptations to compromise does the enemy constantly attack you with?

Conclusion

As godly leaders we must be aware of our enemy's tactics both to protect ourselves and also our communities. What are Satan's tactics to stop the work of God?

1. The enemy's tactic of deception: He is a liar and the father of lies.
2. The enemy's tactic of persistence: He wants to wear believers down with his attacks and temptations.
3. The enemy's tactic of slander and gossip: He will slander God, slander others, and he will slander us.
4. The enemy's tactic of psychological warfare: He works through fear and discouragement.
5. The enemy's tactic of infiltration through false teaching: We must know the Word and our identity to not be deceived.
6. The enemy's tactic of attacking right after a victory: We must be as alert after victory, as before.

7. The enemy's tactic of infiltration through compromise: This might be the most dangerous tactic. It spreads; it removes the blessing of God and hinders intimacy with him.

The Priorities of Godly Leaders

When the wall had been rebuilt and I had positioned the doors, and the gatekeepers, the singers, and the Levites had been appointed, I then put in charge over Jerusalem my brother Hanani and Hananiah the chief of the citadel, for he was a faithful man and feared God more than many do. I said to them, "The gates of Jerusalem must not be opened in the early morning, until those who are standing guard close the doors and lock them. Position residents of Jerusalem as guards, some at their guard stations and some near their homes." Now the city was spread out and large, and there were not a lot of people in it. At that time houses had not been rebuilt. My God placed it on my heart to gather the leaders, the officials, and the ordinary people so they could be enrolled on the basis of genealogy. I found the genealogical records of those who had formerly returned. Here is what I found written in that record: These are the people of the province who returned from the captivity of the exiles, whom King Nebuchadnezzar of Babylon had forced into exile. They returned to Jerusalem and to Judah, each to his own city. They came with Zerubbabel, Jeshua, Nehemiah, Azariah, Raamiah, Nahamani, Mordecai, Bilshan, Mispereth, Bigvai, Nehum, and Baanah...
Nehemiah 7 (NET)

What are the priorities of godly leaders?

If you go through the cities of Europe, you will find many great cathedrals; however, the problem with these cathedrals is that nobody worships there anymore—all the people are gone. Similarly, Nehemiah had rebuilt the walls around Jerusalem in fifty-two days, but only a few people were living in the city (v. 4). Therefore, he began to labor to rebuild and to restore the people. This labor is detailed here in chapter 7 and throughout the rest of the book.

If we are going to build up the people of God, what steps must we take? Many of our churches and Christian communities are just shells of what they used to be. They began with revival and were used to ignite the communities they were in, but now many of them are simply surviving. They are on life support. Many of our Christian schools started off with a mission to send out pastors and missionaries, but now they are secular. If many of us looked at our individual lives, we would see times where we loved God more and were more passionate for him.

How do we rebuild the community we serve and also our own spiritual lives? If we are going to rebuild, it must start out with a renewed focus. It must start out with a change in priorities. I think we see something of this in this chapter.

What are the first things that Nehemiah did in seeking to rebuild the nation of Israel after the completion of the wall? His first actions show us his priorities and, therefore, what our priorities should be in seeking to rebuild our communities, our churches, and our lives. When the first things are first everything else falls into place. Here in this text we will see six priorities of godly leadership in building up a people for God.

Big Question: What are Nehemiah's priorities after the completion of the wall and how can we apply these truths to build up the body of Christ and our spiritual lives?

Godly Leaders Prioritize Worship

> When the wall had been rebuilt and I had positioned the doors, and the gatekeepers, the singers, and the Levites had been appointed,
> Nehemiah 7:1

The first thing that Nehemiah did after the rebuilding of the wall is appoint gatekeepers, singers, and Levites. Why did he do this?

It seems very clear that Nehemiah does this in order to set up the worship of Israel. The Levites were called to maintain the temple, which probably had been neglected while the Israelites were just trying to survive without walls, and they were called to teach the people Scripture.

Nehemiah established the singers to lead Israel's praise. Even the gatekeepers played a role in the worship of Israel. Now it is good to remember the walls that had been rebuilt weren't around Israel, but only around Jerusalem, the capital city, where the worship was supposed to happen. Therefore, people from all over Israel and even other nations would go through the gates of Jerusalem to worship God. In fact, certain gates were particularly important for worship such as the Sheep Gate. This was not just for random sheep but for sheep that were to be sacrificed at the temple.

166

When Nehemiah appointed the gatekeepers, the singers, and the Levites, he was reestablishing the worship of Israel. That was his first priority. In fact, it should be noted that Israel had struggled with worship, especially while they were exiled in Babylon. Listen to what the Jews in Babylon wrote:

> By the rivers of Babylon we sit down and weep when we remember Zion. On the poplars in her midst we hang our harps, for there our captors ask us to compose songs; those who mock us demand that we be happy, saying: "Sing for us a song about Zion!" How can we sing a song to the Lord in a foreign land?
> Psalm 137:1-4

It was hard for them to sing while they were outside the land and being harassed by foreigners, and no doubt, they still struggled while they were back in Jerusalem without walls, similarly being harassed and attacked by their neighbors. Therefore, Nehemiah reestablished the worship of Israel starting with the Levites, singers, and gatekeepers.

In addition, this was also a problem with the church of Ephesus in Revelation 2. Jesus said to them:

> To the angel of the church in Ephesus, write the following: "This is the solemn pronouncement of the one who has a firm grasp on the seven stars in his right hand—the one who walks among the seven golden lampstands: 'I know your works as well as your labor and steadfast endurance, and that you cannot tolerate evil. You have even put to the test those who refer to themselves as apostles (but are not), and have discovered that they are false. I am also aware that you have persisted steadfastly, endured much for the sake of my name, and have not grown weary.
> Revelation 2:1-3

They were doing many good things but neglecting the main thing. They were doing good works, testing false apostles, persevering through hardship; they hated the practice of the Nicolaitans (v. 6) and yet had lost their first love. Consider what Christ said to them:

> But I have this against you: You have departed from your first love! Therefore, remember from what high state you have fallen and repent! Do the deeds you did at the first; if not, I will come to you and remove your lampstand from its place—that is, if you do not repent.
> Revelation 2:4-5

167

The greatest commandment is to love God with all our heart and caring for our neighbor is second. To neglect loving and worshiping God breaks the greatest commandment and invites his judgment. He threatened to remove their lampstand, which meant their ability to be a witness in their community and maybe even destruction. Many churches are no longer effective for Christ because they put some issue, some good cause before him. Their worship is dead, and therefore, their ministry died as well. Worship must be first.

The church should be concerned about many good and worthy causes: feeding the poor, abortion, trafficking, evangelism, missions, etc. However, none of these should come before worship. Worshiping God and seeking his face must be the focus of the church (cf. 1 Peter 2:9). When anything else takes that place in the life of the church, we have lost our first love and are in danger of being disciplined by God.

If we lose our first love, if we neglect the worship of God as the priority of our lives and our communities, then God is just in disciplining us and removing our lampstand. "Man's chief end is to glorify God and enjoy him forever" (Westminster Shorter Catechism). We shouldn't even neglect worship for the sake of ministry. Like Mary, we must daily rush to sit at the feet of Jesus, for it is the one thing needed that will not be taken from us (Luke 10:42).

How do we restore our first love, our worship? Christ said to the Ephesian church that they should remember the height from which they had fallen. Then repent and do the works they did at first (cf. Rev 2:5). We should remember when God was our first love, our delight, and then do what we did then. Were we faithfully reading the Bible, attending a small group, or serving? Then we should do that in order to put God first and restore our worship.

When Nehemiah rebuilt the walls, the first thing he established was worship. As godly leaders, we must always point people back to the Word of God, to corporate worship with the saints, and to seeking the Lord for that must be the priority of every believer.

In what ways has worship ceased to be your priority? What is taking the place of your first love? Is it work, family, hobbies, or ministry? Let us repent and turn our focus back to Christ.

Nehemiah appointed the Levites, singers, and gatekeepers probably because worship had been neglected. The people put their circumstances, their survival, their careers, their families, etc., in front of God, and therefore, worship became a lesser priority.

Is worship your priority? Or are you neglecting God and putting something else first in your life?

Application Question: What are your major distractions from prioritizing the worship of God? How can we help ourselves or those whom we minister to, to re-prioritize worship?

Godly Leaders Prioritize Raising up Leaders

> I then put in charge over Jerusalem my brother Hanani and Hananiah the chief of the citadel, for he was a faithful man and feared God more than many do.
> Nehemiah 7:2

Observation Question: What were the characteristics of Hanani and Hananiah, the two men appointed to leadership by Nehemiah?

The next thing Nehemiah did, after reestablishing the worship of Israel, was choose leadership for Israel. Nehemiah realized he could not lead Israel alone—he needed help. Therefore, he set up two leaders in Jerusalem: Hanani, his brother, and Hananiah.

Obviously, Nehemiah knew Hanani to be a man of God. In chapter 1, Hanani alerted Nehemiah to the problems in Israel, prompting him to go back and initiate the rebuilding of the walls. Hanani was a man with the same heart as Nehemiah.

He also selected Hananiah. Hananiah was the "chief of the citadel." This means he was a military leader who protected the Persian palace, but more than that, he was a "faithful man." Nehemiah also said he "feared God more than many."

Here I think we learn something about the characteristics of those we should consider selecting for leadership positions, those we should mentor for future leadership, and also who we should be. It is good to remember that when Christ came to build up the nation of Israel, he also selected future leaders—the apostles. He trained them throughout his three years of ministry.

Similarly, we are called to make disciples (Matt 28:19-20) and to specifically train up others to serve in the church (cf. Heb 10:24-25, Eph 4:12-16).

The priority of every godly leader should be mentorship and training others for future leadership. But also this should challenge us to make sure we have the qualities of one whom God could raise up into leadership.

Application Question: What can we learn about potential leaders, those we should mentor and raise up, by the characteristics of the men Nehemiah chose?

1. Potential leaders must be faithful.

Hananiah was a faithful man. Certainly, the same was true about Nehemiah's brother, Hanani. He was the one who told Nehemiah about the problems in Israel after returning from a visit. Then he followed Nehemiah back to Israel and served with him. No doubt, he was a faithful man.

When Paul was concerned about raising future leaders for the church, he told Timothy to find "faithful men" to train so they could teach others. He said, "And entrust what you heard me say in the presence of many others as witnesses to faithful people who will be competent to teach others as well" (2 Timothy 2:2).

Faithful can also be translated "integrity," as in the NIV 1984. To have integrity means to be honest or to adhere "to moral and ethical principles."[30] Hananiah and Hanani were people Nehemiah could trust; they were people who followed through with their commitments. Similarly, when God is seeking for someone to use, he finds somebody who is faithful. Christ said this in Luke 16:10: "The one who is faithful in a very little is also faithful in much, and the one who is dishonest in a very little is also dishonest in much."

The person who is faithful with the little God has given him, will be faithful over much. We see these faithful qualities in the requirements for pastors. They must run their household well and their children must be obedient (1 Tim 3:4-5, Titus 1:6). If a husband cannot faithfully oversee the people in his house (little), then he cannot faithfully oversee the people in a church (much). Paul said that they must be hospitable, which means a lover of strangers (1 Tim 3:2). If they care for those they do not know by taking them into their home and providing for them, then they will faithfully care for strangers in the house of God.

This is what Scripture says: if one is faithful with little, then he will be faithful over much. But if one is not faithful with little, then he will be unfaithful with much.

I think one of the faithful things we must look for in future leadership is a consistent and disciplined devotional life. This seems like something little, but it is immensely important. David said he learned that the person who "meditated day and night" on God's law prospered in everything he did (Psalm 1:2-3). If we want to raise up successful leaders, they must be people who are faithful in their devotional lives.

This little thing called meditating on the Bible day and night will make an effective leader. Those who are not faithful in this will not be effective and probably shouldn't be in spiritual leadership at all. If a person is unfaithful in little, they will be unfaithful in much.

I have no doubt when Nehemiah looked at Hananiah, he saw a man who loved the Word of God, faithfully shepherded a believing family, and attended temple. He worked with integrity and honored God in all he did. That's probably why he called him faithful and selected him for leadership. And, no doubt, with Hanani it was the same.

Are you faithful with the little things such as: your devotional life, your care of family and friendships, your work, your studies, etc.? God looks at the little things when selecting leadership. He finds the one who faithfully shepherds his little flock of sheep and raises him up to lead Israel. Are you faithful with little?

2.   Potential leaders must fear God.

It also says Hananiah feared God more than many. That's pretty interesting because "the fear of God" is not something we typically think of as being quantified or added up. But the reality is that some fear God more than others.

Interpretation Question: What does it mean to fear God?

- To fear God means to revere him—to understand and stand in awe of his characteristics—his perfections.

To fear God essentially means to worship him. Hananiah was a man who loved to worship. That's the same characteristic we saw in David, the one God exalted to be king of Israel. He was the primary writer of the book of Psalms, the worship hymnal of Israel. He loved to sing praises to the Lord and honor him. It was David who said, "one day in your temple courts is better than spending a thousand elsewhere" (Psalm 84:10). When God selects a leader, he finds somebody who loves to worship and adore him.

Do you love to worship God? When we look for leaders, we must find people who love to worship and dwell in God's presence. People who are apathetic towards worship are not fit for leadership.

- To fear God means to fear his wrath and discipline.

Scripture says, "For the Lord disciplines the one he loves and chastises every son he accepts" (Hebrews 12:6). Instead of disciplines and chastises, the KJV translates them chastens and scourges. To chasten is to rebuke and to scourge is to whip. The people whom God selects for leadership are afraid of God's discipline—his spankings.

171

Jonah told God, "No" and God sent a storm in his life. He would have drowned in the sea if it wasn't for being swallowed by a big fish. God disciplines his children. He killed Ananias and Sapphira for lying to the church and the Holy Spirit (Acts 5). Some of the members of the Corinthian church were sick, weak, and some had died because they dishonored the Lord's Supper (1 Cor 11:29-30). God is a God of wrath who is angry at sin all day (Psalm 7:11). When God selects a leader, he finds somebody who fears him.

Solomon said the fear of God is the beginning of wisdom (Prov 9:10). Fearing the Lord is important because it enables people to make wise decisions. Because we want wise decision makers in leadership, we must find people who fear God.

A lot of people lack wisdom because they do not fear God. They look at God as their buddy who is simply there to forgive their sins and answer their prayers. There is no fear of a holy God who is a consuming fire (Hebrews 12:29). And this is the very reason so many believers live such foolish and wasteful lives.

In fact, what makes this lack of fear so much worse is that it endangers other people. When Jonah was in sin, it almost killed a bunch of bystanders on a boat with him going to Tarshish (Jonah 2). When David, full of pride, counted the people of Israel, it led to the death of thousands in the nation (2 Sam 24). When Solomon stopped fearing God, it brought the judgment of God leading to a divided kingdom. A leader who does not fear God will lead his people into judgment.

When we look for a leader or someone to disciple, we must find a person who has a genuine fear of God, which makes him live a life of holiness.

Application Question: Why is a lack of the fear of God so common among Christians?

One of the reasons Christians lack fear is because we have so much anemic, feel good preaching in the church these days. There is no reason to fear God. A pastor at one of the biggest churches in the U.S. said on TV that he did not preach on sin anymore because his people were already discouraged, and preaching on sin would only make it worse—they needed encouragement.

Listen, if we do not preach on sin, then we are not teaching the Bible and, therefore, are raising up people who do not fear the Lord and consequently live unwise lives.

Godly leaders must be faithful, and they must fear God. They must be people of character. This is the type of person we must seek to place in leadership. This is the type of person we must mentor for leadership, and the type of person we must become.

172

Application Question: In what ways is God calling you to grow in faithfulness, integrity, and the fear of him? In what ways do you feel God is calling you to help raise up future leaders in the church?

Godly Leaders Prioritize Protecting the People of God

> I said to them, "The gates of Jerusalem must not be opened in the early morning, until those who are standing guard close the doors and lock them. Position residents of Jerusalem as guards, some at their guard stations and some near their homes."
> Nehemiah 7:3

After establishing leadership, Nehemiah focused on the protection of the people by establishing rules for the gates and walls. In those days the gates were typically open at sunrise and closed at sunset[31]; however, Nehemiah established even stricter regulations. He said they should not be opened in the early morning. The NIV 1984 translates this, "The gates of Jerusalem are not to be opened *until the sun is hot*. While the gatekeepers are still on duty, have them shut the doors and bar them." Derek Kidner said this phrase referred "to the morning and evening routine, directing that the gates should be opened late and closed early."[32] Instead of opening at six am, maybe they were opened between ten to noon when the sun was hot. This made sure the people were not asleep when the gates opened. This also probably meant when the sun was going down, no longer hot, that the gates were closed and locked. This meant everybody was still awake when the gates were closed and, therefore, were less vulnerable to attack. Then, he appointed residents throughout Jerusalem to guard the walls at strategic posts and near their houses. Nehemiah's priority was to protect the people of God, and he went to great extremes to do this.

When we look at Nehemiah's priority of protecting the people of God, we, no doubt, see God's priority. Jesus said he was the good shepherd and that when the wolf comes, good shepherds give their lives for the sheep (John 10:11). The good shepherd would always watch the sheep and protect them with his life. As godly leaders, we must aim to do the same.

Application Question: How can we practically apply watching and protecting the people of God to our lives? How can we protect God's people?

1. We watch and protect the people of God by prayer.

Listen to what God said through Isaiah:

I post watchmen on your walls, O Jerusalem; they should keep praying all day and all night. You who pray to the Lord, don't be silent! Don't allow him to rest until he reestablishes Jerusalem, until he makes Jerusalem the pride of the earth.
Isaiah 62:6-7

Here, God set watchman to pray over Jerusalem for the restoration of it and that it may be holy. A watchman typically sat at a strategic place on the wall of the city to alert everybody when an enemy approached. However, the watchmen God set up were primarily called to pray when they saw threats coming towards Jerusalem and ultimately for the nation's prosperity. I believe God still has people praying for Israel until he restores the nation and fulfills his covenants with her.

Similarly, God has called us to be watchmen over his church by being alert and devoted to prayer. Listen to these texts:

With every prayer and petition, pray at all times in the Spirit, and to this end be alert, with all perseverance and requests for all the saints.
Ephesians 6:18

Be devoted to prayer, keeping alert in it with thanksgiving.
Colossians 4:2

We are to be alert watchmen, as we care for the church of God. We should keep our eyes open for any potential threats. If there is division, sickness, weariness, false teaching, etc., we should pray. We should give thanks when there are blessings: open doors, unity, fruitfulness, etc. We should, with all kinds of prayers and requests, keep on praying for Christ's church. These prayers are not only for our local congregation but for "all the saints." We must be alert and intercede for the entire body of Christ.

God seeks to find men and women who will covenant with him in this type of ministry. Remember what he said to Ezekiel: "I looked for a man from among them who would repair the wall and stand in the gap before me on behalf of the land, so that I would not destroy it, but I found no one" (Ezekiel 22:30).

Often God can't find people who are willing to guard and protect others from destruction. Are you willing to stand in the gap and pray for the people of God? This ministry of protecting God's people through prayer is for everybody, but it is especially for leaders.

2.   We watch and protect the people of God by being alert and sounding the alarm when we see the enemy.

Alertness was mentioned in the last point on prayer, but it will be given more attention here. First Peter 5:8 says, "Be sober and alert. Your enemy the devil, *like a roaring lion,* is on the prowl looking for someone to devour."

Christians and Christian leaders, specifically, must be alert to the work of the devil amongst God's people. No doubt, we saw a good picture of this with Christ and Peter right before Peter's denial. The Lord said, "Simon, Simon, Satan has asked to sift you like wheat but I have prayed for you that your faith will not fail" (Luke 22:32, paraphrase). Christ was alert and sensitive to the plan of the evil one and warned his disciple.

Certainly, we should be alert to the plans and activities of the evil one in other people's lives as well. We should be sensitive to any type of decay in their spiritual lives. Have they stopped attending small group or church? Have their conversations changed? Are they hanging around the wrong people, making wrong decisions? It is there we can trust that the evil one is at work. It is there we must aim not only our prayers but also our attention as we warn, rebuke, and encourage so they may be protected.

John the Baptist told the tax collectors to stop stealing and to make right whatever wrongs they committed. He told the wealthy to share their wealth, and he told the Pharisees to repent (Luke 3). He was a watchman over Israel, warning the people and calling them to repent.

Are you willing to be watchful over the church of God? In the same way Nehemiah set watchman over Israel and God set prayer warriors to watch over Israel, we must be willing to take part in this ministry for the church. The church has an enemy called the devil, and his only desire is to steal, kill, and destroy (cf. John 10:10). It is for this reason we must be alert and warn those in danger.

3.   We watch and protect people by being aware of the enemy's tactics.

It must be remembered that if we are going to be watchful, we must be aware of the enemy's tactics (2 Cor 2:11), as mentioned in the previous chapter. We can be sure that is why Nehemiah set specific regulations in Jerusalem. He knew the enemy would attack at certain times and in certain ways. We must, therefore, be aware of our enemy's tactics as well.

Interpretation Question: What are some of the enemy's tactics we can discern from Nehemiah's regulations on the gates?

175

- The enemy likes to attack while people are resting.

Nehemiah told them they must not open the gate until the sun was hot. Again, this probably meant sometime around ten to noon. The people were more vulnerable early in the morning while they were asleep. Therefore, Nehemiah had the gates opened later in the day to decrease their vulnerability to a surprise attack.

Certainly, Satan also likes to attack when Christians are resting. We should be aware of our times of leisure. It is then the enemy likes to attack. He will attack with loneliness, depression, discouragement, lust, anger, etc. It is in our leisure time that addictions are often developed. We are vulnerable at our times of leisure, when we are resting. It is then we often let down our guard and are more susceptible to attack.

As mentioned in chapter 6, the enemy also likes to attack right after a victory. After a victory we typically let down our guard to rest. After finishing some great project, some great work, or after a time of spiritual renewal, those will be strategic times for the enemy to attack. We should be aware of this and, therefore, be especially alert. Satan is a cunning enemy. He has tempted man for thousands of years, and because of this, he understands human nature. He understands the vulnerability of man at times of rests—during our leisure or after a victory. We must watch ourselves and also our people at these times.

- The enemy likes to attack at night.

Enemies commonly attacked while it was dark, and therefore, Nehemiah closed the gates when the sun was no longer hot. Again, the night is often a time of relaxation when a person's inhibitions naturally lower, making us more susceptible to temptation and sin. Certainly, Satan understands how strategic night time is as well. Listen to what Paul said:

> For you all are sons of the light and sons of the day. We are not of the night nor of the darkness. So then we must not sleep as the rest, but must stay alert and sober. *For those who sleep, sleep at night and those who get drunk are drunk at night. But since we are of the day, we must stay sober* by putting on the breastplate of faith and love and as a helmet our hope for salvation.
> 1 Thessalonians 5:5-8

Paul described the world as those who belong to the night. They typically get drunk at night, are less self-controlled at night, and fall into various other temptations. But, Christians should not be characterized by the night but by the day. They should live self-controlled, godly lives. As Christians, we should always be on guard, but at certain times, we should be more alert and one of those is at night.

When do people typically fall to lust on the Internet? At night. When do conversations on the phone with one's girlfriend or boyfriend go astray? At night. When do people have a tendency to get drunk or break the law? At night. Even when people accused Peter and the apostles of drunkenness on the day of Pentecost, he said, "It's only nine in the morning!" meaning that nobody gets drunk this early (Acts 2:15). It was clearly understood those type of activities typically happened at night.

Let us be on guard during the day, but let us especially be on guard in the night hours. Being on guard includes getting a good night's sleep. I would say Satan often wins the battle at night simply by people not getting proper rest. They stay up late, typically neglecting their times of prayer or devotion, and then start off the next day too tired to meet with God. Through a pattern of being undisciplined and frivolous at night, the enemy keeps the gates open to cause havoc in people's lives. Yes, let us guard the night. Nehemiah's strategy certainly applies to us as well.

- The enemy likes to attack the family.

Nehemiah tells them to post guards right by their homes to protect the wall by their houses. This way they would have guards to sound the alarm and alert the city in case of attack. Attacking enemies would often neglect the front gate and try to enter through the side. Listen to what Nehemiah says: "Position residents of Jerusalem as guards, some at their guard stations and some near their homes" (Nehemiah 7:3).

This is significant because our enemy, Satan, also likes to attack our homes. The family is the basic unit of the church and society. When God wanted to start a kingdom, he started it with a husband and wife (a family) in the Garden of Eden. Because of this, Satan realizes if he can destroy the family, he can destroy the foundation of both the church and society. It is a very strategic target. When sin came into the world, one of the consequences was the battle of the sexes. The woman would try to control the husband and the husband would try to dominate her (cf. Gen 3:16).

From that faulty relationship, we later saw the first murder. Cain, the son of Adam, killed his brother, Abel. And this battle in the family continued throughout the rest of Scripture. In fact, the Scripture is a story of dysfunctional families.

Abraham broke the marriage order and married two wives who battled with one another. Isaac, the son of Abraham, favored the oldest son, Esau, and

177

created jealousy with the younger son, Jacob. Jacob cheated the older brother, Esau, out of his inheritance. Jacob, the grandson of the polygamist Abraham, committed the same sin by marrying multiple wives and, similarly, had great marital strife.

Joseph, the son of Jacob, had ten older brothers who sold him into slavery. David, the king of Israel, had a son who raped his daughter Tamar. Absalom, the older brother of Tamar, killed the brother who raped his sister. Absalom, the son of David, eventually overthrew his father's kingdom.

One of the major themes in the narrative of the Bible is how Satan continually attacked the family, and it is no different today. Not only does Satan commonly attack while people are resting and when it's dark, he loves to attack the home—our families.

Therefore, we must guard and protect our families. We must especially protect our children from the godlessness taught through TV, music, and the Internet. Satan often destroys homes through the media. We must guard our homes by saturating them with prayer, the study of Scripture, and being involved in a Bible preaching church. We must not be unaware of Satan's tactics.

When God sent John the Baptist to prepare Israel for Christ's coming, one of his jobs was to restore the family. He was called to turn the fathers back to the sons and the sons back to the fathers (Mal 4:6 NIV 1984). This must be one of our priorities as well, as we seek to build up the people of God. Godly leaders must protect the family, as that is one of the enemy's primary targets.

Application Question: In what ways have you seen Satan use the tactic of attacking during times of rest (times of leisure and after victories) and at night in your spiritual life or others? In what ways do you feel God is calling you to better protect yourself and others from the works of the enemy?

Godly Leaders Prioritize Discerning God's Voice

> My God placed it on my heart to gather the leaders, the officials, and the ordinary people so they could be enrolled on the basis of genealogy.
> Nehemiah 7:5

One of the common themes seen throughout Nehemiah's memoirs is his discernment of the voice of God. He said in verse 5, "My God placed it on my heart to gather the leaders, the officials, and the ordinary people so they could be enrolled on the basis of genealogy." He said something similar in Nehemiah

178

2:12 as he surveyed the broken down walls of Jerusalem. He said, "I did not tell anyone what my God was putting on my heart to do for Jerusalem." Nehemiah was a man who sought to discern the voice of God.

This is an essential priority for every godly leader. They must be committed to discerning God's voice if they are going to effectively lead the people of God. This is important because God is the head of the church, and we are simply his under-shepherds. Some leaders abuse their leadership because they think they are the head. However, godly leaders prioritize discerning the voice of God so they can lead people according to God's will. We see this in Nehemiah, as he discerned God's voice and assembled the families for registration.

Application Question: How do we discern God's voice?

1.   We discern God's voice by knowing the Word of God.

Throughout the book it is very clear that part of the way Nehemiah discerned God's voice was by knowing Scripture. When he prayed in chapter 1, he talked about how God promised to scatter Israel for their disobedience and to restore them if they were obedient (v. 8, 9). In that prayer, he was praying the promises in Deuteronomy 30:1-5, which are reaffirmed in many other Old Testament passages. He knew it was God's will to restore Israel's fortunes if they repented.

When he rebuked the nobles in chapter 5, he rebuked them because they broke the law (5:9). The Jews were not allowed to charge one another interest on loans (cf. Exodus 22:25). Even in this text, as he felt led to create a census, it seems also prompted by his knowledge of Scripture.

The census was something very important. In the book of Joshua, the tribes of Israel were each given a part of the promised land (chapters 14-17). The census was necessary to establish the family rights. This was especially important for the Levites and priests who didn't receive an allotment of the land but instead worked at the temple in Jerusalem and lived off the offerings of the people. The census or genealogy was needed to prove what tribe a person was from so they could receive their allotment and to determine the priests and Levites for service at the temple.

Again, Nehemiah's actions show that he was a man who thoroughly knew the Scripture. In fact, at the end of the book, he rebuked Israel for intermarriage with the pagans and also for letting Tobiah, an Ammonite, live in the temple. This was another departure from God's law. Nehemiah was clearly a man who knew God's law and was zealous in keeping it.

In the same way, if we are going to know God's voice, we must know Scripture. Many times, the Scripture tells us exactly what to do, and at other times, it gives us principles to make wise decisions. When we live in the Word of God, we, like Nehemiah, often will discern exactly what God's will is. David said, "Your word is a lamp to walk by, and a light to illumine my path" (Psalm 119:105). God's Word gives us direction.

2.   We discern God's voice by putting him first.

Proverbs 3:6 says, "Acknowledge him in all your ways, and he will make your paths straight."
Nehemiah was a man who prioritized God and, therefore, heard his voice. When we make God our priority, when we acknowledge him in every way, he will also show us what paths to take.
When putting God first, you will not only find that God directs you, but he will also commonly use you to give direction to others. When they are seeking direction for their path, you will find that God gives you words of wisdom to help them discern which path to take.
As godly leaders we must know God's voice in order to continually build others up and help them walk in God's best for their lives.

3.   We discern God's voice by not being conformed to the world culture.

Romans 12:2 says, "Do not be conformed to this present world, but be transformed by the renewing of your mind, so that you may test and approve what is the will of God—what is good and well-pleasing and perfect."
Many people can't discern the will of God because the voice of the world is in their mind. They know what culture would tell them to do, what friends and family would tell them to do, but they can't hear the voice of God. We must continually get rid of sin and the lies of the world culture to be able to test and approve what God's will is. God's will is often the opposite of culture, since Satan is the ruler of this world (cf. John 12:31, 2 Cor 4:4).

Application Question: What is God currently putting in your heart as you continually seek his face? In what ways does the culture of the world often hinder us from hearing the voice of God?

Godly Leaders Prioritize the Assurance of the People of God

> Now the city was spread out and large, and there were not a lot of people in it. At that time houses had not been rebuilt. My God placed it on my heart to gather the leaders, the officials, and the ordinary people so they could be enrolled on the basis of genealogy. I found the genealogical records of those who had formerly returned. Here is what I found written in that record
> Nehemiah 7:4-5

Interpretation Question: What was the significance of the genealogical records for Nehemiah and the Israelites?

Again, Israel rebuilt the walls, but the city itself needed to be rebuilt. It was large and spacious but had only a few people in it. God put into Nehemiah's heart to have a registration by families of those living in Israel.

This was important to establish who was Jewish, as there were some privileges in worship that only Jews could enjoy. In fact, some priests could not minister because their records were lost. They had to wait until a priest could seek the Lord through the Urim Thummim (cf. Neh 7:63-65). It was also important to establish what tribes they were from because of certain land rights. God gave parts of the land to certain tribes as an enduring inheritance. We see that they had their own towns in Nehemiah 7:73:

> The priests, the Levites, the gatekeepers, the singers, some of the people, the temple servants, and all the rest of Israel lived in their cities. When the seventh month arrived and the Israelites were settled in their cities,

The registration was also important to establish the line of the messiah. We see genealogies used in Matthew and Luke to establish the lineage of Christ.

In fact, this list of names Nehemiah used is almost the exact list found in Ezra 2, which documented the initial people who came back to Israel from Babylon. There are slight differences, but this is probably because the list was updated, as the people were registered. Some have speculated that the "minor discrepancies are possibly due to Ezra listing those who intended to depart [from Babylon to Israel], while Nehemiah listed those who actually arrived."[33]

The fact we see two lists repeated in Scripture shows how special these people and their names were. They were the faithful families who came back to Israel to worship. The list marks them as such. God did not need the list, for he knew who were his. However, the Jewish people needed to know.

They needed the genealogies to prove they were part of God's chosen people in order to enjoy the rights given them.

It is good to remember that being Jewish, especially in the Old Covenant, was special. Listen to what Paul said:

> For I could wish that I myself were accursed—cut off from Christ—for the sake of my people, my fellow countrymen, who are Israelites. To them belong the adoption as sons, the glory, the covenants, the giving of the law, the temple worship, and the promises. To them belong the patriarchs, and from them, by human descent, came the Christ, who is God over all, blessed forever! Amen.
> Romans 9:3-5

It was through this nation God was going to reach the world; they were to be lights to the Gentiles.

Application Question: How can we as Christians apply the need for the people to have an official census to prove they were Jewish and the tribe they were from?

Similar to Old Testament Israel, the church is now the people of God, and he has called us to be lights to the world (cf. 1 Peter 2:9-10). We can be assured that God knows who are his and that he knows us by name. John 10:3 says, "The doorkeeper opens the door for him, and the sheep hear his voice. He calls his own sheep by name and leads them out." However, like the Jews needing to take the census to prove their lineage in order to enjoy their privileges, we also need to know that we are God's. We need to have assurance of salvation.

God knew who were his and this Jewish census wasn't important for God. It was important for the people, so they could have the rights to their land, to work in the temple as priests, or to enjoy certain elements of worship only allowed for the Jew.

Scripture teaches a similar principle about our salvation. God knows who are truly saved, but we must know as well. Therefore Scripture teaches the necessity of believers having assurance of salvation. Second Peter 1:10 says, "Therefore, brothers and sisters, make every effort to be sure of your calling and election."

Though we don't have a genealogical list, we still have the command to make our election sure and to test whether Christ is in us (cf. 2 Cor 13:5). This is the doctrine of assurance of salvation.

Are you sure you are saved? It is the most important thing you can be sure about in your life. How can we be sure?

Well, after accepting Jesus as our Lord and Savior, the primary test for our salvation is growing in righteousness. Peter calls all believers to make their election sure in 2 Peter 1:10 but tells us how in the previous verses:

> For this very reason, make every effort to add to your faith excellence, to excellence, knowledge; to knowledge, self-control; to self-control, perseverance; to perseverance, godliness; to godliness, brotherly affection; to brotherly affection, unselfish love. For if these things are really yours and are continually increasing, they will keep you from becoming ineffective and unproductive in your pursuit of knowing our Lord Jesus Christ more intimately. But concerning the one who lacks such things—he is blind. That is to say, he is nearsighted, since he has forgotten about the cleansing of his past sins. Therefore, brothers and sisters, make every effort to be sure of your calling and election. For by doing this you will never stumble into sin.
> 2 Peter 1:5 -10

Peter says make every effort to add to your faith, excellence; to excellence, knowledge; to knowledge, self-control; to self-control, perseverance; to perseverance, godliness; to godliness, brotherly affection, and to brotherly affection, love. Peter essentially commands them to grow and says if you are not growing in these things you might not be saved. Make your election sure by growing. We are not saved by growing in righteousness but bearing these fruits proves our election. They prove we are in the Lamb's Book of Life—registered citizens of heaven (cf. Rev 21:27).

John the Baptist and Paul taught similar things. Listen to what they said:

> Therefore produce fruit that proves your repentance, and don't begin to say to yourselves, 'We have Abraham as our father.' For I tell you that God can raise up children for Abraham from these stones! Even now the ax is laid at the root of the trees, and every tree that does not produce good fruit will be cut down and thrown into the fire."
> Luke 3:8-9

> but I declared to those in Damascus first, and then to those in Jerusalem and in all Judea, and to the Gentiles, that they should repent and turn to God, performing deeds consistent with repentance.
> Acts 26:20

One of the things that was common in Peter's teaching, John the Baptist's teaching, and Paul's was the necessity of proving one's salvation by good deeds. Listen, nobody is saved by works, but works are necessary to prove one's salvation. If we are without the necessary fruits, then we might not be saved. I think this is a fair application to the Jews needing to prove their Jewishness in order to enjoy the rights that came with it.

Many of the rights and blessings that come in Christ can only be taken by those who have assurance they are saved, and this assurance is more than just a confession. Listen to what Christ said:

> "Not everyone who says to me, 'Lord, Lord,' will enter into the kingdom of heaven—only the one who does the will of my Father in heaven. On that day, many will say to me, 'Lord, Lord, didn't we prophesy in your name, and in your name cast out demons and do many powerful deeds?' Then I will declare to them, 'I never knew you. Go away from me, you lawbreakers!'
> Matthew 7:21-23

These people had some type of faith because they called him Lord and served him on the earth. However, they never bore fruit; they continued to practice sin as a lifestyle and that is why Christ said, "I never knew you. Go away from me, you lawbreakers!" They were never truly saved.

Christ knew them because he knows all things, but he didn't know them personally. Are you making your election sure? I worry about Christians who stay in the church twenty years but never grow. They may simply be stagnant, but if so, they lose assurance of whether they are truly saved since they aren't growing.

God wants his children to have assurance. They are his and that proof will be evident if they are truly saved. They will grow in love for God, love for his Word, love for others, peace, patience, faith, endurance, good works, etc. All these will prove the reality of their faith.

In Israel, a Jewish person without a genealogy would miss out on many of the privileges of his Jewishness, and I think Christians do as well. They miss the joy and the assurance that comes from knowing they are children of God and also significant protection from the evil one.

One of Satan's primary attacks is on the Christian's assurance of salvation. He works hard to cause those who are truly born again to doubt their salvation. That is why Paul commands believers to put on the "helmet of salvation" in the armor of God (Ephesians 6:17). The "helmet of salvation" is assurance. In spiritual warfare, Satan often aims for the head. If true Christians

184

doubt their salvation, they will not be very productive for the kingdom. They probably won't evangelize and serve others. They will be too worried about their own salvation to be concerned with others.

For people with false professions, Satan instead assures them that their faith is true. He promotes a false assurance. Therefore, we must make our election sure. We must test ourselves to see if we are in the faith (cf. 2 Corinthians 13:5).

This was a priority of Nehemiah with Israel, and it should be with us as well. We must know we are his and we must help those we disciple know. Assurance is important in order to walk in the full blessings of God.

Are we on the list (cf. Rev 21:27)? Have we been born again into the family of God? Does our continual progress in the faith prove this to be true or are we stagnant and living in rebellion towards God?

Are you making your election sure? Do you have assurance of your salvation?

Application Question: Do you ever struggle with assurance of salvation? What are some other texts that teach us how we can have assurance of salvation (cf. 1 John 5:13, Matthew 5:3-10)?

Godly Leaders Prioritize Giving

It also seems that Nehemiah reestablished the worship, not only by setting up the gates, the Levites and the singers, but by working on the temple. It says the leaders gave to the temple work at the end of the chapter. Look at what it says:

> Some of the family leaders contributed to the work. The governor contributed to the treasury 1,000 gold drachmas, 50 bowls, and 530 priestly garments. Some of the family leaders gave to the project treasury 20,000 gold drachmas and 2,200 silver minas. What the rest of the people gave amounted to 20,000 gold drachmas, 2,000 silver minas, and 67 priestly garments.
> Nehemiah 7:70-72

Some scholars estimated that the nobles gave over 5 million dollars in today's currency.[34] No doubt, this was partially at Nehemiah's urging, as he reestablished the worship of Israel.

Certainly, Scripture teaches that one of the priorities of a godly leader should be giving—supporting the work of the Lord financially—and encouraging others to do so as well. Paul also urged the Corinthians to give in support of the church in Jerusalem. He encouraged them with the many promises of God to those who are faithful givers. Let us hear these promises:

> My point is this: The person who sows sparingly will also reap sparingly, and the person who sows generously will also reap generously. Each one of you should give just as he has decided in his heart, not reluctantly or under compulsion, because God loves a cheerful giver. And God is able to make all grace overflow to you so that because you have enough of everything in every way at all times, you will overflow in every good work.
> 2 Corinthians 9:6-8

The promise to a giver is "all grace" in verse 8. This grace shows up in God providing for all our needs, but it also shows up in us overflowing in every good work.

Giving is a priority for a leader because God promises to meet the needs of his people and also open the door for more righteousness in accordance to our giving. Some people may be anemic in their serving, evangelism, intercession, knowledge of Scripture, etc., and it could all be attributed to a lack of giving. God promises we will abound in righteousness if we are cheerful givers.

Consider what Paul said to the Philippians whom he was thanking for their financial support: "I do not say this because I am seeking a gift. Rather, I seek the credit that abounds to your account" (Phil 4:17). Paul says, "I want you to give because I want you to be credited." No doubt, this meant receiving riches in heaven and also grace on earth.

Are you a giver? This is the priority of godly leadership. When rebuilding the lives of others, we must train them to give for this opens the door for "all grace" in their lives.

Application Question: In what ways have you experienced "all grace" from God in response to faithful giving? In what ways has God been challenging you to grow in your giving (cf. 2 Corinthians 8:7)?

Conclusion

What are the priorities of a godly leader? How do we build up the people of God? As we look at the first things Nehemiah did after rebuilding the wall, we learn something about the godly leader's priorities in building up the people of God and also his or her own life.

1. Godly leaders prioritize worship.
2. Godly leaders prioritize raising up leaders.
3. Godly leaders prioritize protecting the people of God.
4. Godly leaders prioritize discerning the voice of God.
5. Godly leaders prioritize the assurance of the people of God.
6. Godly leaders prioritize giving.

When Revival Continues

All the people gathered together in the plaza which was in front of the Water Gate. They asked Ezra the scribe to bring the book of the law of Moses which the Lord had commanded Israel. So Ezra the priest brought the law before the assembly which included men and women and all those able to understand what they heard. (This happened on the first day of the seventh month.) So he read it before the plaza in front of the Water Gate from dawn till noon before the men and women and those children who could understand. All the people were eager to hear the book of the law...
Nehemiah 8 (NET)

What are characteristics of revival in worship?

In Nehemiah 3, we saw God revive the hearts of the people to start rebuilding the walls. They worked while mocked and attacked, and yet they still completed the wall in fifty-two days as seen in chapter 6.

In chapters 7-13, we see the continuation of this revival in the people. Previously, God had revived their hearts to rebuild ruins that had been there for over 140 years (586 BC-445 BC). But here in chapter 8, God revives, not just their hearts, but their worship.

This began in Nehemiah 7:1. After finishing the wall, the first thing Nehemiah did was establish gatekeepers, singers, and Levites. By establishing them, Nehemiah was showing the priority of worship. Even the gatekeepers had a role to play in worship, as all the Israelites and Gentiles would come to the city through the gates to worship the Lord. In fact, certain gates were specifically for worship like the Sheep Gate. It was there that the sacrificial sheep would be led through to be offered to God.

The implication of Nehemiah establishing gatekeepers, singers, and Levites is the fact that the Israelites were no longer worshiping or no longer worshiping as they should have been. Maybe in their trials and difficulties, they had forgotten or turned away from God. Therefore, their worship needed to be restored.

At times, we also have lost our worship in the midst of trials, in the midst of busyness, and sometimes in the midst of personal sin. Many of our churches and Christian communities are dying spiritually. The majority of our churches are decreasing in numbers and barely surviving. Many of them have a great number of older people but very few young people. The majority of our youth, when they get to college, fall away from the faith. In addition, the majority of our historically Christian universities have become secular.

The church is in a crisis. Many of our spiritual lives are in a state of crisis. How do we restore our worship? How can we experience revival?

In this text, we see characteristics of revival in worship as Israel is restored to the worshiping nation it was always meant to be. As we go through this study, we must ask ourselves this question, "Am I experiencing the characteristics of revival in my own personal worship and in my church?" Also, we should ask, "How can I as a leader help bring revival in my community?"

Big Question: What are characteristics of the revival in Israel? How can we begin to experience revival in our lives and in our church communities?

In Revival, God Restores Unity amongst the People of God

> All the people gathered together in the plaza which was in front of the Water Gate. They asked Ezra the scribe to bring the book of the law of Moses which the Lord had commanded Israel.
> Nehemiah 8:1

The first thing that we notice is how "all the people gathered together." There was no division amongst the people. We talked about this in Nehemiah 3 as Nehemiah motivated the people to work together to rebuild the wall. But even in chapter 3, they were not completely unified. We saw how some of the nobles would not submit to their supervisors (cf. 3:5). However, here they gathered "together."

This is true of every great revival. When God revives the people of God, it spans gender, race, socio-economic status, and theological differences. The people of God come together to pray, to study the Word, and to serve together, and in the midst of this, God moves. This is exactly what David said about unity in Psalm 133:

> Look! How good and how pleasant it is when brothers live together! It is like fine oil poured on the head which flows down the beard Aaron's beard, and then flows down his garments. It is like the dew of Hermon,

which flows down upon the hills of Zion. Indeed, that is where the Lord has decreed a blessing will be available—eternal life.

Wherever people are unified, God blesses. How should we respond to this?

We must respond to this individually by forgiving anybody who has hurt us, especially in the body of Christ, and seeking reconciliation. Corporately as churches, we must seek to unify with other parts of Christ's body so that the body of Christ can be more effective.

Where there is unity, there is God's blessing. And where there is division, the enemy is in the midst (cf. Eph 4:26-27). Therefore, we must labor together to keep the unity of the Spirit (cf. Eph 4:3).

Application Question: How can the churches labor for unity both within their own local congregation and with other congregations? How should the church handle theological differences?

In Revival, God Restores Devoted Teachers of the Word of God to Leadership

All the people gathered together in the plaza which was in front of the Water Gate. They asked Ezra the scribe to bring the book of the law of Moses which the Lord had commanded Israel. So Ezra the priest brought the law before the assembly which included men and women and all those able to understand what they heard. (This happened on the first day of the seventh month.) So he read it before the plaza in front of the Water Gate from dawn till noon before the men and women and those children who could understand. All the people were eager to hear the book of the law... Jeshua, Bani, Sherebiah, Jamin, Akkub, Shabbethai, Hodiah, Maaseiah, Kelita, Azariah, Jozabad, Hanan, and Pelaiah—all of whom were Levites—were teaching the people the law, as the people remained standing.
Nehemiah 8:1-3, 7

The next thing that we see is Ezra and the Levites teaching the law to the people. Ezra was called a scribe and a priest, as seen in Nehemiah 8:1-2. As a scribe, he meticulously copied the Scripture, and as a priest, he studied and taught it. Listen to what Ezra 7:10 said about him: "Now Ezra had dedicated himself to the study of the law of the Lord, to its observance, and to teaching its statutes and judgments in Israel."

191

Ezra had devoted his life to studying, copying, and teaching the Scripture. After the second group of Jews returned to Israel from the exile, God had previously used Ezra to turn Israel back to the Word of God and repentance in the book of Ezra (chapters 9, 10). However, it is clear that the initial revival didn't last, and God again called Ezra to help revive Israel.

Again, Ezra was not alone; thirteen helpers were on the platform with him (v. 4) who may have been priests.[35] And then, another thirteen Levites taught the Scripture as well. Nehemiah 8:7-8 says this:

> Jeshua, Bani, Sherebiah, Jamin, Akkub, Shabbethai, Hodiah, Maaseiah, Kelita, Azariah, Jozabad, Hanan, and Pelaiah—all of whom were Levites—were teaching the people the law, as the people remained standing. They read from the book of God's law, explaining it and imparting insight. Thus the people gained understanding from what was read.
> Nehemiah 8:7-8

We see that these Levites were used in making the Scripture clear by "explaining it and imparting insight. Thus the people gained understanding from what was read." There is some dispute over what this means. The NASB translates it differently. It says, "translating to give the sense so that they understood the reading."

No doubt, many of the Jews while living in Babylon for over 140 years had lost their Hebrew language and were now speaking Aramaic.[36] Therefore, the Levites might have had to translate the passages first into Aramaic and then explain the meaning. Also, it is good to remember that even ancient Hebrew probably went through many changes. At that point, it had been 1000 years since Moses wrote the law. Even if we studied the original KJV, which is only around 400 years old, we would see that there are many words we don't use anymore. Therefore, the Levites might have had to explain archaic words, even to those who spoke Hebrew.

Whatever it means, we can assume there was some amount of translating. This might have been done in smaller groups led by the Levites after Ezra read to the entire congregation. But the part we will focus on is the "imparting insight" so that people could understand.

Ezra and the Levites were called to teach the Word of God and to stir up the people's love and affection for God's Word. However, it must be noted that this is nothing new; this has happened in every revival. When God brings a revival, he raises up people who have been devoted to the studying and teaching of God's Word.

God did the same thing with John the Baptist. He was raised by a priestly family in the wilderness, and, when God chose to turn Israel back to himself before the coming of the messiah, he called for a man who knew the Word and would preach it. He showed up in the Gospels preaching repentance and turning Israel back to God.

Was this not true of Joshua as well? Joshua was called to lead Israel in the conquering of the Canaanites. You would think that as a military general, he would need to focus his study on the doctrine of war or military tactics. But no, God called him to make his focus the Word, and, when he did that, he would prosper. Look at what God said:

> Be strong and very courageous. Be careful to obey all the law my servant Moses gave you; do not turn from it to the right or to the left, that you may be successful wherever you go. Do not let this Book of the Law depart from your mouth; meditate on it day and night, so that you may be careful to do everything written in it. Then you will be prosperous and successful.
> Joshua 1:7-8 (NIV 1984)

When God said, "Do not let the Book of the Law depart from your mouth," he was calling Joshua not just to meditate but to teach. He was to meditate on it and teach the Word of God, and God would prosper him and make him successful. We are all called to be teachers of the Scripture in some form or another, as we make disciples of all nations (Matt 28:19-20).

Hear what God said in 2 Chronicles 16:9: "Certainly the Lord watches the whole earth carefully and is ready to strengthen those who are devoted to him." He searches for people who are fully devoted to him, so he can strengthen them. What does a person look like who is fully devoted to him? They are people of his Word, like Joshua, like David, and like John the Baptist. He looks for people who are devoted to his Word so he can use them greatly for his kingdom.

When God looks for someone to revive the people of God, he finds someone who is devoted to the Word of God. Here God called Ezra and the Levites, who had been prepared in the quiet place of study, to bless and lead others.

When there is national revival, revival in a local church, or a community, it first starts with individuals. God uses those who have devoted themselves in the secret place to set people free from depression, worry, anxieties, and the bondage of habitual sins. He uses them to motivate others to seek his face. Like with Ezra and the Levites, God is always seeking faithful teachers to help stir up revival.

193

A Catalyst for Spiritual Decay

It should also be noted that decay in a community, a church or a nation will result from a lack of devoted teachers of God's Word. Look at what Paul said about the end times:

> For the time will come when men will not put up with sound doctrine. Instead, to suit their own desires, they will gather around them a great number of teachers to say what their itching ears want to hear.
> 2 Timothy 4:3 (NIV 1984)

In the end times, probably, the majority of the church will have teachers who will not teach the Word. They will not teach sound doctrine, and therefore, the church will fall further away from God. We must be aware of this.

However, when God brings revival, he finds those who are devoted to the study and teaching of God's Word and he uses them to turn others back to himself.

The Need for Persistence in Revival

Another aspect of this devotion is persistence. As mentioned previously, God had used Ezra to revive Israel earlier after the second return from exile; however, that revival must have quickly fizzled out. A weaker man would have become discouraged and given up. In fact, it must be noted that up to 1,500 pastors leave the ministry every month in the United States.[37] Many of them got burnt out, got discouraged, and eventually gave up.

However, Ezra had been both on the mountain top in revival and in the valley when there was rebellion. And yet, he was still faithful. We must have this type of resiliency and perseverance if we are going to see revival around us because there will be many discouragements.

Paul said this: "So we must not grow weary in doing good, for in due time we will reap, if we do not give up" (Galatians 6:9). Let us not give up or get discouraged when we teach people and they do not respond or they backslide. We must be faithful in seasons of plenty and in seasons of lack. God is the one who makes the seed grow (cf. 1 Corinthians 3:6). We are just called to be faithful sowers of the seed.

Are you willing to devote yourself to the study and teaching of Scripture? This is a necessary aspect of revival. God looks for those who are devoted to the study and teaching of his Word, and he uses them mightily to revive his people.

Application Question: What is your daily discipline like in studying Scripture? In what ways is God calling you to be more faithful in your study? Why is persistence so important in bringing revival?

In Revival, God Renews Reverence for the Word of God

Observation Question: In what ways do we see the people's reverence for the Word of God in Nehemiah 8?

The previous characteristic of revival had to do with the teachers; this one has to do with the people. Throughout this narrative, we see the great reverence that the people had for the Word of God. This is seen in many ways. Listen to Nehemiah 8:1-3:

> All the people gathered together in the plaza which was in front of the Water Gate. They asked Ezra the scribe to bring the book of the law of Moses which the Lord had commanded Israel. So Ezra the priest brought the law before the assembly which included men and women and all those able to understand what they heard. (This happened on the first day of the seventh month.) So he read it before the plaza in front of the Water Gate from dawn till noon before the men and women and those children who could understand. All the people were eager to hear the book of the law.

(1) We see the people's great reverence in the fact that they approached Ezra to bring out the Book of the Law and teach it to them. It was also seen in how (2) they listened to the Word of God from "dawn till noon." This means that they listened to the Scripture being read and taught for about six hours. But more startling than that is the fact that it says (3) "All the people were eager to hear the book of the law" while standing. Nehemiah 8:5 and 7 say this:

> Ezra opened the book in plain view of all the people, for he was elevated above all the people. When he opened the book, all the people stood up... Jeshua, Bani, Sherebiah, Jamin, Akkub, Shabbethai, Hodiah, Maaseiah, Kelita, Azariah, Jozabad, Hanan, and Pelaiah—all of whom were Levites—were teaching the people the law, as the *people remained standing*.

Now for people who have served in teaching ministry, specifically that of the Word of God, this might be hard to believe. Most would say, "What? Are

195

you kidding me? No, not possible. It's hard to keep somebody's attention for thirty minutes. You mean to tell me that these people listened attentively for six hours, while standing!"

This may seem like a shock, but this is happening all over the world in places where there is revival. In places like China, it is not uncommon to hear stories of all day worship services with three to six hour sermons. In fact, during much of the Great Reformation, the sermons were at least one hour and usually longer.[38]

When there is revival happening, people tend to have a tremendous reverence for the Word of God. Later, we see this reverence in how they responded with weeping and rejoicing (v. 9, 12). They obeyed it, as they practiced the Feast of Booths (v. 14-17), and they came back every day for more (v. 18). These people reverenced the Word of God.

Erosion of the People of God

In the same way that we see reverence for the Word of God in revival, we also see a decrease in reverence for the Word of God when moral and spiritual decay has crept in. This is what you will typically see in churches around the world today, not this growing reverence, but a growing disdain. Again, listen to what Paul said about the preaching of the Word of God in the last days:

> Preach the Word; be prepared in season and out of season; correct, rebuke and encourage—with great patience and careful instruction. For the time will come when men will not put up with sound doctrine. Instead, to suit their own desires, they will gather around them a great number of teachers to say what their itching ears want to hear. They will turn their ears away from the truth and turn aside to myths.
> 2 Timothy 4:2-4 (NIV 1984)

Previously, we looked at these verses and considered the teachers, but now we will consider the congregations. Paul said a time will come (and it has been here a long time) when people will not stand "sound doctrine," which can be translated "healthy doctrine." They won't want to hear it and so they will hire pastors and teachers who itch their ears and make them feel good. These pastors won't talk about sin, they won't talk about repentance, and they won't talk about taking up one's cross. But they will heap teaching upon the audience that will make them feel good. The pastors will do this because this is what the people want.

196

We see this not only in Paul's warning to Timothy, but we see it in his teaching to the church of Thessalonica. Listen to what he said to them: "Do not extinguish the Spirit. Do not treat prophecies with contempt" (1 Thessalonians 5:19-20). Now when we hear the word prophecy, we tend to think of "foretelling"—someone telling the future. However, that is not fully correct. The majority of "prophecy" written by the prophets in the OT was "forthtelling,"— authoritatively preaching the Word of God and calling people back to following the law.

Seventy-five percent of prophecy in the Bible is forthtelling, preaching an authoritative word from God and calling the people to turn from sin. The prophets did this all the time, as they told Israel to stop worshiping idols, to stop partnering with the foreign nations, to stop abusing and neglecting the poor, and to practice the Sabbath.

In the same way, there is a tendency in the church to show contempt for the prophetic preaching of God's Word, and when we do this, we put out the Spirit's fire. The Spirit can't revive us if we despise or neglect his Word. The Spirit is the author of Scripture, and he works through it.

Sadly, we see what was forbidden in this text happening in most churches around the world. In many congregations when the sermon goes over thirty minutes, it incites great anger amongst the congregants. People commonly despise the preaching of the Word of God and, therefore, lose the Spirit's power.

In a sporting event, when the game goes into overtime, it is an exciting thing. The crowd roars and people start high-fiving. But when the Word of God goes into overtime, people start fidgeting and some even get mad. There is something wrong with our worship when we don't adore hearing and studying the Word of God.

During the Middle Ages (approximately 500 AD to 1500 AD), before the Reformation, the preaching of the Word of God was all but lost from the church. Charles Terpstra said this in his article "The Reformation: A Return to the Primacy of Preaching":

> Many of the established clergy, bishops, and priests, simply did not preach at all. It is said that the lay people could not expect any preaching from the priests in the local parish. Weeks and even months could go by without their hearing any sermon from the pulpit of their local church.[39]

Similarly, the primacy of the Word of God is being lost today. No doubt, if we looked at surveys of preaching length over the last hundred years, I am sure we would see a continual decline towards shorter and shorter messages.

197

In many congregations around the world, the sermon has shrunk to a five or ten minute devotional message, while all the other elements of worship are much longer. In many congregations the exposition of the Word of God is nonexistent.

Do I mean to say longer sermons are better than shorter sermons? No, but I do mean to point out the fact that if we don't want to stay in the Word of God a long time, it says something about our hearts, just as Israel desiring to hear it for six hours said something about their hearts. They really reverenced the Word of God.

Jesus said, "God is seeking those who will worship God in spirit and in truth" (John 4:23, paraphrase). This truth is the Word of God; we can't have worship without the Word.

Interpretation Question: Why is reverence for the Word of God so important?

Remember Jesus prayed this in John 17:17 (NIV 1984): "Sanctify them by the truth; your word is truth." Reverence of the Word of God is important because it is primarily through the Word of God that God sanctifies us. He makes us holy, he changes us into his image, and he gets rid of sin. However, when there is a decrease in the reverence of the Word of God, there will always be a decrease in holiness. People will start to fall away from God because the Word is absent.

It is for this reason that Satan works overtime to undermine the Scripture. In the beginning, one of Satan's first attacks was on the "Word of God." He said to Eve, "Did God really say?" He sought to undermine the Word of God, and he does that today through liberal teachings. He whispers to the church, "Did God really say that?" He tries to rob the church of the inerrancy of Scripture, the sufficiency of Scripture, and, consequently, the authority of Scripture.

If people aren't sure that it's true or they think that only part of it is true, then why would someone reverence something that is full of errors? Why reverence something that might be a lie? In fact, Matthew 13:19 says that wherever the seed of the Word of God is sown, the evil one shows up to steal it. The enemy works hard to stop the Word of God from taking root in the lives of those who have heard it. This stops them from growing and sometimes from even being saved.

And, therefore, where there is decay in the people's "reverence" of the Word of God, you will find a falling away from God, since Scripture reveals who God is. But, listen. We don't just see this in the church at large, but we see this in our individual lives as well.

You can be sure that when there is decay in your time in the Word and in your passion for the Word of God that your sanctification will decay. Where the Word is not exalted, you will find that sin is not lacking.

Do you still revere the Word of God? God said this: "I show special favor to the humble and contrite, who respect what I have to say" (Isaiah 66:2).

Application Question: How have you seen a general decay in the reverence of the Word amongst God's people? How is your reverence for the Word of God? How can we increase our reverence for God's Word both corporately and individually?

In Revival, God Renews Corporate Prayer

> Ezra opened the book in plain view of all the people, for he was elevated above all the people. When he opened the book, all the people stood up. Ezra blessed the Lord, the great God, and all the people replied "Amen! Amen!" as they lifted their hands. Then they bowed down and worshiped the Lord with their faces to the ground.
> Nehemiah 8:5-6

Verses 1-4 seem to be a summary of Ezra's ministry, as it describes the gathering of the people and Ezra's reading. However, verses 5-6 tell us how it happened. He began the reading with prayer, as he praised the Lord. The people responded by lifting their hands and saying, "Amen, Amen" which means "so be it, so be it" or "truly, truly."

This prayer was not just a formality before the reading of God's Word. It was genuine corporate worship and adoration of God. Corporate prayer and worship are a necessary part of revival.

Listen to what Christ taught:

> Again, I tell you the truth, if two of you on earth agree about whatever you ask, my Father in heaven will do it for you. For where two or three are assembled in my name, I am there among them."
> Matthew 18:19-20

We commonly hear this verse quoted, "For where two or three are assembled in my name, I am there among them." We often apply this to any time people are gathered for fellowship, but the context of this is prayer and the wider context is church discipline. The previous verse says, "if two of you on earth agree about whatever you ask, my Father in heaven will do it for you" (v. 19).

I think Christ is trying to teach that there is a tremendous power in corporate prayer. It brings the presence of God, which ultimately brings transformation, repentance, and revival. We experience God in a special way in corporate prayer, and it is through corporate prayer that we will see God move in a special way. For those who have truly experienced the benefits of it, they cannot live without it.

They cannot but be in a small group lifting up one another's prayer requests; they cannot but be part of the church's prayer ministry for it is there they have experienced him and seen his hand move in amazing ways. It is no wonder that soon after the prayer and the reading of the Word, we see Israel in this text weeping, rejoicing, and following God in obedience. God was there when they brought their prayers before him, and he moved in response.

In fact, we see a promise of revival connected to corporate prayer in 2 Chronicles 7:14:

If my people, who belong to me, humble themselves, pray, seek to please me, and repudiate their sinful practices, then I will respond from heaven, forgive their sin, and heal their land.

This is God's response to Solomon's prayer for God to bless the temple (cf. 2 Chronicles 6:13-42). God said that when Israel was unified in humble prayer and repentance, he would hear and heal their land. Corporate prayer is necessary for revival.

Do we not see the need for corporate prayer? Do we not see the need to gather together and intercede over the church, government policies, and over our nation? It is there where God's presence is manifest, and he moves on behalf of his people.

It is no wonder that every revival began with people gathering together to pray. They gathered, prayed, and God moved to restore the land. Even the great revival in Acts began with people waiting on the Lord in prayer. Acts 1:14 says, "All these continued together in prayer with one mind." The small band of disciples prayed and the Spirit of God fell and brought a revival. After Pentecost, the early church continued to gather daily to devote themselves to Scripture and prayer (Acts 2:42). Furthermore, the apostles declared their dependence on it. They would not neglect the discipline of prayer and the Word, not even for social service like caring for widows (Acts 6:4).

Sadly, when we are lacking revival in our own lives and in the church, we are too busy to pray. We are too busy to pray individually and too busy to pray corporately. Therefore, revival tarries both individually and corporately.

How is God calling you to restore or grow in your prayer life? How is God calling you to gather with others to intercede for revival?

Application Question: How is God calling you to protect and cultivate your prayer life both individually and corporately?

In Revival, God Renews Genuine Mourning over Sin

> Then Nehemiah the governor, Ezra the priestly scribe, and the Levites who were imparting understanding to the people said to all of them, "This day is holy to the Lord your God. Do not mourn or weep." For all the people had been weeping when they heard the words of the law.
> Nehemiah 8:9

As the people listened to the Word of God, they began to weep. Nehemiah rebuked them because this was supposed to be a day of celebration; God had rebuilt their walls and taken away their reproach before their enemies. However, as the Word of God was listened to, people had genuine remorse, which resulted in genuine obedience to God.

In every revival, there have been great waves of repentance. People were cut to the heart over their sins and repented. This is the natural response of somebody who has seen or experienced God. When Isaiah saw God he cried, "Too bad for me! I am destroyed, for my lips are contaminated by sin, and I live among people whose lips are contaminated by sin. My eyes have seen the king, the Lord who commands armies."' (Isaiah 6:5). Isaiah essentially called himself a dead man. "Too bad" can also be translated "Woe," which was used for dead people. Peter, when he recognized Christ, said, "Go away from me, Lord, for I am a sinful man!" (Lk 5:8).

Because in revival we experience God, genuine mourning and repentance will be involved. Listen to what James said to scattered Jewish Christians in James 4:8-10:

> Draw near to God and he will draw near to you. Cleanse your hands, you sinners, and make your hearts pure, you double-minded. Grieve, mourn, and weep. Turn your laughter into mourning and your joy into despair. Humble yourselves before the Lord and he will exalt you.

As we come near God, he comes near us. Then, we, by necessity, mourn and repent of our sins, and then he lifts us up. He revives us; he strengthens us; he renews us.

201

However, the opposite of mourning is laughter. When the church or an individual Christian is unhealthy, instead of mourning over sin, they laugh at it. They pump it in their music; they watch it on their TV; they make jokes about it with their friends. An unhealthy church or individual believer enjoys sin instead of mourning and repenting over it.

Are you still mourning over your sin and the sin of your community? Or have you just accepted it or, even worse, are you rejoicing in it, like the world?

In describing the characteristics of those who are part of the kingdom of God, Christ said, "Blessed are those who mourn, for they will be comforted" (Matt 5:4). True believers are mourners, and they also receive the comfort of God. He comforts them as he forgives their sin. He comforts them as he turns their church or their community around in revival. He comforts them, ultimately, when he destroys sin and the evil one at his second coming. Oh Lord, comfort your church.

Application Question: In what ways have you seen a lack of mourning over sin in the church, your community, or in your own life? How is God calling you to become a mourner?

In Revival, God Renews Obedience to the Word of God

On the second day of the month the family leaders met with Ezra the scribe, together with all the people, the priests, and the Levites, to consider the words of the law. They discovered written in the law that the Lord had commanded through Moses that the Israelites should live in temporary shelters during the festival of the seventh month, and that they should make a proclamation and disseminate this message in all their cities and in Jerusalem: "Go to the hill country and bring back olive branches and branches of wild olive trees, myrtle trees, date palms, and other leafy trees to construct temporary shelters, as it is written." So the people went out and brought these things back and constructed temporary shelters for themselves, each on his roof and in his courtyard and in the courtyards of the temple of God and in the plaza of the Water Gate and the plaza of the Ephraim Gate. So all the assembly which had returned from the exile constructed temporary shelters and lived in them. The Israelites had not done so from the days of Joshua son of Nun until that day. Everyone experienced very great joy.
Nehemiah 8:13-17

202

Finally, we cannot but notice Israel's obedience to the Word of God. The heads of all the families came back to Ezra on the second day of the month to give further attention to the words of the law (v. 13). They wanted more of the Word of God. The leaders got into a small group with Ezra and actually rediscovered the Feast of the Booths, which Israel had neglected.

After learning this, the leaders called all the people of Israel to practice this feast. They placed tents on their roofs and in their courtyards and lived in them, as the nation once did in the wilderness. This was a reminder of God's faithfulness to provide for the nation after leaving Egypt, where they were previously slaves. In fact, Scripture says they did it in such a way that had never been done since the days of Joshua. Israel was obedient to the Word of God. Obedience to Scripture is a necessary part of revival.

Application Question: Why is obedience a common experience in revival?

Genuine Conversion

One of the reasons that obedience is a common characteristic of revival is because obedience is a characteristic of genuine conversion. In the church, we often find extremes in one's affection for the Word: some people love to hear and respond to the Word, and yet many are extremely apathetic towards it. Christ talks about this tendency in the Sermon on the Mount.

In Matthew 7:24-27, he described those who hear and obey the Word, as those who build their house on a strong foundation and the house stands in the storm. But, those who hear and do not obey it are like those who build their house on the sand, and it falls during the storm. When he gives this illustration, he is really describing those who are converted and those who are not. In Matthew 7:21-23, he had previously described those in the church who say "Lord, Lord," but live a life of disobedience and he says to them, "I never knew you."

One's continual response to the Word of God is a picture of one's salvation. James taught the same thing. He said, "But be sure you live out the message and do not merely listen to it and so deceive yourselves" (James 1:22).

What does he mean by one being self-deceived? He is talking about the genuineness of his salvation. He speaks directly to these people in James 2:17 and says, "So also faith, if it does not have works, is dead being by itself" He says, even the demons believe in God (v.19), but they are not saved.

He spoke to Christians who listened but weren't responding, and therefore, he challenged the reality of their salvation. Remember even Herod enjoyed listening to John the Baptist (Mk 6:20), but he didn't obey the Word of

God. Herod wasn't born again. In fact, he later murdered John the Baptist. Part of the reason why so many churches are dead is because so many listeners don't practice God's Word—proving they are not truly born again.

Similarly, the apostle John said, "Now by this we know that we have come to know God: if we keep his commandments" (1 John 2:3). When people are obeying God, it proves that they are saved.

In revivals, genuine conversion brings about great repentance and obedience. People start following Christ, and it changes their life. Sadly, most churches are full of people who call him, "Lord," and yet practice a lifestyle of disobedience (cf. Matt 7:21-23).

God's Blessings

With that said, James gives another fruit of obedience. He says, "But the one who peers into the perfect law of liberty and fixes his attention there, and does not become a forgetful listener but one who lives it out—he will be blessed in what he does" (James 1:25).

God blesses those who do the will of God. That is what we see happening in Nehemiah 8. The Israelites had a celebration of the Feast of Booths that was greater than any feast since the days of Joshua (v. 17). God blessed them because they were obedient. Obedience will characterize corporate revival and also revival in our own lives.

In the days of Nehemiah, Israel had been in rebellion towards God's Word. They were no longer celebrating the festival and many other commandments. However, when they heard the preaching of God's Word, they were cut to the heart and responded. They turned away from their sin and practiced what God's Word said. This has characterized revivals throughout history: people repented—turning away from sin and the things of this world—and submitted to God.

Are we obedient to the Word of God? Do we practice obedience as a lifestyle? Obedience gives us assurance of salvation, but it also brings God's blessings on his people. Revivals have always been characterized by obedience because it is proof of genuine conversion and it also brings God's blessing.

Are you practicing obedience? Or are you choosing the world and sin over God?

Application Question: In what ways is God challenging you to greater obedience? In what ways have you seen his blessing when you were obedient and the removal of his blessings when you were not?

Conclusion

What are characteristics of a revival of worship amongst God's people or in our individual lives?

1. In revival, God restores unity amongst the people of God.
2. In revival, God restores devoted teachers of the Word of God to leadership.
3. In revival, God restores reverence for the Word of God.
4. In revival, God restores corporate prayer.
5. In revival, God restores genuine mourning over sin.
6. In revival, God restores obedience to the Word of God.

Application Question: As a leader, in what ways is God calling you to help restore revival in your life and in your community?

Characteristics of Acceptable Worship

On the twenty-fourth day of this same month the Israelites assembled; they were fasting and wearing sackcloth, their heads covered with dust. Those truly of Israelite descent separated from all the foreigners, standing and confessing their sins and the iniquities of their ancestors. For one-fourth of the day they stood in their place and read from the book of the law of the Lord their God, and for another fourth they were confessing their sins and worshiping the Lord their God. Then the Levites—Jeshua, Binnui, Kadmiel, Shebaniah, Bunni, Sherebiah, Bani, and Kenani—stood on the steps and called out loudly to the Lord their God. The Levites—Jeshua, Kadmiel, Bani, Hashabneiah, Sherebiah, Hodiah, Shebaniah, and Pethahiah—said, "Stand up and bless the Lord your God!" "May you be blessed, O Lord our God, from age to age. May your glorious name be blessed; may it be lifted up above all blessing and praise. You alone are the Lord. You made the heavens, even the highest heavens, along with all their multitude of stars, the earth and all that is on it, the seas and all that is in them. You impart life to them all, and the multitudes of heaven worship you....
Nehemiah 9 (NET)

What are characteristics of acceptable worship, worship that God desires and honors?

In Nehemiah 1-6, the focus is the rebuilding of the wall around Jerusalem, and, in Nehemiah 8-12, the focus is the spiritual revival in Israel. Nehemiah, with the help of Ezra and the Levites, began to rebuild the people of God. In Nehemiah 9, we learn a great deal about worship specifically. On the 24th day of the same month that the Israelites celebrated the feast of booths in Nehemiah 8, the Israelites gathered together for a day of national repentance and worship.

In John 4:23, Jesus said this: "But a time is coming—and now is here—when the true worshipers will worship the Father in spirit and truth, for the Father seeks such people to be his worshipers."

207

The reality that God the Father is seeking worshipers who worship in spirit and truth, implies that there is both a wrong and right way to worship God. In fact, we see the importance of proper worship early on in Scripture. Cain and Abel both brought offerings before the Lord but Cain's was rejected (Gen 4).

Similarly, we see rejected worship throughout much of Israel's history. God derailed Israel for their fasting in the book of Isaiah and said that it would not be accepted. He shared their unrighteous complaints and then answered them. In Isaiah 58:3-4 it says:

> They lament, 'Why don't you notice when we fast? Why don't you pay attention when we humble ourselves?' Look, at the same time you fast, you satisfy your selfish desires, you oppress your workers. Look, your fasting is accompanied by arguments, brawls, and fistfights. Do not fast as you do today, trying to make your voice heard in heaven.

Israel noticed that their fasting was unprofitable and they asked, "What good is it?" God rebuked them and said that the type of worship they were offering was unacceptable. How could they be living in quarreling and strife and expect their offering to be accepted by God? God said their voices (i.e. their prayer and worship) would not even be heard by him. In Malachi 1, God rejected the offerings of the priests because they were offering the lame and the blind, instead of offering a lamb without blemish.

Many people in the church have the same dilemma. They recognize that their devotions aren't profitable, the church services they attend aren't alive, and they wonder why it is so. Sometimes the problem is that their worship has been rejected by God.

As we consider this reality, we must ask the question, "How can we have a worship that is acceptable to God?" Jesus said God is seeking proper worship; he looks for it.

In this text, we learn characteristics of acceptable worship by looking at the revival that happened in Israel. This is especially important for leaders, as they seek to guide people in a worship that is pleasing to God and edifying for them.

Big Question: What characteristics of acceptable worship can we discern from Nehemiah 9, and how can we apply these characteristics to our spiritual lives?

Acceptable Worship Includes Preparation

On the twenty-fourth day of this same month the Israelites assembled; they were fasting and wearing sackcloth, their heads covered with dust. Those truly of Israelite descent separated from all the foreigners
Nehemiah 9:1-2

We cannot but notice that the Israelites prepared for worship. Clearly, they did not just fall out of bed and head to service, as often happens in church today. Many Christians give no thought to preparation for worship, small group, or even daily devotions. No wonder many people leave these activities saying, "I didn't get anything out of that."

Why does this happen? It happens in part because most believers don't prepare for worship. As demonstrated in the Parable of the Sowers (Matt 13), nothing is wrong with the seed of the Word sown in worship; the problem is with the ground of our hearts. Therefore, as with farming, the ground of our hearts must be cultivated to worship God. An unprepared worship is an unacceptable worship.

Observation Question: How did Israel prepare for worship in verses 1 and 2?

1.   They prepared for worship by fasting.

On the twenty-fourth day of this same month the Israelites assembled; they were fasting and wearing sackcloth, their heads covered with dust.
Nehemiah 9:1

This meant they neglected eating food for some period of time before they came to worship. Fasting is never given as a command in the New Testament, but it is given as an expectation. Christ said to his disciples, "When you fast, do not look sullen like the hypocrites ..." (Matt 6:15). Also, when John's disciples asked why Christ's disciples didn't fast, Jesus replied that when he was taken away, they would fast (Matt 9:15). It seems that God expects each of us to fast in some form or another. Fasting is meant to help focus our heart, mind, and spirit on God by neglecting some great priority in our lives. Fasting doesn't necessarily have to be food; it can be anything that demands a tremendous amount of our time, focus, or energy.

Some of the greatest ways we can fast may be giving up time on the Internet, Facebook, TV, hobbies, etc. Even Scripture condones married couples fasting from the practice of physical intimacy to focus on prayer. Paul said this in 1 Corinthians 7:5, "Do not deprive each other, except by mutual agreement for a specified time, so that you may devote yourselves to prayer. Then resume your relationship, so that Satan may not tempt you because of your lack of self-control."

There is often a need to fast in order to prepare for worship because our hearts are so prone to be divided, distracted, and hard. For example, for a season of my life, I made a covenant that I wouldn't do anything before I got into the Word in the morning. This included getting on the Internet, studying, eating, or anything else.

I remember being in seminary and on Saturdays sometimes I would stay in the bed till one pm, not because I was tired, but just because I didn't want to read the Bible. I had decided to fast from everything else before I spent time in the Word of God and prayer as a discipline. I made that commitment while I was in college, and I stayed with it for many years. I still practice it but just not as legalistically. This is a form of fasting, letting go of something else to focus on God.

Jesus said we should consider fasting with anything that we consider a treasure in our lives. Look at what he said in Matthew 6:19-21:

> "Do not accumulate for yourselves treasures on earth, where moth and rust destroy and where thieves break in and steal. But accumulate for yourselves treasures in heaven, where moth and rust do not destroy, and thieves do not break in and steal. For where your treasure is, there your heart will be also.

Jesus said not to accumulate treasures on the earth, not because they are sin, but because they have a tendency to steal our hearts away from God. He said, "For where your treasure is, there your heart will be also."

This is something we must consider with such things as our phones, Internet, cable television, hobbies, etc. We must ask ourselves, "What is my treasure?" because it is our treasures that have the ability to quench our worship, as they steal our hearts away from God.

For some, this may mean giving up certain treasures all together. That's what Christ demanded of the rich man (Matt 19:21). He was called to sell all his riches and follow Christ. For others it may mean to practice rigorous discipline with those treasures in order to protect their hearts. In 1 Corinthians 7:31 (NIV 1984), Paul said that those who use the things of this world should not be "engrossed in them."

For some, a fast could be as simple as going to bed early so that they can have time with God in the morning. That would mean neglecting time given to other things in order to prepare one's mind and body to seek God the next day. This can be a form of fasting.

210

Application Question: What are some other practical ways we can fast to prepare for worship?

2. They prepared for worship by mourning as they put on sackcloth and dust.

    On the twenty-fourth day of this same month the Israelites assembled; they were fasting and wearing sackcloth, their heads covered with dust.
    Nehemiah 9:1

Again this seems to be something they did before coming to the service; they put on sackcloth, which is a cheap, uncomfortable type of clothing, and put dust on their heads. Obviously, the sackcloth and dust was meant to be a picture of their hearts before God. This practice was associated with mourning and would typically be done at funerals. In this case, the Israelites were mourning over their sins and the neglect of the law.

Essentially, they prepared their hearts for worship by mourning over sin in their personal lives and that of the community. Mourning is not only preparation for worship, it is part of worship. Look at how Isaiah responded when he saw God in Isaiah 6:5: "I said, 'Too bad for me! I am destroyed, for my lips are contaminated by sin, and I live among people whose lips are contaminated by sin. My eyes have seen the king, the Lord who commands armies.'"

The natural reaction for a person who truly sees God will be mourning. When Peter encountered Christ he fell down and cried, "Go away from me, Lord, for I am a sinful man!" (Lk 5:8). We mourn because our sin and the sin of our communities appear so ugly, as we look at God's beauty and perfect righteousness. Mourning is a part of worship because it is the natural response of meditating on God, who is perfect.

In fact, Scripture declares that God blesses those who mourn. Jesus said, "Blessed are those who mourn, for they will be comforted" (Matt 5:4). God blesses those who mourn over their own sin and the sin of the world. With Isaiah, God comforted him by forgiving his sin and, soon after, calling him to the ministry of prophet (cf. Isaiah 6).

Application Question: How do we prepare to worship by mourning?

-   Mourning comes from genuine contemplation on God.

Isaiah mourned as he saw God. He said, "Too bad for me! I am destroyed, for my lips are contaminated by sin, and I live among people whose lips are contaminated by sin. My eyes have seen the king, the Lord who commands armies." (Isaiah 6:5).

It is clear that Israel was contemplating God, even before coming to public worship. They came with hearts that had been looking at God, which revealed their sinful condition. Therefore, they dressed with sackcloth and dust. In the same way, we must prepare our hearts for worship by contemplating God and his holiness.

- Mourning comes from genuine contemplation of the human condition.

Mourning happens not only when we look at God but also by contemplating the human condition in view of God. It means to look at ourselves and society in comparison to God's character and revealed will. Man was made in the image of God, and therefore, any time we fail to practice God's commands, we are sinning. Isaiah's time with God drew him to mourn over his condition and that of his people. It showed him their need for God's grace. In Nehemiah 8, Israel listened to the Word of God read and taught for six hours and while listening they wept because of their sin (v. 9).

We cannot truly worship God unless we know how much we desperately need him. Contemplation of God and the human condition prepares us to draw near him for his grace and mercy (cf. Heb 4:16). Many are not prepared for worship because they have not properly contemplated the human condition and their need.

I think we see this struggle often in small groups. At the end or beginning of many small groups there is a time of sharing praises and prayer requests. However, often during these times many will have nothing to share. They won't have a prayer request, and they won't have any praises. This aspect of worship only comes when we have contemplated God and the human condition. Without this contemplation, many show up before God without any expectation—any faith in him to do something—and without anything really to offer. They come to church or small group not really seeking God for anything or seeking to give God anything, and therefore, many times, they leave without anything. Similarly, Christ said he couldn't do very many miracles in his hometown because they had so little faith (cf. Matt 13:58). Often, it is the same in our corporate worship.

Contemplation of the human condition will typically bring praise or mourning. Praise, when we see God moving and transforming people. Mourning, as we see how far we fall short. Contemplation of God and the human condition is needed for us to truly worship.

212

When I was young, I used to show up to church with no preparation; the concept of preparing for worship never dawned on me. I thought only pastors, teachers, and the worship teams prepared. However, I began to realize that what I received from God on Sundays or in a small group was often proportional to my preparation. Jesus said, "Blessed are those who hunger and thirst for righteousness, for they will be satisfied" (Matt 5:6). The only people who are hungry are the ones who have contemplated God and their condition, which reveals their needs. And it is those people who God fills during worship. They come to church with an expectation because they recognize their great need and that of their community, and therefore, God satisfies their hunger.

What else did Israel do in preparation for worship?

3. They prepared for worship by separating themselves from all foreigners.

    Those truly of Israelite descent separated from all the foreigners.
    Nehemiah 9:2

Why did Israel separate from the foreigners? They separated, in part, because the foreign nations were leading them into sin. God called the nation of Israel to separate from the Canaanites because of their sexual immorality, false worship, and lack of morals. If they were not living separately, they would be tempted to intermarry, worship their gods, and be drawn into all types of sin. Yes, they were still called to be a light to the nations, but, in order to do that, they needed to be separate from anything that might contaminate (cf. James 1:27). That is why the nation of Israel initially fell under Solomon. Solomon married many foreign wives who influenced him to take their gods, and his stumble brought the judgment of God on Israel and eventually the exile. When Israel separated from the foreigners before worship, it was a protection from temptation and a consecration of themselves to God alone.

In a similar way, God calls the church to be separate from the world (cf. 2 Cor 6:17). He has established it as a necessary aspect of true worship. James 1:27 says, "Pure and undefiled religion before God the Father is this: to care for orphans and widows in their misfortune and to keep oneself unstained by the world." A religion that is not separate is a worship that is not acceptable to God. This must be our necessary practice as well.

A person trying to live for God and walk with the world is a "double-minded individual." James 1:7-8 says that this person will receive nothing from God. We must be single minded because it is the "pure in heart" who will see God (Matt 5:8).

213

In what ways is God calling you to separate in order to better worship him? In what ways is he calling you to be different from the world in order to have more intimacy with him?

If we are going to worship God, we must prepare through fasting, mourning, and separating, and we must lead others to do the same. An unprepared worship is an unacceptable worship.

Application Question: What are some other practical ways to prepare for daily worship? In what ways is God challenging you to be more prepared to come into his presence?

Acceptable Worship Includes Confession of Sin

> Those truly of Israelite descent separated from all the foreigners, standing and confessing their sins and the iniquities of their ancestors. Nehemiah 9:2

The next thing we see is that when the Israelites came together, they stood and confessed their sin and the iniquities of their fathers. Confession is also a necessary aspect of acceptable worship.

Interpretation Question: Why is confession of sin so important in worship?

1. Confession of sin is important for worship because sin hinders the reception of the Word of God.

It must be noticed that this prayer of confession was offered right before hearing the Word of God. Nehemiah 9:2-3 says,

> Those truly of Israelite descent separated from all the foreigners, standing and confessing their sins and the iniquities of their ancestors. For one-fourth of the day they stood in their place and read from the book of the law of the Lord their God

This was an ideal place because sin always affects our ability to receive God's Word. Listen to what James 1:21 says: "So put away all filth and evil excess and humbly welcome the message implanted within you, which is able to save your souls."

It says get rid of all moral filth and evil and humbly accept the word planted in you. James says getting rid of sin must come before the Word of God

214

is received. For the believers James was ministering to, the Word of God was already present. He said, "welcome the message implanted within you." As in the Parable of the Sower (Matt 13), the seed was in the soil, but it was not producing any fruit. Most believers know what God's Word says; however, it has no effect on their lives. They are not being changed by it. They have not truly accepted the Word planted in them.

How do we remedy this? One of the ways is by confessing our sins and turning away from them. This is necessary for us to truly accept the Word of God. If we have unconfessed sins in our lives, it will choke the Word and keep it from being fruitful. Matthew 13:22 (NIV 1984) says, "The one who received the seed that fell among the thorns is the man who hears the word, but the worries of this life and the deceitfulness of wealth choke it, making it unfruitful." In the example of the thorny ground, worry and the deceitfulness of wealth choked the Word and made it unfruitful. Worry is sin because it essentially says, "God, I don't trust you." Wealth is deceptive because it has a tendency to draw people into trusting it over God and pursuing it over God. It also has a tendency to deceive people into pride (cf. 1 Tim 6:17), once again creating a lack of dependence upon God. Sin chokes the Word of God and makes it unfruitful.

It has been said, "Sin will either keep you out of the Word of God or the Word of God will keep you out of sin." It's one or the other. When you find the Word of God decreasing in your life, sin will increase. When the Word of God is increasing in your life, sin, by necessity, will decrease. They always affect one another.

Peter says the exact same thing as James:

So get rid of all evil and all deceit and hypocrisy and envy and all slander. And yearn like newborn infants for pure, spiritual milk, so that by it you may grow up to salvation
1 Peter 2:1-2

We must rid ourselves of evil, deceit, hypocrisy, envy, and slander in order for us to even yearn for the milk of the Word of God. If you don't yearn for it, you won't eat it. Part of true worship is confession of sin because it enables us to desire, receive, and produce fruit from the Word of God.

2. Confession of sin is important to worship because it will hinder our prayer life.

Listen to what David said: "If I had harbored sin in my heart, the Lord would not have listened" (Psalm 66:18).

Many people have ineffective worship because they have not confessed and turned away from their sin. This not only quenches the effectiveness of the Word of God but it also quenches the effectiveness of prayer.

Interpretation Question: Why did the Israelites confess the iniquities of their fathers?

Israel confessed the sins of their fathers because they were in part under God's judgment because of their sins. Look at Exodus 20:4-6:

> "You shall not make for yourself a carved image or any likeness of anything that is in heaven above or that is on the earth beneath or that is in the water below. You shall not bow down to them or serve them, for I, the Lord, your God, am a jealous God, responding to the transgression of fathers by dealing with children to the third and fourth generations of those who reject me, and showing covenant faithfulness to a thousand generations of those who love me and keep my commandments.

It says God responds to the sins of the fathers to the third and fourth generation but shows covenant faithfulness or love to a thousand generations of those who love God. This does not teach that God will judge children for the sins of the fathers, as made clear by other Scriptures (cf. Deut 24:16). However, it does teach that we are affected by both the sins and righteousness of those who came before us. We see this in Adam's sin as it was passed down generationally. We see it in Christ's righteousness and how we receive life through his act of righteousness. We see this in the Abrahamic covenant as God promises to bless both Abraham's physical and spiritual seed, which we are a part of.

Exodus 20 teaches that generational curses get passed down from our fathers as well as generational blessings. The sins of the fathers will often follow the sons for generations, prompting God's judgment. I don't think it's a coincidence that Abraham lied about his wife being his sister in Egypt and Gerar (cf. Gen 13, 20) and then Isaac did the same thing (Gen 26). Our shortcomings often get passed from generation to generation bringing God's judgment on those generations. Although many had returned from the exile, Israel was still suffering from the sin and consequences of previous generations.

It is for this reason that Israel confessed not only their sins but also their fathers'. Their fathers were idolaters and unfaithful to God, and they, the

216

sons and daughters, had done the same thing and reaped the same harvest of discipline.

Application Question: Should Christians still confess the sins of others today? Is there Scriptural support for this?

Scripture clearly teaches that it is good and proper to pray for and confess the sins of others. Even though much of the church has gotten away from this practice, it is clearly a biblical doctrine.

How else do we see this in Scripture? Listen to what Samuel said:

> All the people said to Samuel, "Pray to the Lord your God on behalf of us—your servants—so we won't die, for we have added to all our sins by asking for a king."... As far as I am concerned, far be it from me to sin against the Lord by ceasing to pray for you! I will instruct you in the way that is good and upright.
> 1 Samuel 12:19, 23

When Israel sinned by asking for a king, Samuel said he would not sin by ceasing to pray for the people. The context of this praying is for Israel's forgiveness as seen by their request in verse 19. Similarly, it is a sin for us to not pray for our nation, to not pray for forgiveness and grace over our church.

In addition, we are clearly commanded in the Lord's Prayer to ask for forgiveness for others' sins (Matt 6:12). It does not say "forgive my debt," it says, "forgive us 'our' debts" (Matt 6:12). Similarly, Jesus prayed for his persecutors, "Father, forgive them, for they don't know what they are doing." We should do the same.

Therefore, we must see that proper worship includes confession of our sin and the sin of others. As a priestly nation, we bring the sins of the world before God and seek his forgiveness and grace (cf. 1 Peter 2:9). We do this both because Scripture teaches us to pray this way and also because we are affected by the sins of others. Abraham's nephew, Lot, almost died because of the sins of his neighbors in Sodom. In Genesis 18, Abraham petitioned for God's mercy on the nation.

This is especially important for leaders. Leaders will often need to lead people to repentance over sin and that of their nations and communities.

Application Question: How is God calling you to get rid of any sins so you can more effectively worship him? Are there any national, church, familial, or individual sins you feel impressed to intercede over?

Acceptable Worship Includes Hearing and Responding to the Word of God

> For one-fourth of the day they stood in their place and read from the book of the law of the Lord their God, and for another fourth they were confessing their sins and worshiping the Lord their God.
> Nehemiah 9:3

The next thing they did was read from the book of the law for one-fourth of the day. The day is probably referring to daylight hours. Therefore, Israel read from Scripture for three hours, then for another three hours they confessed and worshipped.[40] The reading of Scripture was probably intermingled with teaching, as seen in the previous chapter (cf. Neh 8:3, 7).

Hear we see the priority given to the Word of God in this service. It was read for three hours, and after, they responded with more confession of sins and worship to God. This is important to hear because we have a tendency to hear the Word of God on Sunday and then quickly leave and go about our business.

Often in our services, very little time is given to actually reflect and respond to the Word of God in prayer. The preacher preaches and closes in prayer, we sing a quick hymn and the service is over. However, I think it is a very healthy practice to have time to respond to God, right after the Word of God has been given. This was the principle behind the "altar call," which many churches have discarded. It is wise to take time to meditate and respond to what God has spoken, even if only through an extended time of corporate prayer and worship.

With that said, I think the main principle we should take from this text is the need to hear and respond to the Word of God as a part of our worship. Listen to what James says:

> But be sure you live out the message and do not merely listen to it and so deceive yourselves. For if someone merely listens to the message and does not live it out, he is like someone who gazes at his own face in a mirror.
> James 1:22-23

James commanded the church to not merely listen to the Word of God but to live it out. He said the person who simply listens and doesn't respond is deceived.

218

What does he mean by deceived? In the context of the book of James, it means to be deceived about their salvation. In James 2:17, he said, "faith, if it does not have works, is dead being by itself." A person who merely listens to the Word of God is not truly born again. Jesus said the same thing in Matthew 7:24-29. He said the person who heard his words but didn't obey them, was like a person who built his house on a foundation of sand, and when the storm came, the house was destroyed (cf. Matt 7:21-23).

James went on to describe hearing the Word and not doing it as a person looking in a mirror and seeing the problems but going away without doing anything about it. This person's worship is pointless. Yet, many people do this each Sunday and every time they hear or study the Word of God. Their worship is pointless. It doesn't change their lives at all.

However, James declared the blessing of God on the person who hears the Word and responds. He said: "But the one who peers into the perfect law of liberty and fixes his attention there, and does not become a forgetful listener but one who lives it out—he will be blessed in what he does" (James 1:25).

This person will be blessed by God. Blessing has to do with approval and favor. When people respond to the Word of God as Israel did, with true confession of sin and worship, it is worship God approves of and blesses. Praise the Lord!

Leaders must continually call their people to hear and respond to God's Word. Jesus said, "If you continue to follow my teaching, you are really my disciples" (John 8:31). Only those who continue to follow Christ's words are truly saved. Therefore, leaders must also warn those they lead of the tendency towards self-deception. It is possible to be a hearer and not a doer and be deceived about one's faith.

Application Question: How can churches similarly give greater honor to the Word of God in our services and also an opportunity to respond? How is God challenging you to be both a hearer and a doer of God's Word?

Acceptable Worship Includes the Leadership of Righteous Leaders

> The Levites—Jeshua, Kadmiel, Bani, Hashabneiah, Sherebiah, Hodiah, Shebaniah, and Pethahiah—said, "Stand up and bless the Lord your God!" "May you be blessed, O Lord our God, from age to age. May your glorious name be blessed; may it be lifted up above all blessing and praise

Nehemiah 9:5

In this text, it says that the Levites led Israel in the worship of God. In the law, God had commanded that a certain tribe should lead the worship of Israel, the tribe of Levi. Within the tribe of Levi, the priests came from the lineage of Aaron who also led specific acts of worship at the temple. Levites were given commands on how to keep themselves holy in order to approach the Lord and lead in worship (Lev 10). They were commanded to be holy and to lead the people in holiness. If the Levites were not holy, it would have drawn the people away from God instead of towards him. It is the same for our spiritual leaders.

Scripture teaches that leaders cannot positively affect people without having holy lives. Remember what Paul said to Timothy: "Be conscientious about how you live and what you teach. Persevere in this, because by doing so you will save both yourself and those who listen to you" (1 Timothy 4:16). If leaders don't have a right life and right doctrine, they will not save the hearers; they will, in fact, destroy them. Acceptable worship includes righteous leaders.

In fact, the requirements for leaders in the New Testament have nothing to do with race, ethnicity or tribe; the requirements are primarily righteous character traits. Take a look at the requirements for an overseer in 1 Timothy 3:1-3:

> This saying is trustworthy: "If someone aspires to the office of overseer, he desires a good work." The overseer then must be above reproach, the husband of one wife, temperate, self-controlled, respectable, hospitable, an able teacher, not a drunkard, not violent, but gentle, not contentious, free from the love of money.

The qualifications for an overseer are primarily character traits—they are to be above reproach, the husband of one wife (a one-woman man), self-controlled, hospitable (a lover of strangers), etc. They are to be people with godly character. Other than the requirements of them being male and apt to teach, the other requirements are all character traits. Therefore, worship must be led by godly leaders.

When God called someone to write the hymnal of Israel—the Psalms—he called a godly leader named David. Acceptable worship is led by godly leaders. We can have little to no doubt that the Levites leading the worship of Israel were godly as well.

Application Question: Why else is it important for the leaders to be holy and righteous?

220

Listen to what James 5:16 says: "So confess your sins to one another and pray for one another so that you may be healed. The prayer of a righteous person has great effectiveness." While encouraging the church to bring their sick to the elders for prayer, James said, "the prayer of the righteous person has great effectiveness." When a righteous man or woman prays, the power of God moves.

Similarly, when the leadership of the church is ungodly and unrighteous, then it removes the power and blessing of God. We saw this with Israel while Christ was on the earth. The spiritual leaders of Israel, the Pharisees and the Sadducees, were ungodly. Consequently, they led the people away from God with both their teachings and their actions. Ultimately, this brought the judgment of God.

In the Old Testament, God often rebuked the spiritual leaders of Israel for their corruption and leading Israel astray. Listen to what he said through Jeremiah:

> "That is because, from the least important to the most important of them, all of them are greedy for dishonest gain. Prophets and priests alike, all of them practice deceit. They offer only superficial help for the harm my people have suffered. They say, 'Everything will be all right!' But everything is not all right! Are they ashamed because they have done such shameful things? No, they are not at all ashamed. They do not even know how to blush! So they will die, just like others have died. They will be brought to ruin when I punish them," says the Lord.
> Jeremiah 6:13 -15

Jeremiah said the prophets and the priests both practiced sin and that God was going to judge both them and the people. They were still worshiping God, but their worship was not acceptable. The leaders were leading them into sin. A characteristic of acceptable worship is having godly leaders.

Jesus said, "It is enough for the disciple to become like his teacher, and the slave like his master" (Matthew 10:25). It is our leaders who set the ceiling for our development. If a leader is ungodly, then he will hinder the worship and development of a congregation. But, when a leader is righteous and growing, he sets the standard for the congregation's development.

A characteristic of acceptable worship is godly leadership. When the church is under God's judgment, you will typically find ungodly people in leadership. Isaiah 3:1-7 describes how, when God judges a people, he removes godly leaders and gives them the leaders they deserve. Consider what it says:

Look, the sovereign Lord who commands armies is about to remove from Jerusalem and Judah every source of security, including all the food and water, the mighty men and warriors, judges and prophets, omen readers and leaders, captains of groups of fifty, the respected citizens, advisers and those skilled in magical arts, and those who know incantations. The Lord says, "I will make youths their officials; malicious young men will rule over them. The people will treat each other harshly; men will oppose each other; neighbors will fight. Youths will proudly defy the elderly and riffraff will challenge those who were once respected. Indeed, a man will grab his brother right in his father's house and say, 'You own a coat— you be our leader! This heap of ruins will be under your control.' At that time the brother will shout, 'I am no doctor, I have no food or coat in my house; don't make me a leader of the people!'"

Isaiah 3:1-7

Godly leadership is an important aspect of worship and receiving God's blessing. In this text, the Levites, those chosen by God to prepare themselves uniquely for worship, were called to lead the people in praising God. Similarly, the leadership of the church should be people of character in order to receive and dispense the blessing of God.

This is a reminder for us, as leaders, to cultivate holy lives so we can lead people in righteousness and not bring God's judgment. But also, it is a reminder for us to help raise up other godly leaders so that people can be led into true worship.

Application Question: In what ways have you seen the leadership of a church or ministry affect its worship either negatively or positively?

Acceptable Worship Includes God-Centered Prayer

After the Israelites had heard the Word of God for ¼ of the day, they confessed and prayed for another ¼ of the day. During this confession, the Levites led them in the longest prayer written in the entire Bible.[41] In this prayer, we see characteristics that should be implemented in every prayer as we worship God. Acceptable worship is God-centered, as we will see throughout this prayer.

Interpretation Question: What can we learn about prayer through Israel's prayer?

222

1. God-centered prayer primarily exalts and honors God.

As we look at the prayer of the Israelites, we should notice how God-centered it was. Look at the first eight verses of the prayer:

> You alone are the Lord. You made the heavens, even the highest heavens, along with all their multitude of stars, the earth and all that is on it, the seas and all that is in them. You impart life to them all, and the multitudes of heaven worship you. "You are the Lord God who chose Abram and brought him forth from Ur of the Chaldeans. You changed his name to Abraham. When you perceived that his heart was faithful toward you, you established a covenant with him to give his descendants the land of the Canaanites, the Hittites, the Amorites, the Perizzites, the Jebusites, and the Girgashites. You have fulfilled your promise, for you are righteous. "You saw the affliction of our ancestors in Egypt, and you heard their cry at the Red Sea. You performed awesome signs against Pharaoh, against his servants, and against all the people of his land, for you knew that the Egyptians had acted presumptuously against them. You made for yourself a name that is celebrated to this day. You split the sea before them, and they crossed through the sea on dry ground! But you threw their pursuers into the depths, like a stone into surging waters. You guided them with a pillar of cloud by day and with a pillar of fire by night to illumine for them the path they were to travel. "You came down on Mount Sinai and spoke with them from heaven. You provided them with just judgments, true laws, and good statutes and commandments. You made known to them your holy Sabbath; you issued commandments, statutes, and law to them through Moses your servant.
> Nehemiah 9:6 -14

One cannot but notice the repetition of "you" in only the first eight verses, referring to God. I counted over twenty in the first eight verses of this prayer. In verses 6-14, the content is primarily about honoring God and remembering his works. This is the same thing Christ taught us to do in the Lord's Prayer. Remember what he said in Matthew 6:9: "So pray this way: Our Father in heaven, may your name be honored,'"

When Jesus said we should pray "may your name be honored," he was saying that we should prioritize glorifying and worshiping God in our prayers. One's name in ancient Israel was a reflection of a person's character. That is what Israel focused on in their prayer. They said, "You alone are the Lord...You impart life...You performed awesome signs...You issued

223

commandments." The Levites led Israel in exalting God and his works in prayer, and the focus of our prayers should be the same.

Whatever we do first shows our priority. For many our prayer life simply shows how we are the priority of our lives. Our prayers are primarily about ourselves. Listen to what James said: "you ask and do not receive because you ask wrongly, so you can spend it on your passions" (James 4:3).

James says selfish prayers will not be answered for they care nothing about God and his will. That is the prayer life of many people. Prayer should glorify and exalt God's name and his characteristics.

2. God-centered prayer remembers God's works with thanksgiving.

Part of worship is thanksgiving and that is exactly what we see in the longest prayer in the Bible. Israel recounted many of God's blessings. They declared how God provided for them throughout history by making a covenant with Abraham (9:7), delivering them from Egypt through miraculous signs (10), giving them laws on Mount Sinai (13), etc.

In our prayers, we should also take time to recount God's faithfulness and his works with thanksgiving. Look at what Paul said in 1 Thessalonians 5:18: "in everything give thanks. For this is God's will for you in Christ Jesus."

In order for us to give thanks in all circumstances, we must contemplate God's grace in everything that has happened. Prayer should not only glorify God's name—his characteristics, it should recount his faithful works with thanksgiving.

3. God-centered prayer offers continual confession of sin to God.

In this prayer they confess both the sins of their fathers and also their sins (9:26). But notice that they had already confessed their sins in verse 2. They confessed their sins and the wickedness of their fathers, and then they read for one-fourth of the day. They then confessed again and spent time in worship. This prayer by the leaders is probably a description of how they confessed their sins for one-fourth of the day. It is clear that the Israelites were continually confessing their sins before God, and this must be true of us as we worship God as well. Look at some of their confession:

"Nonetheless they grew disobedient and rebelled against you; they disregarded your law. They killed your prophets who had solemnly admonished them in order to cause them to return to you. They committed atrocious blasphemies.
Nehemiah 9:26

224

Its abundant produce goes to the kings *you have placed over us due to our sins.* They rule over our bodies and our livestock as they see fit, and we are in great distress!
Nehemiah 9:37

As mentioned before, in viewing God we cannot but see how great our sins are. We saw this with Isaiah when he saw God. He confessed both his sin and that of his people (Isaiah 6).

Similarly, confession is a natural part of worship to God as we are sinners in need of grace. We must not just confess, but we must confess continually because we sin so often and so do those around us.

4. God-centered prayer should often be done corporately.

Nehemiah 9:5 says,

The Levites—Jeshua, Kadmiel, Bani, Hashabneiah, Sherebiah, Hodiah, Shebaniah, and Pethahiah—said, "Stand up and bless the Lord your God!" "May you be blessed, O Lord our God, from age to age. May your glorious name be blessed; may it be lifted up above all blessing and praise.

We see the leaders leading in corporate prayer. They called for everybody to stand and praise God and then led them into corporate prayer. Remember, tremendous power is in this kind of prayer. Christ said, "Again, I tell you the truth, if two of you on earth agree about whatever you ask, my Father in heaven will do it for you" (Matthew 18:19).

When two or more agree, Jesus says, the Father moves. There is a power in corporate prayer that we should not neglect. We should commonly bring our prayer requests before one another and pray in agreement for God to move.

In 1 Timothy 2, Paul was giving a description of how the house of God should be run (cf. 1 Tim 3:15), and it included corporate prayer. First Timothy 2:1-3 says,

First of all, then, I urge that requests, prayers, intercessions, and thanks be offered on behalf of all people, even for kings and all who are in authority, that we may lead a peaceful and quiet life in all godliness and dignity. Such prayer for all is good and welcomed before God our Savior

225

When the body of Christ gathers together, there should be corporate prayer.

5.   God-centered prayer is biblical.

Another practical principle we can learn from Israel's prayer is how biblical it was. It is a biblical prayer recounting the Lord's past faithfulness and their sin. It recounts God's works and promises in Genesis, Exodus, Numbers, Deuteronomy, Judges, Kings, etc.

When you look at many of the prayers of Scripture, you will find how biblical they are. When Jonah is in the belly of the whale in Jonah 2, much of what he prayed came from the Psalms. Jesus, while he was being crucified, cried out, "My God, my God, why have you abandoned me?" which is Psalm 22. And also, "Into your hand I entrust my life," which is Psalm 31.

In prayer we should use the Bible, because when we praying God's words, we can be confident that we are praying in line with the Spirit and the will of God. Much prayer is awry because it is not in line with the revelation of God's Word.

Jesus said this: "If you ask me anything in my name, I will do it" (John 14:14). When Jesus promises to answer every prayer prayed in his name, he was not promising that if we tacked his name on every request that it would be answered. He was talking about praying things that are in line with his character, as revealed in the term "name." The primary way we do this is by praying what he has said in his Word. Our prayers should be full of the Word of God and full of theology. We see this throughout Israel's prayer.

Prayer that is full of Scripture and in line with what Scripture says is acceptable worship. Godly leaders must lead their people in God-centered prayer as the Levites did. Selfish prayers will not be answered, but prayers that honor God and seek his will, will be honored.

Application Question: In what ways does looking at the longest prayer in the Bible encourage you in your prayer life? What aspects of this prayer do you commonly neglect?

Conclusion

As we look at Israel and the continual revival happening in the nation, we learn a lot about worship that pleases God. What are aspects of acceptable worship,

worship that our God seeks and desires? How can we as leaders, lead our people into acceptable worship?

1. Acceptable worship includes preparation. We need to prepare our spiritual sacrifices so that they may be received by God.
2. Acceptable worship includes confession. Sin will hinder our worship, and therefore, we must continually confess before God.
3. Acceptable worship includes hearing and responding to the Word of God. God blesses those who hear and do his Word.
4. Acceptable worship includes righteous leaders. Leadership affects our worship. Our leaders must be godly.
5. Acceptable worship includes God-centered prayer. Selfish prayers are not acceptable to God (cf. James 4:3). Prayer is primarily to honor God and to get his will done on the earth.

Application Question: In what ways is God challenging you to offer worship that is acceptable to him?

Marks of True Repentance

On the sealed documents were the following names: Nehemiah the governor, son of Hacaliah, along with Zedekiah... "Now the rest of the people—the priests, the Levites, the gatekeepers, the singers, the temple attendants, and all those who have separated themselves from the neighboring peoples because of the law of God, along with their wives, their sons, and their daughters, all of whom are able to understand—hereby participate with their colleagues the town leaders and enter into a curse and an oath to adhere to the law of God which was given through Moses the servant of God, and to obey carefully all the commandments of the Lord our Lord, along with his ordinances and his statutes...
Nehemiah 10 (NET)

What are marks or evidences of true repentance in a Christian's life—repentance that saves? We have all seen people who claim to follow Christ but are lacking the fruits that prove the reality of their faith.

It is very easy to make a claim or to have a profession of faith, but how does one know if it's a reality? Christ said in Matthew 7:21-23 that many would come in his name claiming to have a relationship with him but he would reply, "I never knew you. Go away from me, you lawbreakers!" They had the talk but not the walk.

In fact, bearing fruit is a very important aspect of our faith. We saw this with John the Baptist's and Paul's teaching. Look at what John said when he showed up preaching repentance:

But when he saw many Pharisees and Sadducees coming to his baptism, he said to them, "You offspring of vipers! Who warned you to flee from the coming wrath? Therefore produce fruit that proves your repentance, and don't think you can say to yourselves, 'We have Abraham as our father.' For I tell you that God can raise up children for Abraham from these stones! Even now the ax is laid at the root of

229

the trees, and every tree that does not produce good fruit will be cut down and thrown into the fire.
Matthew 3:7-10

John the Baptist in commanding repentance did not just say simply "confess" or make a declaration. True repentance always has the corresponding fruits. Paul said the same thing. Consider what he said: "First to those in Damascus, then to those in Jerusalem and in all Judea, and to the Gentiles also, I preached that they should repent and turn to God and prove their repentance by their deeds" (Acts 26:20 NIV 1984).

Paul preached the need to repent, but like John, he also preached the necessity of proving one's repentance. It is not enough just to confess; confession must be followed by the proper works. Now this is not a works salvation; it is a salvation that works—a salvation that changes us.

In the context of Nehemiah, we must remember that there was a revival happening. In chapter 8, the people listened and responded to Ezra's reading and teaching of the Word of God. In chapter 9, the people put on sackcloth and ashes and repented of their sins and the sins of their fathers. But in this chapter, they responded by renewing their covenant with God and committing to prove their repentance by their deeds. Listen to what they said in Nehemiah 9:36-10:1:

> "So today we are slaves! In the very land you gave to our ancestors to eat its fruit and to enjoy its good things—we are slaves! Its abundant produce goes to the kings you have placed over us due to our sins. They rule over our bodies and our livestock as they see fit, and we are in great distress! "Because of all of this we are entering into a binding covenant in written form; our leaders, our Levites, and our priests have affixed their names on the sealed document." On the sealed documents were the following names: Nehemiah the governor, son of Hacaliah, along with Zedekiah,

They made a commitment to God by renewing the Mosaic covenant. Eighty-four leaders of the community signed a document—a binding agreement. This document showed the priorities of their commitment to God. Even though we are not a part of Israel, we as Christians should have these same commitments. These same fruits will prove the reality of our repentance and relationship with Christ.

What are marks of true repentance—genuine faith?

230

Big Question: What commitments did Israel make in this chapter as a fruit of their repentance? How can we practice true repentance in our lives?

True Repentance Includes a Commitment to God's Word

> "Now the rest of the people—the priests, the Levites, the gatekeepers, the singers, the temple attendants, and all those who have separated themselves from the neighboring peoples because of the law of God, along with their wives, their sons, and their daughters, all of whom are able to understand—hereby participate with their colleagues the town leaders and enter into a curse and an oath to adhere to the law of God which was given through Moses the servant of God, and to obey carefully all the commandments of the Lord our Lord, along with his ordinances and his statutes.
> Nehemiah 10:28-29

What is the primary focus of this covenant community as seen in the signed document? The primary focus was to submit to the law of God. Israel had disobeyed God's covenant, which was given in the Pentateuch. But, in this text, they renewed their commitment to God's Word. Look at what they said:

> "Now the rest of the people—the priests, the Levites, the gatekeepers, the singers, the temple attendants, and all those who have separated themselves from the neighboring peoples because of the law of God, along with their wives, their sons, and their daughters, all of whom are able to understand—hereby participate with their colleagues the town leaders and enter into a curse and an oath to adhere to the law of God which was given through Moses the servant of God, and to obey carefully all the commandments of the Lord our Lord, along with his ordinances and his statutes.
> Nehemiah 10:28-29

Here Israel committed to follow God's Word. Jesus taught that practicing God's Word was a proof of true faith in the Sermon on the Mount. He taught that there were two types of people who listened to his words. One listened and built the foundation of his house on these words, and his house stood in the storm. But, the other did not build his house on Christ's words, and his house was destroyed. He said this in Matthew 7:24-26:

"Everyone who hears these words of mine and does them is like a wise man who built his house on rock. The rain fell, the flood came, and the winds beat against that house, but it did not collapse because it had been founded on rock. Everyone who hears these words of mine and does not do them is like a foolish man who built his house on sand.

It is very easy for us to look at the Scripture and say with awe, "No one ever spoke like this" as those in John 7:46 did, when listening to Christ, and yet not submit to him. It is also possible for us to pick and choose what we like about the Scriptures instead of submitting to the whole counsel of it.

The apostle John said the same thing as Christ. Listen to what he said: "Now by this we know that we have come to know God: if we keep his commandments. The one who says 'I have come to know God' and yet does not keep his commandments is a liar, and the truth is not in such a person" (1 John 2:3-4). He said obeying God's commands marks genuine faith and repentance. If we are not committed to God's Word and following it, we are not truly saved and our repentance is false.

True saving faith and true repentance recognizes Scripture as God's Word and commits to studying it and submitting to it. This should be the focus of the Christian life, and it is an evidence of true repentance.

Here Israel renewed their covenant to follow the laws of God which demonstrated true repentance. Do we need to renew our covenant to God's Word as well?

Application Question: What are your thoughts about commitment to knowing and obeying God's Word as a proof of genuine repentance? Why do so few Christians demonstrate this commitment in their lives? In what ways is God challenging you to both study and obey his Word more?

True Repentance Includes a Commitment to Fearing God

hereby participate with their colleagues the town leaders *and enter into a curse* and an oath to adhere to the law of God which was given through Moses the servant of God, and to obey carefully all the commandments of the Lord our Lord, along with his ordinances and his statutes.
Nehemiah 10:29

Not only did they commit to following God's Word but they also put themselves under a curse if they failed to follow it. In those days when people made covenants, they would often slay an animal and walk through the parts of the animal. By doing this they were saying, "Let this happen to me if I don't fulfill what I have committed to." This is what God did in confirming his covenant with Abraham in Genesis 15. He walked through the cut-up bodies of animals, committing to fulfill his covenant with Abraham.

It is possible these leaders did the same thing. But more than likely, they "bound themselves to a curse" by reading Deuteronomy 27 and 28. God had essentially promised Israel that if they did not obey his words, he would severely discipline them. Look at what he said:

> But you must not turn away from all the commandments I am giving you today, to either the right or left, nor pursue other gods and worship them. But if you ignore the Lord your God and are not careful to keep all his commandments and statutes I am giving you today, then all these curses will come upon you in full force: You will be cursed in the city and cursed in the field. Your basket and your mixing bowl will be cursed. Your children will be cursed, as well as the produce of your soil, the calves of your herds, and the lambs of your flocks. You will be cursed when you come in and cursed when you go out. The Lord will send on you a curse, confusing you and opposing you in everything you undertake until you are destroyed and quickly perish because of the evil of your deeds, in that you have forsaken me.
> Deuteronomy 28:14-20

By binding themselves to the curse, they recognized that God was faithful to his words and that he would curse, discipline, and even destroy them for disobedience. Now, under the New Covenant we are not under the curse of the Mosaic Law (cf. Gal 3:13); however, the fear of the Lord should still be a motivating factor in our lives.

Interpretation Question: Where do we see the necessity of fearing the Lord taught in the New Testament?

In contradiction to how some say God was a God of wrath in the Old Testament and a God of grace in the New, he is gracious and wrathful in both. Listen to what Philippians says: "Therefore, my dear friends, as you have always obeyed—not only in my presence, but now much more in my absence—continue to work out your salvation *with fear and trembling*" (2:12 NIV 2984).

Why should we have fear while working out the completion of our salvation (sanctification, becoming like Christ)? We should fear because God is a God of discipline. Listen to 2 Corinthians 7:1: "Therefore, since we have these promises, dear friends, let us cleanse ourselves from everything that could defile the body and the spirit, and thus *accomplish holiness out of reverence for God.*"

We must remember our God killed Ananias and Sapphira for lying about their offering in Acts 5. Our God brought sickness and death to some of those who were abusing the Lord's Supper in 1 Corinthians 11. Our God is still a God of discipline.

And ultimately, it is good to remember that even though we are not under the law, we are still bound by the spiritual principle of "sowing and reaping" which God oversees. We will reap what we sow, whether in this life or after. Galatians 6:7-8 says,

> Do not be deceived. God will not be made a fool. For a person will reap what he sows, because the person who sows to his own flesh will reap corruption from the flesh, but the one who sows to the Spirit will reap eternal life from the Spirit.

When the Jews were recommitting, they recommitted not only to the Word of God but to fearing the Lord, which should be a sobering motivation for all Christians. Hebrews 12:6 says, "for the Lord disciplines the one he loves." Discipline is a major aspect of our sanctification, and we should recognize this everyday as we are confronted with temptation and opportunities to sin.

Do you still fear God? Solomon said it is the beginning of wisdom—the beginning of living a wise life (Proverbs 9:10). Therefore, we must fear him if we are going to live a wise life, which is a holy life.

Application Question: Why should the fear of the Lord be a motivation in the Christian life? How would you describe your fear of God's discipline? How do we find a balance between the motivation of God's love (cf. 2 Cor 5:12) and fearing his discipline?

True Repentance Includes a Commitment to Holiness

> "Now the rest of the people—the priests, the Levites, the gatekeepers, the singers, the temple attendants, and all those who have separated themselves from the neighboring peoples because of the law of God, along with their wives, their sons, and their daughters, all of whom are able to understand… "We will not give our daughters in marriage to the neighboring peoples, and we will not take their daughters in marriage for our sons. We will not buy on the Sabbath or on a holy day

234

from the neighboring peoples who bring their wares and all kinds of grain to sell on the Sabbath day. We will let the fields lie fallow every seventh year, and we will cancel every loan.
Nehemiah 10:28, 30-31

Another focus of the Christian life and evidence of true repentance is the practice of holiness. Where do we see this commitment in Israel? Look at what they committed to:

"Now the rest of the people—the priests, the Levites, the gatekeepers, the singers, the temple attendants, and all those who have separated themselves from the neighboring peoples because of the law of God, along with their wives, their sons, and their daughters, all of whom are able to understand—hereby participate with their colleagues the town leaders and enter into a curse and an oath to adhere to the law of God which was given through Moses the servant of God, and to obey carefully all the commandments of the Lord our Lord, along with his ordinances and his statutes. "We will not give our daughters in marriage to the neighboring peoples, and we will not take their daughters in marriage for our sons. We will not buy on the Sabbath or on a holy day from the neighboring peoples who bring their wares and all kinds of grain to sell on the Sabbath day. We will let the fields lie fallow every seventh year, and we will cancel every loan.
Nehemiah 10:28-31

This holiness was seen in two ways. They would not intermarry with the neighboring nations, and they would not sin against God by buying and selling from the foreigners on the Sabbath.

Israel lived amongst neighboring nations that wanted to interact with them spiritually by drawing them to worship their gods. They wanted to interact with them socially through marriage and the practice of other cultural norms. And they wanted to interact with them economically through trade, which was often done on the Sabbath.

However, God had called Israel to be holy and separate from the neighboring nations primarily so they would not be led into sin. Listen to the command about not marrying in Exodus 34:15-16:

Be careful not to make a covenant with the inhabitants of the land, for when they prostitute themselves to their gods and sacrifice to their gods, and someone invites you, you will eat from his sacrifice; and you then take his daughters for your sons, and when his daughters

235

prostitute themselves to their gods, they will make your sons prostitute themselves to their gods as well.

The call to not interact or marry with the surrounding nations was never racial but spiritual. They were called to be separate and holy in order to not be drawn into sin with them or to worship their gods. This is what happened with Solomon, who led the kingdom of Israel into God's judgment.

It's good to remember that Ruth and Rahab were both Gentiles, and yet they both married into Israel and were put into the lineage of Christ. However, they both were converts to Judaism—they worshiped the God of Israel. Moses also married an Ethiopian woman. Jonah was sent to prophesy to the Gentiles in Nineveh. They were not to be totally separate from the Gentiles but to be separate in the sense that they would not be influenced to sin.

It is no different for us. Second Corinthians 6:14 says to not be "partners with those who do not believe," and James declares that this practice of not being polluted by the world is a religion God accepts. Listen to what he said: "Pure and undefiled religion before God the Father is this: to care for orphans and widows in their misfortune and to keep oneself unstained by the world" (James 1:27).

A religion our God accepts is one that keeps itself unstained from the world. You must be careful of the music you listen to, the TV shows you watch, and the friendships you cultivate. We must not adopt the ideals and practices of the world.

Scripture says that in the same way that the neighboring nations were seeking to lead Israel astray, the world does the same with us. Listen to Romans 12:2:

Do not be conformed to this present world, but be transformed by the renewing of your mind, so that you may test and approve what is the will of God—what is good and well-pleasing and perfect.

The word "conform" has the connotation of being acted upon. We are being pressed and molded into the image of the world. We are being pressured into having the same passions, the same desires, and the same worldview, rather than that of the inhabitants of the kingdom of God (cf. Matt 5:3-10, Phil 3:19-21).

Scripture also commands us to not love the world, for whoever loves the world, the love of the father is not in him (1 John 2:15). There is a principle in the world system working to draw us away from the love of God.

Yes, our priority must be holiness. Are you living out a life of separation from the world? Or are you trying to love God and love the world as well?

In fact, John says that if we have not committed to holiness and are still living in sin, we are not truly born again. It is a genuine fruit of repentance and if we lack this desire and practice of being holy, then we are not truly saved. Listen to what he says: "If we say we have fellowship with him and yet keep on walking in the darkness, we are lying and not practicing the truth" (1 John 1:6).

Israel committed to being separate from the nations in order to be holy unto God. We must make this commitment as well. Separation is necessary in order for us to not be influenced by this world, and it is also necessary for us to influence the world (cf. Matt 5:13). We must be different in order to influence the world.

Application Question: How can we reconcile the tension of being in the world and not of the world? In what ways is God challenging you to practice separation?

True Repentance Brings a Commitment to the House of God

Observation Question: In what ways did the people of Israel commit to supporting the temple ministry as seen in Nehemiah 10:32-39?

In the next verses, Nehemiah 10:32-39, we see the house of God mentioned nine times, referring to the restored temple.[42] As a fruit of their repentance, the people of God committed to support the ministry of the temple in four different ways.

1. The temple tax (Neh. 10:32–33). The annual census of the people twenty years of age and older was accompanied by the collecting of a half-shekel tax to be used to support the ministry of the house of God (Ex. 30:11–16).

2. The wood offering (Neh. 10:34). Since the fire on the brazen altar was to be kept burning constantly (Lev. 6:12–13), it required a steady supply of wood; and wood was a precious commodity.

3. The firstfruits (Neh. 10:35–37a). The Jews were taught to give God the first and the best, and this is a good example for us to follow today.

"Honor the Lord with your wealth, with the firstfruits of all your crops" (Prov. 3:9 NIV 1984).

4. The tithes (Neh. 10:37b-39). The word tithe means "a tenth." The Jews were to bring a tenth of their produce to the Lord each year for the support of the Levites (Lev. 27:30–34). The Levites then gave a "tithe of the tithe" to the priests (Num. 18:25–32).[43]

Application Question: What can we learn from the commitment of the people of Israel to support the work of the temple? How can we apply this?

1. Israel's commitment to the house of God reminds us of our need to support the work of the Lord with our finances.

Israel committed to give the temple tax, the wood offering, the first fruits, and the tithe. In the New Testament, we are not under the Old Testament tithe or giving system, but we are commanded to practice faithful giving. We learn about New Testament giving in Paul's command to the Corinthian church in 1 Corinthians 16:1-2. It says:

> With regard to the collection for the saints, please follow the directions that I gave to the churches of Galatia: On the first day of the week, each of you should set aside some income and save it to the extent that God has blessed you, so that a collection will not have to be made when I come.

We are called to give "to the extent that God has blessed you"; other versions say, "as the Lord prospers you." What makes this harder than the Old Covenant is the fact that many people should be giving way more than 10% because God has prospered them so much. This may be especially true for the Western church, which is very wealthy in comparison to the rest of the world.

Christians are called to not store up riches on this earth (Matthew 6:19), and we are called to be cheerful in giving (2 Corinthians 9:7). Also, we are called to seek to excel in the act of giving in the same way we do in acts of love or mercy. Second Corinthians 8:7 says this: "But as you excel in everything—in faith, in speech, in knowledge, and in all eagerness and in the love from us that is in you—make sure that you excel in this act of kindness too."

In the practice of grace giving, we are not called to give our 10% and then say we have fulfilled the law. No, we are called to seek to increase our giving at all times, just as we are always trying to love more.

238

How does this look practically? Personally, every year or at certain times during a year, my wife and I will look at our finances and see how we are doing. We have a fixed giving each year but our priority is always to see if we can increase it. Can we give 5% or 10% more this year or semester based on our income? Or, should we consider lowering it because of new costs?

That's one way we can apply the practice of grace giving and trying to continually grow in this grace. As Israel committed to support the work of God, we must continually make this commitment as well.

How else can we apply Israel's commitment to the house of God?

2. Israel's commitment to the house of God reminds us of our need to give our best to God.

Israel committed to give God their firstfruits. The firstfruits were considered the best and a picture of the future harvest. In what ways can we give God our best?

In Malachi, which was written to Israel during the days of Nehemiah,[44] God accused Israel of bringing lambs which were blind and lame, and he rejected them. Look at what God said to Israel in Malachi 1:6-8:

> "A son naturally honors his father and a slave respects his master. If I am your father, where is my honor? If I am your master, where is my respect? The Lord who rules over all asks you this, you priests who make light of my name! But you reply, 'How have we made light of your name?' You are offering improper sacrifices on my altar, yet you ask, 'How have we offended you?' By treating the table of the Lord as if it is of no importance! For when you offer blind animals as a sacrifice, is that not wrong? And when you offer the lame and sick, is that not wrong as well? Indeed, try offering them to your governor! Will he be pleased with you or show you favor?" asks the Lord who rules over all.

Many times we do this with God. We give him the last five minutes of the day and sometimes nothing at all. We give him our left-overs, not our best. We also should give God our firstfruits because he is our King. How can we give our King anything less? Are you giving God your best?

Application Question: In what ways is God calling you to give him your best practically? How does this affect your time management, your priorities, and your future goals?

3. Israel's commitment to the house of God reminds us that we should labor to build up God's church.

Another application we can take from this is our need to build up God's church. Today, God does not live in temples built with hands, but he indwells the people of God—the living temple. Listen to what Peter said: "you yourselves, as living stones, are built up as a spiritual house to be a holy priesthood and to offer spiritual sacrifices that are acceptable to God through Jesus Christ" (1 Peter 2:5).

Similarly, Paul teaches that we are the temple of God both corporately (1 Cor 3:16) and individually (1 Cor 6:19). Therefore, one of the ways we build God's house is by being committed to the church and serving his people there.

God has uniquely given each believer a spiritual gift for the purpose of building up the body of Christ (1 Cor. 12:7). Just as each person brought wood, firstfruits, etc., to build up the house of God, we must use our gifts and our time to build up God's people as well. This is a true fruit of genuine repentance: serving the house of God.

John said this: "We know that we have crossed over from death to life because we love our fellow Christians. The one who does not love remains in death" (1 John 3:14). Love always results in service. If anybody does not serve the church—Christ's body—he has not passed from life to death. They lack a fruit of true repentance.

Application Question: In what ways do you feel called to serve the people of God? What are your spiritual gifts and what sacrifices do you feel called to make in building God's house?

General Applications

As we look at the covenant Israel renewed with God in Nehemiah 10, we learn a lot about our spiritual commitments and how we should continually practice them. As seen with New Year's commitments, many people feel that making them is pointless. "We are just going to break them anyway," they say. However, commitments are very important to any aspect of society and especially to our spiritual life. We make commitments when we sign a job contract, when we buy a house, and even when we get married. Commitments are important.

Application Question: What can we learn about commitments from Israel in Nehemiah 10?

1. We should not hesitate to make or renew biblical commitments to God. It doesn't matter if we failed in the past; we can start over at any time.

What commitments is God calling you to make or renew with him today?

2. We should practice sharing our commitments with others in order to have accountability.

It seems that because only eighty-four leaders signed the document, the leaders were not only committing themselves but committing to help Israel keep their commitments. They were the nation's representatives, and the contract was an accountability system for Israel. It also may be wise for us to share our commitments with spiritual leaders or those we trust so they can help hold us accountable.

Who are your accountability partners? What commitments are they helping you keep with God?

3. We should practice writing down our commitments.

The Jews wrote down their commitments to God and had the leaders sign and seal it (cf. Neh 9:38-10:1). There is something powerful about both verbalizing our commitments and writing them down.

Writing them down helps us clarify them and make sure they are attainable. This is another form of accountability for us. This helps increase our faith as we watch God's faithfulness in helping us fulfill these commitments. This may be done with a journal or even a contract like Israel's.

Application Question: In what ways have you found accountability helpful in your spiritual life? Why is it so important?

Conclusion

What are marks of true repentance and, therefore, saving faith? In this chapter, Israel followed up their repentance in chapter 9 with a renewal of the Mosaic covenant. They made many commitments to God, and, in many ways, these should be our commitments today.

1. The people of God must be committed to the Word of God. How is God calling you to renew a commitment to studying and practicing his Word?

2. The people of God must be committed to the fear of the Lord. Israel put themselves under the curse of the Mosaic law for breaking the covenant. They essentially committed to recognizing and allowing it to motivate them to faithfulness. Does the fear of the Lord motivate you?

3. The people of God must be committed to holiness. Israel separated from the neighboring nations and their ways of life. In what ways are you practicing separation?

4. The people of God must be committed to building the house of God. The house of God is not the temple anymore but it is our bodies (1 Cor 6:19) and the people of God (I Peter 2:5). We should be committed to serving and seeing God's kingdom come in our own lives and the lives of others.

Application Question: In what ways is God challenging you to be more committed to him and/or to challenge others through this study on true repentance?

Characteristics of Honored Servants

So the leaders of the people settled in Jerusalem, while the rest of the people cast lots to bring one out of every ten to settle in Jerusalem, the holy city, while the other nine remained in other cities. The people gave their blessing on all the men who volunteered to settle in Jerusalem...
Nehemiah 11 (NET)

What are qualities of those who will be honored by God for their service to him?

In Nehemiah 11, we see the repopulating of the city of Jerusalem, but not only that, we see those who are honored and commended for taking the leap of faith in moving there. By reminder, chapters 1-6 focused on the rebuilding of the wall. In chapter 7, a census was taken of all the people living in Israel. But in that census there was clearly a problem with the city. Nehemiah 7:4 says, "Now the city was spread out and large, and there were not a lot of people in it. At that time houses had not been rebuilt."

They had rebuilt the walls of Jerusalem, but only a few people were living in the city and the buildings needed to be rebuilt. In chapters 8-10, there was a spiritual revival in Jerusalem; the people met often to hear the Word of God and recommitted to following it.

Nehemiah 11 is especially important because the worship of God was integrally connected to the city of Jerusalem. We must remember that not only did God call Israel to be his priests, but he had called for Jerusalem to be his capital city. It was in Jerusalem that the temple was located, God's presence dwelled, and people from throughout the world would come to offer sacrifices in worship of the living God. In fact, in Nehemiah 11:1, Jerusalem is called the "holy city."

In this text, the narrator honors those who sacrificed—left home and land to build up the holy city—by recording their names. They and their families were honored as the record of their names would have been read before the nation of Israel. But these people were also honored when they initially volunteered to serve in Jerusalem. Nehemiah 11:2 says, "The people gave their blessing on all the men who volunteered to settle in Jerusalem."

243

Similarly, this has applications for God's church. One day God will honor everyone who has labored to build his church and spread his kingdom on the earth. Consider what Paul said in 1 Corinthians 4:4-5:

> For I am not aware of anything against myself, but I am not acquitted because of this. The one who judges me is the Lord. So then, do not judge anything before the time. Wait until the Lord comes. He will bring to light the hidden things of darkness and reveal the motives of hearts. Then each will receive recognition from God.

Paul said a day is coming in which God will honor those who have served him with a right heart and right motives. Then each person will receive their praise from the Lord. Christ taught that even the giving of a glass of water in his name would receive a reward (Matt 10:42).

In the same way that the narrator honored those who faithfully served in rebuilding and populating Jerusalem, God will one day honor those who faithfully served in the populating of the New Jerusalem, heaven's capital city (cf. Rev 21:1-2).

With that said, it is important to recognize that not every servant will have the same honor in heaven. Consider what Christ taught:

> So anyone who breaks one of the least of these commands and teaches others to do so will be called least in the kingdom of heaven, but whoever obeys them and teaches others to do so will be called great in the kingdom of heaven.
> Matthew 5:19

Jesus taught there will be those who are called great in the kingdom of heaven and those who will be called least. Not everybody in the kingdom of heaven will have the same honor.

In Nehemiah 11, we learn something about those who faithfully populated Jerusalem in order to help restore the worship of God in Israel. These people were honored by Israel publicly and, ultimately, by God, as he chose to include their names in his Holy Word. In the same way, God will one day publicly honor all his servants who have faithfully built his kingdom on this earth.

As we study this passage, we must ask, "What are the qualities of those who will be honored for their service to the Lord?" There is coming a day when those who have served God faithfully will be honored before all. God is still looking for people to restore the worship of God around the world and those who take up this call will be honored by him.

Big Question: What were the qualities of those who were honored for repopulating and rebuilding Jerusalem? How can we apply this to those whom God will honor eternally?

Honored Servants Are Willing to Lead by Example

So the leaders of the people settled in Jerusalem
Nehemiah 11:1

Interpretation Question: Why did the leaders of the people settle in Jerusalem first, before anybody else?

What initially stands out about the repopulation of Jerusalem is that the leaders settled there first. No doubt, this included Nehemiah, Ezra, and other leaders. This is normal for most capital cities. The leadership dwells in the capital, since all the major decisions typically happen there.

However, this represents more than the fact that they needed to be in Jerusalem—they were setting the example for others to follow. Very shortly after they settled, others were recruited to help in the repopulation process. If Jerusalem was going to be repopulated, the leaders had to lead the way.

Similarly, this is true for the church as well. If worship is going to be restored in our churches, our communities, and our cities, it must begin with spiritual leadership. Consider how Paul challenged the Corinthians. He said: "Be imitators of me, just as I also am of Christ" (1 Corinthians 11:1).

Paul was willing to set the example for others to follow. Likewise, those who are honored by God will always be those who are willing to be examples. They set the example in their devotional lives, in their work, in their dating relationships, in their marriage, in their finances, etc. They do this so they can say, "Imitate me," just as Paul did, in order to ultimately help people look more like Christ.

Similarly, Paul told Timothy this: "Let no one look down on you because you are young, but set an example for the believers in your speech, conduct, love, faithfulness, and purity" (1 Timothy 4:12). He challenged Timothy to set an example for others.

In response to this reality, we must ask ourselves, "Are we willing to be godly examples for others?" This is an essential qualification for those who serve in any ministry. "Do we have a spiritual life that is worthy to be modeled?" "Can we give others a plan on how to faithfully practice their devotional lives?" "Can we demonstrate to others how to practice purity both in our thought life and our relationships?"

Those who lead must set the example, but, not only that, many times those who lead must often give up their rights to better serve others. In order to set the example, Nehemiah and the leaders had to give up their right of living outside of Jerusalem. Yes, it would have been safer, less work, and more comfortable if they would have lived outside of Jerusalem. But, they instead gave up their rights in order to lead others into what was best.

Paul said this: "For this reason, if food causes my brother or sister to sin, I will never eat meat again, so that I may not cause one of them to sin" (1 Corinthians 8:13). Surely, eating meat is a freedom and a biblical right, but if someone was offended because of a weak conscience, then he would have stopped rather than allow that person to be hurt by his freedom. This attitude is a must for leaders; they must think of others before themselves (cf. Phil 2:3-4) and, at times, even give up their rights in order to set the example.

Am I free to go to the movies? Am I free to drink alcohol or smoke cigarettes? Certainly, Scripture does not clearly forbid such things. However, in my freedom, I must ask, "Could my freedom harm someone who is weaker than me in the faith and has less discipline than me?" This is the type of question people in leadership must ask.

Paul said, "'Everything is lawful,' but not everything is beneficial" (1 Corinthians 10:23). Everything is a freedom for me that Scripture doesn't clearly forbid, but I must ask the right questions before I use my freedom such as: "Will this practice build others up? Will it build me up?" This is what keeps many from being good examples. The only question they ask is, "Is it my right?" or "Can I do this?" When they should ask, "Is this best for others?" and "Will this be best for me?"

Are you willing to be a godly example for others? Nehemiah and the leaders could have stayed outside of Jerusalem where the housing was better and it was safer, but they, instead, chose to set the example for others in order to accomplish God's work. And they, therefore, were honored because of it.

Application Question: In what specific ways do you feel God is calling you to set the example for others? In what ways has God called you to give up freedoms to set an example?

Honored Servants Are Committed to Seeking God's Will

So the leaders of the people settled in Jerusalem, while the rest of the people cast lots to bring one out of every ten to settle in Jerusalem, the holy city, while the other nine remained in other cities. The people

246

gave their blessing on all the men who volunteered to settle in Jerusalem.
Nehemiah 11:1-2

Interpretation Question: Why did the Israelites cast lots? What did it represent?

The next step in repopulating Jerusalem was getting one out of ten Israelites to move into the land. How did they select these people? They cast lots, which is a lot like rolling dice. Some have called this a draft, but it is not a draft. It is more than that.

In ancient Israel, the casting of lots was a form of seeking the will of the Lord. In fact, we see the apostles use this form of seeking God's will in Acts 1, when they chose the replacement for Judas. Look at what they did:

> So they proposed two candidates: Joseph called Barsabbas (also called Justus) and Matthias. Then they prayed, "Lord, you know the hearts of all. Show us which one of these two you have chosen to assume the task of this service and apostleship from which Judas turned aside to go to his own place." Then they cast lots for them, and the one chosen was Matthias; so he was counted with the eleven apostles.
> Acts 1:23-26

They chose the replacement by having all the disciples propose two men who had been with Christ from the beginning of their ministry. After two people were selected, they prayed for God to make his choice clear. God's will was discerned by the casting of the lot, as it fell on Matthias. This was a common method of seeking God's will used by Israel.

The Israelites had a very strong understanding of the sovereignty of God. They believed that God was in control of all things. Listen to what Proverbs says: "The dice are thrown into the lap, but their every decision is from the Lord" (Proverbs 16:33).

Every time a person throws a dice and it lands on six or three, the Jew would say that is of the Lord. There is no random chance in life; God is in control of all events. In fact, we see this with Job when Satan tested him by bringing poverty and death in his family. Even though we know Satan did it, as revealed in chapter 1, Job said, "God did it." He cried out, "Even if he slays me, I will hope in him; I will surely defend my ways to his face!" (Job 13:15).

Some today would say, "No, Job, your doctrine is all wrong. Sickness and trials do not come from God. It was Satan alone." But Scripture teaches that God works all things in conformity with the purpose of his will. Our God is

247

sovereign. Ephesians 1:11 says, "In Christ we too have been claimed as God's own possession, since we were predestined according to the one purpose of him who accomplishes all things according to the counsel of his will."

Paul said our God accomplishes "all things" according to the counsel of his will. This is a mystery. I don't claim to fully understand it, but somehow this includes the Fall, sin, Satan, and everything else. Somehow all things fall into God's sovereign will.

Peter actually told the Jews who killed Christ that they did it according to the predetermined plan of God. Acts 2:23 says, "this man, who was handed over by the predetermined plan and foreknowledge of God, you executed by nailing him to a cross at the hands of Gentiles." Peter essentially said that this was under God's sovereign control too. The worse thing that ever happened on the earth was part of God's plan.

Now this is just a side point of showing how these Jews sought the will of God by casting lots. With that said, I am not promoting making decisions by rolling dice. My point is that those who will be honored by God for their service are those who continually seek God's will, even when it hurts or is uncomfortable. They lay down their plans and their desires and cry out like Christ, "Yet not my will but yours be done" (Luke 22:42).

Application Question: How do we seek the Lord's will so we can faithfully submit to it?

Let it be known that the primary way that we seek God's will is through studying his Word. David said this: "Your word is a lamp to walk by, and a light to illumine my path" (Psalm 119:105).

David said that when he was seeking direction from the Lord, he realized that all he needed to do was turn the lights on in his life by getting into the Word. Those who live in the Word of God have the lights on. If we are not living in God's Word, we do so to our own peril. It is impossible to properly navigate this dark world without the light of Scripture.

How does Scripture help us determine God's will? Scripture either gives clear direction in doing God's will or it gives us principles to help us make decisions. Even if that principle is something as simple as, "but the one who listens to advice is wise" (Proverbs 12:15). Wise people don't make decisions on their own about marriage, career, or life without allowing wise, godly people to speak into their life.

Yes, those who will be honored by God for their service are those who seek God's will, and those who seek God's will live in his Word. A person who does not live in the Word of God is not even fit to serve in ministry. It is the Word of God that equips the man of God for all righteousness (cf. 2 Tim 3:17). Without God's Word, they will constantly harm others and themselves.

Just as Israel sought the Lord through casting lots, we must seek the Lord through studying the full revelation of God's Word, something the Israelites did not have. How much more should we live in it and allow it to guide our decisions? It should guide what career path we go on, who we should marry, and even the kind of car we drive. Scripture gives us principles to help guide the man or woman of God in all those decisions.

These are the kind of servants that will be honored by God. They continually seek the Lord's will in every aspect of life. Sadly, most Christians are not like this. Listen to what Paul said to the Philippians:

> I hope in the Lord Jesus to send Timothy to you soon, that I also may be cheered when I receive news about you. I have no one else like him, who takes a genuine interest in your welfare. For everyone looks out for his own interests, not those of Jesus Christ.
> Philippians 2:19 -21 (NIV 1984)

That's how most Christians are. They seek their own interest instead of the interests of Jesus Christ. Paul said that he had no one else like Timothy (who sought the will of Christ), even though he worked with many churches and many Christians. Those who look out for the interests of Christ are still in small supply today. However, these are the ones who will be honored by God.

Application Question: In what ways is the Word of God sufficient to guide the man of God in all righteousness (cf. 2 Tim 3:17)? In what ways has God used his Word to help you make major decisions?

Honored Servants Are Willing to Obey the Lord's Commands

> So the leaders of the people settled in Jerusalem, while the rest of the people cast lots to bring one out of every ten to settle in Jerusalem, the holy city, while the other nine remained in other cities. The people gave their blessing on all the men who volunteered to settle in Jerusalem.
> Nehemiah 11:1-2

Interpretation Question: Why does the narrative say the people volunteered to live in Jerusalem? How does this correspond with them being selected by the casting of lots?

The next thing we must notice is that not only did the leaders and the people in this narrative seek the will of the Lord, but they obeyed by volunteering. Now this may seem kind of strange. It says that they cast lots (v.1), and then the people volunteered (v. 2). This is why it's clearly not a draft. They cast lots to see who God had chosen, but the people still had the ability to say, "No."

Hypothetically, if a person said, "No," they would have simply cast the lots again to see who God chose next. However, there was no need to re-cast the lot since each person who God chose volunteered. Therefore, the people commended them for it.

Yes, it is one thing to seek the will of the Lord, but it is another thing to obey the will of the Lord. These people were obedient.

Listen to this: God is always calling people to serve him. He calls them to go to missions. He calls to use them in great ways, but, if they turn him down, God may at times give the opportunity to somebody else.

We saw this with Saul. God called him to be king and to obey God as his vice-regent over Israel. But, Saul disobeyed God and refused to serve him, and therefore, Scripture says, "The Lord has sought out for himself a man who is loyal to him" (1 Sam 13:14).

Yes, God calls many to serve him, to serve in working with the children in the church, to share the gospel with friends, but when they choose to be disobedient, many times God will simply call another.

The good thing about God is that he is gracious and merciful. One of the most wonderful verses in Scripture is Jonah 3:1. After Jonah had said "No" and God had disciplined him through a storm, it says: "The Lord said to Jonah a second time."

God's Word came to Jonah a second time, and this time Jonah obeyed. Are you willing to obey the Lord? Those who will be honored by God are those who live lifestyles of obedience.

Application Question: In what ways is God calling you to serve and build his kingdom? What are common hindrances to doing God's will?

Honored Servants Are Willing to Sacrifice and Be Uncomfortable

So the leaders of the people settled in Jerusalem, while the rest of the people cast lots to bring one out of every ten to settle in Jerusalem, the holy city, while the other nine remained in other cities. The people gave their blessing on all the men who volunteered to settle in Jerusalem.
Nehemiah 11:1-2

All these people would have to leave their homes and move to a city that was broken down. Moving to Jerusalem essentially meant moving to the ghetto. The city was filled with ruins (cf. Neh 7:4). It was dangerous and susceptible to attack. Typically an attack would have been on the capital city. It was where the leaders and the wealth were. To move to Jerusalem meant to be uncomfortable.

Similarly, the very reason many people cannot serve the Lord and will not be honored by him is because they aren't willing to be uncomfortable. They are not willing to step out of their comfort zone to serve and do God's will.

Listen, any time God calls us, he calls us to step out of our comfort zone. He is not calling us to do something we could do in our own power, but something that could only be done through him. Therefore, following God always leads us out of our comfort.

It is no surprise then to see in Scripture so many people make excuses when they were called. Moses said, "I can't speak." Gideon said "I'm from the smallest tribe." If God calls, he calls us to do something God-sized and outside of our ability.

In what ways is God calling you to sacrifice and to leave your comfort zone? I have no doubt that God is calling many to leave their home country and go to a place with a different language, culture, and standard of living. He may even call some of us to sacrifice our lives for him, as he did with Peter and the majority of the apostles. But even though there is a call, we still must be willing to submit to it. We must be willing, like the Israelites, to volunteer.

In Luke 9:57-58, one would-be disciple approached Christ and said, "I will follow you wherever you go." Christ responded, "Foxes have dens and the birds in the sky have nests, but the Son of Man has no place to lay his head." Essentially, Christ said, "Are you sure? Are you sure you can handle the cost of following me? It will mean being a wanderer in the world I created."

We hear nothing from this man who zealously raised his hand and said, "I'll go." It seems the cost was too much. Similarly, many do the same thing today at the opportunity to follow Christ in ministry. The cost is too much. Giving up dreams, retirement, and security is not in their plans. They vehemently declare, "I cannot," and therefore, they cannot serve the Lord in ministry and won't be honored by him.

What is God calling you to sacrifice? In what way is he calling you to be uncomfortable in order to do his will and build his kingdom?

In this text, the leaders and those who volunteered all would be leaving the comfort of their homes to serve the Lord in a broken down city that needed to be rebuilt. However, it was God's will for their lives and the best place they could be. And because they obeyed, they were honored by the people and ultimately by God.

Application Question: In what ways has God led you into uncomfortable situations to grow your faith and build his kingdom? Are there any ways that you feel God is calling you to be uncomfortable and trust him now to do his work?

Honored Servants Are Committed to Building God's House

> From the priests: Jedaiah son of Joiarib, Jakin; Seraiah son of Hilkiah, the son of Meshullam, the son of Zadok, the son of Meraioth, the son of Ahitub, supervisor in the temple of God … and their colleagues who were carrying out work for the temple…Shabbethai and Jozabad, leaders of the Levites, were in charge of the external work for the temple of God; Mattaniah son of Mica, the son of Zabdi, the son of Asaph, the praise leader who led in thanksgiving and prayer
> Nehemiah 11:10-12, 16-17

What else can we learn about the people who volunteered to serve the Lord by populating Jerusalem? It is clear that the majority of them focused their attention on serving the temple. The priests, Levites, and the temple workers are named next in the narrative (Neh 11:10–24), and obviously their ministry was focused on the temple. However, it must be remembered that not only did they focus on the temple, but apparently, so did everybody else. Remember what the last verse of Nehemiah 10 said:

> The Israelites and the Levites will bring the contribution of the grain, the new wine, and the olive oil to the storerooms where the utensils of the sanctuary are kept, and where the priests who minister stay, along with the gatekeepers and the singers. We will not neglect the temple of our God."
> Nehemiah 10:39

As part of the revival, they promised to not neglect the house of God. It was to be a permanent focus of their life and ministry, whether they lived in Jerusalem or not.

In the same way, those who serve the Lord today and will be honored by him must focus their attention on the temple, the church. Today, God's temple is not a building as in the Old Covenant—it is a people. First Corinthians 3:16 says this: "Do you not know that you are God's temple and that God's Spirit lives in you?" And Scripture also says that God has given each person a spiritual gift to serve in his temple (1 Corinthians 12:7). God's plan to change the world is through a people using their spiritual gifts to serve God, one another, and the world.

Therefore, no matter where God calls you to serve, if he calls you to serve as a doctor, a lawyer, a professor, or a teacher, you still have a call from God to serve in his temple, which is the church. Even though God has given you a ministry in the world, he wants you to reach the world by being involved with your local church.

In talking specifically about serving the church, Paul taught that each man will receive a reward for his faithful service to her. Listen to what he said:

> We are coworkers belonging to God. You are God's field, God's building... If anyone builds on the foundation with gold, silver, precious stones, wood, hay, or straw, each builder's work will be plainly seen, for the Day will make it clear, because it will be revealed by fire. And the fire will test what kind of work each has done. If what someone has built survives, he will receive a reward.
> 1 Corinthians 3:9, 12-14

After describing the people of God as God's building, he says that each one of us will be rewarded based on the way we build up the church. If we give our time, if we are willing to invest, as represented by costly stones, we will be rewarded. But if we give God our scraps—service with wrong motives or a lack of service—as represented by wood, hay, and straw, we will not be rewarded—we will not be honored.

Scripture clearly teaches that those who will be honored by God are those who have served faithfully in building up God's temple. In fact, they are consumed with God's temple (cf. John 2:17, Rom 12:11, 1 Cor 15:58). This is a characteristic of those God honors.

Our tendency as Christians is to have our job, attend our church, care for our family, but not use our gifts to serve the church. Most Christians don't feel a need to. However, the people who were honored in this narrative all were focused on serving the house of God, and previously, in chapter 10, all of Israel swore not to neglect it.

How has God called you to serve the church? Are you giving him your best or are you neglecting God's work? Just as God honored these volunteers who sacrificed and served the temple, he also will honor those who have volunteered to faithfully serve God's church with eternal rewards.

Application Question: What are your spiritual gifts? In what ways do you feel God has called you to serve the church? How can we balance serving God in the church with all our other responsibilities?

Honored Servants Are Willing to Serve without Receiving Glory Here on Earth

> The sum total of the descendants of Perez who were settling in Jerusalem was 468 exceptional men. These are the descendants of Benjamin: Sallu son of Meshullam, the son of Joed, the son of Pedaiah, the son of Kolaiah, the son of Maaseiah, the son of Ithiel, the son of Jeshaiah, and his followers, Gabbai and Sallai—928 in all. Joel son of Zicri was the officer in charge of them, and Judah son of Hassenuah was second-in-command over the city. From the priests: Jedaiah son of Joiarib, Jakin, Seraiah son of Hilkiah, the son of Meshullam, the son of Zadok, the son of Meraioth, the son of Ahitub, supervisor in the temple of God, and their colleagues who were carrying out work for the temple—822
> Nehemiah 11:6 -12

It is important to note that many of the people who served were unnamed. We see this throughout the text:

> The sum total of the descendants of Perez who were settling in Jerusalem was 468 exceptional men. These are the descendants of Benjamin: Sallu son of Meshullam, the son of Joed, the son of Pedaiah, the son of Kolaiah, the son of Maaseiah, the son of Ithiel, the son of Jeshaiah, and his followers, Gabbai and Sallai—928 in all.
> Nehemiah 11:6-8

Many of the people who settled in Jerusalem are unnamed in this narrative. There were priests, Levites, descendants of certain tribes, etc., but

254

the names of most of the people were not mentioned. There were 468 men from Perez, 928 people from Benjamin, etc., who volunteered to serve the Lord.

It is like that in every church and ministry. Some names are often in lights—the pastor, the worship leaders, and the elders. However, there are many people whose names are never mentioned but who are just as important, if not more important than those whose names everybody knows.

Listen to how Paul talks about these people in describing the church as a body in 1 Corinthians 12. He describes the head, the arm, and the feet—all parts that are visible. But he then says the parts that seem "to be weaker are essential." More important than a leg, an arm, or a face is the heart or the liver. The body cannot function without these, and, when they shut down, the body shuts down. First Corinthians 12:21-23 says this:

> The eye cannot say to the hand, "I do not need you," nor in turn can the head say to the foot, "I do not need you." On the contrary, those members that seem to be weaker are essential, and those members we consider less honorable we clothe with greater honor, and our unpresentable members are clothed with dignity
> 1 Corinthians 12:21-23

In the same way, each ministry has hidden parts that may not receive great honor here on earth, but, in heaven, they will be exalted. These often are women who never preach a sermon, but they labor in prayer for the preaching and in service of the people with needs in the church. They are the heart, the liver, and other internal organs. Without them, the whole body would shut down. They might not get applause here on earth, but we can have no doubt that they will receive great applause in the kingdom of heaven.

Jesus said, "But many who are first will be last, and the last first" (Matthew 19:30). In heaven there will be great surprises. No doubt, many times the people we think will be exalted will not be, and those who have been overlooked will be. Listen to what the writer of Hebrews says: "For God is not unjust so as to forget your work and the love you have demonstrated for his name, in having served and continuing to serve the saints" (Hebrews 6:10).

He will not forget those who are unnamed, for he sees their hard work, and they will be greatly rewarded.

No doubt, many of these unnamed people served without ever needing applause or a thank you. Christ actually taught this as a necessary quality of all his disciples. He said this:

> "Would any one of you say to your slave who comes in from the field after plowing or shepherding sheep, 'Come at once and sit down for a

meal'? Won't the master instead say to him, 'Get my dinner ready, and make yourself ready to serve me while I eat and drink. Then you may eat and drink'? He won't thank the slave because he did what he was told, will he? So you too, when you have done everything you were commanded to do, should say, 'We are slaves undeserving of special praise; we have only done what was our duty.'"
Luke 17:7-10

In describing a servant serving his master, he said, "He won't thank the slave because he did what he was told, will he?" The answer to the rhetorical question was, "No." He was a servant doing what he was supposed to do. He says in the same way, we should be like that servant. We are servants who should serve without a need for applause or thanksgiving. We are simply doing our duty.

Are you willing to serve without ever being named, without ever receiving applause or earthly recognition?

God is looking for people who are willing to serve whether they receive recognition or not. It is no surprise that when God often called people in Scripture, he often found the people who were not looking for acclaim or applause. He often called the reluctant leaders to serve and do great things.

Moses said, "No, not me." Gideon said, "No, I'm last in my father's house." These people were not looking to be great or honored. They were just people willing to obey God. God takes those not looking for acclaim or applause, and he makes them great. This is how God works. The people in Babel were trying to make a name for themselves, trying to make themselves great, and God brought them low (cf. Gen 11:4-8). But with Abraham, he found a man not looking to make a name for himself and said to him, "I will make your name great" (Gen 12:2). When David wanted to build God a house, God said to him, "I will build you a dynastic house" (2 Sam 7:27).

God opposes the proud but exalts the humble (James 4:6). This is a characteristic of those who are exalted. They are the humble who ultimately want to honor and glorify God. Because of this, God exalts them.

Application: Why is it important to be able to serve God without earthly recognition? How can we develop the type of humility that doesn't need to be seen or heard?

Honored Servants Are Committed to Respecting and Serving the Authorities

Next, we also must notice that the singers and others, though following God, were also serving the king of Persia. We see this in Nehemiah 11:23-24. It says:

> For they were under royal orders which determined their activity day by day. Pethahiah son of Meshezabel, one of the descendants of Zerah son of Judah, was an adviser to the king in every matter pertaining to the people.
> Nehemiah 11:23-24

How did this happen? In the book of Ezra, when King Darius had initially ordered the building of the temple, the people of Israel were commanded to give the elders daily support for the rebuilding and maintenance of the temple. He also commanded that "they may be offering incense to the God of heaven and may be praying for the good fortune of the king." Ezra 6:8-10 says this:

> "I also hereby issue orders as to what you are to do with those elders of the Jews in order to rebuild this temple of God. From the royal treasury, from the taxes of Trans-Euphrates the complete costs are to be given to these men, so that there may be no interruption of the work. Whatever is needed—whether oxen or rams or lambs for burnt offerings for the God of heaven or wheat or salt or wine or oil, as required by the priests who are in Jerusalem—must be given to them daily without any neglect, so that they may be offering incense to the God of heaven and may be praying for the good fortune of the king and his family.

Therefore, the singers not only were submitting to God in their worship and prayers, but they were also honoring the king of Persia.

In addition, Pethahiah, who was the "king's adviser" (v. 24), probably advised the king on Israel's affairs.[45]

Now in many nations, there is a separation of church and state, which is a different model of government than in Israel and most of the ancient world. However, Scripture still commands Christians to honor and submit to those in authority (cf. Rom 13:1-7) and also to pray for them. First Timothy 2:1-3 says this:

> First of all, then, I urge that requests, prayers, intercessions, and thanks be offered on behalf of all people, even for kings and all who are in authority, that we may lead a peaceful and quiet life in all godliness and dignity. Such prayer for all is good and welcomed before God our Savior

In fact, while Israel was in Babylon, they also were commanded by God to pray for, not only the king, but the whole pagan nation. Look at what he told the Jews to do: "Work to see that the city where I sent you as exiles enjoys peace and prosperity. Pray to the Lord for it. For as it prospers you will prosper'" (Jeremiah 29:7).

Peter said it this way: "Honor all people, love the family of believers, fear God, honor the king" (1 Peter 2:17).

Similar to those who were honored in Israel, Christians must still seek to be good citizens, good employees, and good neighbors. We are commanded to honor those in authority, to pray for the king, and to pray for godliness and holiness in our nation.

Serving the Lord does not mean to neglect the government or our community. It is very much a Christian's job to be involved with the affairs of the state and nation.

In fact, I was listening to a former governor in the United States who is an ordained Southern Baptist pastor. In an interview, someone asked him if he regretted leaving the ministry, and how he felt about those who looked down on him for working in politics. His response was along the lines of:

> I never got out of ministry. This is what Romans 13:4 says about those serving in government: "For he is God's servant to do you good. But if you do wrong, be afraid, for he does not bear the sword for nothing. He is God's servant, an agent of wrath to bring punishment on the wrongdoer." I am still serving God in a very important ministry.

Scripture calls the rulers of government, God's servants—his ministers. Yes, one can still serve the Lord as a governor or a president. God selected David to serve in leadership as the king of Israel. He promoted Joseph to vice-president of Egypt. He also exalted Daniel to what we might call the "Senate" in Babylon. These people served the Lord, but they honored the king and blessed their nation through their good works.

Serving the Lord does not mean we are only to think about heaven and spiritual things. No, we must still be very much concerned with our state, our nation, our community, and our job. This includes voting; it includes seeking the prosperity of the nation in serving in the school systems, businesses, etc. It also includes seeking to promote righteousness in areas like serving the poor, working for human rights, etc.

This is important because for many Christians serving God means to not care about practical things such as one's community or nation, but Scripture

258

calls us to honor the king, to pray daily for those in leadership, and to care for the poor (cf. 1 Peter 2:17, 1 Tim 2:1-3, James 1:27).

Sometimes while serving God, he may also call us to serve in the government in order to better serve the world and promote Christian values. Are you willing to allow God to use you in government, education, health care, politics, social work, etc.?

The singers and Pethahiah served the Lord but also served the government. These people were honored by Israel and by God. We must be willing to do the same.

Application Question: In what ways is God calling you to be a better citizen including such areas as studies, business, social justice, voting, etc.? Why are Christians so prone to neglect these practical aspects of the Christian life for more "spiritual endeavors"?

Conclusion

What are necessary qualities of those who will be honored for their service to the Lord?

1. Honored servants are willing to lead by example.
2. Honored servants are committed to seeking God's will.
3. Honored servants are willing to obey the Lord's commands.
4. Honored servants are willing to sacrifice and be uncomfortable.
5. Honored servants are committed to building God's house.
6. Honored servants are willing to serve without receiving glory here on the earth.
7. Honored servants are committed to respecting and serving the government.

Application Question: In what ways is God calling you to develop the qualities of a servant who will be honored by God? What areas do you struggle with the most?

Living a Life of Celebration

...At the dedication of the wall of Jerusalem, they sought out the Levites from all the places they lived to bring them to Jerusalem to celebrate the dedication joyfully with songs of thanksgiving and songs accompanied by cymbals, harps, and lyres. The singers were also assembled from the district around Jerusalem and from the settlements of the Netophathites...
Nehemiah 12, 13:1-3 (NET)

Application Question: Why is it important to practice the discipline of celebration?

How can we live a life of celebration? Celebration is an essential aspect of one's spiritual life. Richard Foster in his classic book, *Celebration of Discipline*, said this:

> Celebration is central to all the Spiritual Disciplines. Without a joyful spirit of festivity the Disciplines become dull, death-breathing tools in the hands of modern Pharisees.[46]

We see celebration not only here in Nehemiah 12, as Israel dedicated the wall, but we also see celebration throughout the Bible. The shepherds, wise men, and angels celebrated the birth of Jesus with gifts, songs, and prayer. God gave Israel many celebrations in the Old Covenant such as the Feast of Booths, year of Jubilee, etc. In the New Covenant, he has given us the Lord's Supper and baptism. We also see future celebrations such as the wedding of the Lamb and the wedding feast with Abraham.

It is clear from Scripture that celebration is a spiritual discipline that God desires for us to practice. It was never his will for Christians to live dry, boring lives and that is why we see celebrations both commanded and practiced throughout the Bible. Scripture says that Christ came so that we may have life and life more abundantly (cf. John 10:10). This abundant life includes celebration. In Nehemiah 12, the Israelites have a great celebration when dedicating the wall, and from it, we can learn many principles about how we can live a life of celebration?

Big Question: What can we learn about practicing the discipline of celebration from Israel's dedication of the wall?

Christians Practice the Discipline of Celebration by Planning

> At the dedication of the wall of Jerusalem, they sought out the Levites from all the places they lived to bring them to Jerusalem to celebrate the dedication joyfully with songs of thanksgiving and songs accompanied by cymbals, harps, and lyres
> Nehemiah 12:27

In this text, Israel had set up a special time of celebrating the Lord's faithfulness by dedicating the wall to him. They sought out the Levites to celebrate in Jerusalem with songs and also later set up two choirs (v. 27, 31). It is clear that there was planning involved in this process. They decided who would come and how they would lead. The celebration was meticulously planned.

This celebration was not commanded by God; however, it was special for the people of Israel and something they needed to do in order to express their joy. Sometimes Christians have problems with celebrations that are not specifically given in the Bible or commanded for Christians to practice such as: Christmas, Thanksgiving, Lent, etc. Sure, we are not commanded to practice these, but the celebration of them can encourage renewed focus and joy in the Lord, if allowed.

It is good and proper to have routine times to celebrate the Lord, as we do on the Lord's Day—Sunday. But, it is also good to have special times of devotion or celebration both on a personal level and a community level. It is easy to live a life of routine, which can eventually become dry and mundane. These devotions at special times often aid us in living a life of celebration and worship.

In the same way that it is good and healthy for a married couple to set special dates and special trips to revive and restore their relationship, sometimes we need to do this with God. We should consider establishing special times of celebration to enrich our relationship with him and our joy. It could be a retreat—a week of prayer and worship—to celebrate God's goodness. Or it could be a celebration of some great success, like a graduation, the launch of a church or a business, where one gathers with others to give thanks to God.

God's faithfulness can be celebrated in many ways; however, none of these will come to fruition without deliberate planning—both short-term and long-term planning.

Application Question: In what ways do you practice the discipline of celebration? Why is celebration important?

Christians Practice the Discipline of Celebration by Dedicating Everything to God

> At the dedication of the wall of Jerusalem, they sought out the Levites from all the places they lived to bring them to Jerusalem to celebrate the dedication joyfully with songs of thanksgiving and songs accompanied by cymbals, harps, and lyres.
> Nehemiah 12:27

The primary purpose of the celebration was to dedicate the wall to God. This dedication was done by bringing in worshipers, walking around the wall, and offering sacrifices to God.

Certainly, we have dedications today. We have baby dedications; we have weddings, which are formal dedications of a couple, both to one another and to God. We have dedications of buildings, companies, etc., which are all offered to the Lord. And these are great things to practice. However, dedications are just special ceremonies which should picture what we practice every day of our lives. Everything we do should be dedicated to the Lord and for his glory— our school work, our marriage, our friendships, our eating and drinking. Consider what Paul taught:

> So whether you eat or drink, or whatever you do, do everything for the glory of God.
> 1 Corinthians 10:31

> Whatever you are doing, work at it with enthusiasm, as to the Lord and not for people
> Colossians 3:23

As Israel dedicated the wall to God, we also should find ways to dedicate everything in our lives to him. A life without dedication is really a life without true celebration. We only celebrate what we are dedicated to. We celebrate good grades because we were dedicated to work for them. We celebrate someone's life only when we have some type of dedication or commitment to the person.

In the same way, only a life that is dedicated to God can truly be a life of celebration and joy.

Application Question: In what ways can we practice dedicating everything to the Lord?

1. We dedicate everything to God by offering our bodies, our time, our relationships, and our projects to God through prayer.

2. We dedicate everything to God by thanking him for everything. This means that we recognize that everything is from him and for him.

3. We dedicate everything to God by working at it with all of our hearts (Col 3:23). We cannot dedicate our scraps to God—only our best.

Application Question: How do you personally practice dedicating things to the Lord?

Christians Practice the Discipline of Celebration when Leaders Serve Joyfully

> At the dedication of the wall of Jerusalem, they sought out the Levites from all the places they lived to bring them to Jerusalem to celebrate the dedication joyfully with songs of thanksgiving and songs accompanied by cymbals, harps, and lyres... I brought the leaders of Judah up on top of the wall, and I appointed two large choirs to give thanks. One was to proceed on the top of the wall southward toward the Dung Gate. Going after them were Hoshaiah, half the leaders of Judah... and the priests—Eliakim, Maaseiah, Miniamin, Micaiah, Elioenai, Zechariah, and Hananiah, with their trumpets—and also Maaseiah, Shemaiah, Eleazar, Uzzi, Jehohanan, Malkijah, Elam, and Ezer. The choirs sang loudly under the direction of Jezrahiah. And on that day they offered great sacrifices and rejoiced, for God had given them great joy. The women and children also rejoiced. The rejoicing in Jerusalem could be heard from far away.
> Nehemiah 12:27, 31-32, 41- 43

In order to live a life of celebration, godly leaders must lead joyfully. One of the things that we must notice in this narrative is that the Levites, the singers, the priests, Nehemiah, and Ezra were all called to lead the celebration. Nehemiah 12:27 says that the Levites were brought "to Jerusalem to celebrate the dedication joyfully." Nehemiah also called the leaders of Judah to help lead in the celebration (v. 31). Nehemiah knew that it was important for the leaders to lead the celebration in order for it to affect everybody else. Nehemiah 12:43 notes the response of the people. It says: "And on that day they offered great sacrifices and rejoiced, for God had given them great joy. The women and children also rejoiced. The rejoicing in Jerusalem could be heard from far away."

As the leaders led with joy, the women and children also rejoiced and the sound of rejoicing could be heard from far away. This means the Jews living in the suburbs and villages near Jerusalem could hear the sheer joy. It also probably reached their Gentile neighbors as well. The people of Israel were very responsive to the leaders' joy, causing a great celebration. We see their joyful response in several ways:

Observation Question: How did the people respond to their leaders and the dedication in Nehemiah 12:47-13:4?

1. The people responded by contributing the daily portions for the singers and gatekeepers.

    Nehemiah 12:47 says,

    So in the days of Zerubbabel and in the days of Nehemiah, all Israel was contributing the portions for the singers and gatekeepers, according to the daily need. They also set aside the portion for the Levites, and the Levites set aside the portion for the descendants of Aaron.

2. The people responded by gathering to read the Word of God and by excluding the foreigners from Israel in order to properly approach God.

    It seems that the beginning of chapter 13 is in response to the dedication. Nehemiah 13:1 says "On that day" meaning it was probably a continuation from the previous chapter. It reads:

    On that day the book of Moses was read aloud in the hearing of the people. They found written in it that no Ammonite or Moabite may ever

enter the assembly of God, for they had not met the Israelites with food and water, but instead had hired Balaam to curse them. (Our God, however, turned the curse into blessing.) When they heard the law, they removed from Israel all who were of mixed ancestry
Nehemiah 13:1-3

Nehemiah shared all this after the dedication and the worship of the leaders to show how it affected Israel. Their joy affected others and the rest of Israel was prompted to give, read the Word, and separate from the foreigners. In order to live a life of celebration, we must have godly leaders who lead joyfully.

Application Question: How can we practically apply the effect of the leaders' joy on others?

The rest of Scripture would similarly teach that our joy, and especially that of leaders, affects others. Proverbs 17:22 says, "A cheerful heart brings good healing, but a crushed spirit dries up the bones."
A cheerful heart is good medicine. Now certainly, this applies to us. Having joy in our life, no doubt, will help us heal and protect us from physical disease. Studies support the effect of joy on our lives. But our cheerful heart is also like good medicine to others.
See, the leaders in Israel got excited, and it affected everybody else's commitment to God as seen in Israel's response. In the same way, our joy, our life of celebration, especially as people in leadership, will encourage the faith of others. It will encourage them to be faithful to the Lord.
Our joy for the Lord, our joy in worship, our joy in evangelism, and our joy in a difficult situation is contagious. It brings healing to broken bones and hearts of those around us. Similarly, Solomon said this: "A joyful heart makes the face cheerful, but by a painful heart the spirit is broken" (Proverbs 15:13).
A happy heart makes the face cheerful. It is contagious. It brings a smile to others, and this is especially important for leaders. I think that's part of the reason why Satan is so aggressive in seeking to discourage the leadership of the church. When elders, small group leaders, deacons, etc., are discouraged, it negatively affects everybody else. Instead of bringing healing, it crushes the spirit of others.
I remember briefly serving at an Army medical hospital in San Antonio, Texas, as a Navy Reserve chaplain. A soldier was flown in from Germany who had previously been injured in Afghanistan. If I remember correctly, a bomb had gone off causing an electric wire to fall on him. This caused electricity to shoot

through his body, out of his fingers, and out of his toes. He had third degree burns everywhere and was missing a few limbs.

I went in thinking, *"How am I going to comfort this guy?"* However, I was encouraged to learn that this nineteen year old soldier was a man of faith. He was joyful and focused on the prospects of his future. He could see how God was going to use this unfortunate situation for his good. And instead of comforting him, he comforted me.

I left there inspired because of the joy and mature perspective of this young man. I went there hoping to give some spiritual medicine, but, by God's grace, I was on the receiving end. A happy heart makes the face cheerful.

I think we also see how a joyful leader affects others in the fact that David is mentioned six times throughout this narrative. It continually says, "as specified by David the man of God." Consider a few of these verses:

> And the leaders of the Levites were Hashabiah, Sherebiah, Jeshua son of Kadmiel, and their colleagues, who stood opposite them to offer praise and thanks, one contingent corresponding to the other, as specified by David the man of God.
> Nehemiah 12:24

> and his colleagues—Shemaiah, Azarel, Milalai, Gilalai, Maai, Nethanel, Judah, and Hanani—with musical instruments of David the man of God. (Ezra the scribe led them.)
> Nehemiah 12:36

His name is mentioned in verses 24, 36, 45 and 46. When it says Israel followed his prescription of worship, it probably refers to the Psalms he wrote, which included songs to sing and also instructions for instruments. He had also probably set up an order of worship that had been passed down throughout the generations in Israel.

I bring up the continual references to David because David was a godly leader, a man after God's own heart, who loved to worship and celebrate God. One time he danced so vigorously before the Lord that he took off his princely robes and looked like a common man (2 Sam 6:14). He was a leader who led with joy and his worship affected all of Israel. Even today, his joy and worship are still contagious. We still use many of his Psalms in our contemporary worship music, and we commonly read them, as part of the Holy Scripture, to encourage our hearts when we are down.

Are you a joyful leader? The Levites and other leaders were called to lead with joy (v. 27), and God has called you to lead with joy as well. It's like a medicine that cheers others up and draws them into a life of celebration.

267

Likewise, a discouraged leader creates discouraged followers. We develop a discipline of celebration as a community by having leaders who lead with joy and by being leaders who lead with joy.

Application Question: In what ways have you seen joyful leaders lead others into joy or celebration? In what ways have you experienced discouraged leaders who lead others into discouragement? How is God calling you to lead with joy?

Christians Practice the Discipline of Celebration by Corporate Worship

> At the dedication of the wall of Jerusalem, they sought out the Levites from all the places they lived to bring them to Jerusalem to celebrate the dedication joyfully with songs of thanksgiving and songs accompanied by cymbals, harps, and lyres. The singers were also assembled from the district around Jerusalem and from the settlements of the Netophathites and from Beth Gilgal and from the fields of Geba and Azmaveth, for the singers had built settlements for themselves around Jerusalem... I brought the leaders of Judah up on top of the wall, and I appointed two large choirs to give thanks. One was to proceed on the top of the wall southward toward the Dung Gate.
> Nehemiah 12:27-29, 31

In this text, we see that not only were the Levites sought out to participate in the worship, but many others as well—the singers from the region around Jerusalem (v. 28-29), the leaders of Judah, two large choirs (v. 31), and many other neighboring Israelites, including women and children (v. 43). The women and children were mentioned in verse 43 to show that everybody was worshiping, even those who had the lowest status in Israel. They all came together to worship God and dedicate the wall to him.

Similarly, in order to live a life of worship, we must be part of a community of worship. We need to meet with the people of God to worship. That is why they all came together from all over Israel.

Can't we worship by ourselves?

Certainly, and we should, but there are special things that God does when the people of God are gathered together. Jesus said that when two or more are gathered in his name he is in the midst of them (Matt 18:20). In fact, Scripture commands us to faithfully participate in the public gathering of the saints. Hebrews 10:24-25 says,

And let us take thought of how to spur one another on to love and good works, not abandoning our own meetings, as some are in the habit of doing, but encouraging each other, and even more so because you see the day drawing near.

The writer of Hebrews taught that gathering into a worshiping community is necessary for stirring up love, good works, and for finding encouragement. Yes, we need each other to practice a lifestyle of celebration. We cannot live a lifestyle of celebration alone. We need the gathering of the saints.

Application Question: How can we practice community worship in order to live a life of celebration?

- We practice community worship by being faithfully involved in weekly church worship and small groups.

- We practice community worship by involving the body of Christ in our personal celebrations. We can do this by strategically inviting church members to our celebrations in order to increase our worship and theirs.

- We practice community worship by participating in the celebrations of others. Romans 12:15 says, "Rejoice with those who rejoice."

Application Question: Why is corporate worship so important to living a life of celebration? How is God challenging you to grow in corporate worship?

Christians Practice the Discipline of Celebration by Giving Thanks in Everything

At the dedication of the wall of Jerusalem, they sought out the Levites from all the places they lived to bring them to Jerusalem to celebrate the dedication joyfully with songs of thanksgiving and songs accompanied by cymbals, harps, and lyres... I brought the leaders of Judah up on top of the wall, and I appointed two large choirs to give thanks. One was to proceed on the top of the wall southward toward the Dung Gate.
Nehemiah 12:27, 31

The leaders of Israel led the people in "songs of thanksgiving" (v. 27), and the two choirs Nehemiah set up gave thanks (v. 31). The dedication of the wall was full of thanksgiving. In the same way, if we are going to live a life of celebration, we must continually give thanks to God.

It is good for us to remember that one of the ways that nonbelievers are characterized in Scripture is by not giving thanks to God. Listen to what Paul said when describing the pagan world: "For although they knew God, they did not glorify him as God or give him thanks, but they became futile in their thoughts and their senseless hearts were darkened" (Romans 1:21).

They are described as a people who knew God through the witness of creation but neither glorified him nor gave thanks to him. The world is characterized by not being thankful. Sadly, many people in the church "know God" but yet refuse to glorify him and give thanks to him.

As Christians we are commanded to give thanks in everything. Paul said this in 1 Thessalonians 5:18-19: "in everything give thanks. For this is God's will for you in Christ Jesus. Do not extinguish the Spirit."

He commands us to give thanks in all circumstances and then says for us to not "extinguish the Spirit." What does he mean by this?

It means that when we are unthankful, we lose the Spirit of God's power in our lives. We lose the power to be joyful, the power to do the works he has called us to do, and, in fact, we often bring the discipline of God on our lives. Israel was disciplined in the wilderness for all their complaining (1 Cor 10:10). However, living a life of thanksgiving opens the door for the Spirit to work in our lives and to give us joy (cf. Gal 5:22). It allows us to truly celebrate God and his works.

Many Christians are walking around without power because they neglect the practice of thanksgiving. They are complainers and worriers, and, by their complaining and worrying, they place water on the Spirit's fire, affecting both themselves and whatever community they are a part of.

It's good to remember that we are commanded to "Do everything without grumbling or arguing" (Phil 2:14) and to not be anxious about anything (Phil 4:6). When we choose to complain or be anxious, we put out the Spirit's fire.

If you want to live a life of worship and celebration, you must put logs on the fire of God by living a life of thanksgiving.

Application Question: What are some ways we can practice the discipline of thanksgiving in order to increase our celebration of the Lord?

1. Practicing the discipline of journaling will help increase our thanksgiving. By journaling, we remember God's faithfulness, his

answers to prayer, and his sovereignty over circumstances. As we remember his good works, we will continually be filled with joy and thanksgiving.

2. Practicing the discipline of singing worship will help increase our thanksgiving. This is not just a corporate discipline; it should also be a personal discipline (cf. Eph 5:19).

3. Practicing the discipline of giving thanks to God in all circumstances, both good and bad, will help us develop a natural habit of thanksgiving.

4. Practicing the discipline of giving thanks to others will help us recognize their good works and/or how God has used them in our lives.

Application Question: Why do we so often forget to praise and glorify God throughout the day, even when he has blessed us? How often do you practice giving thanks to God and to others?

Christians Practice the Discipline of Celebration by Confessing Sins

> When the priests and Levites had purified themselves, they purified the people, the gates, and the wall. I brought the leaders of Judah up on top of the wall, and I appointed two large choirs to give thanks. One was to proceed on the top of the wall southward toward the Dung Gate. Nehemiah 12:30-31

It must be noted that before the dedication began, the Levites first purified themselves, the people, and the wall (v. 30). How did they do this? This probably included ceremonial washings and a sin offering, where they sought the Lord to forgive their sins.

Similarly, we cannot live a life of celebration without the continual cleansing of sin. Consider what David said about forgiveness in Psalm 32:2-5 (NIV 1984):

> Blessed is the man whose sin the LORD does not count against him and in whose spirit is no deceit. When I kept silent, my bones wasted away through my groaning all day long. For day and night your hand was heavy upon me; my strength was sapped as in the heat of summer. Selah Then I acknowledged my sin to you and did not cover

271

up my iniquity. I said, "I will confess my transgressions to the LORD"—
and you forgave the guilt of my sin. Selah

He declared how "Blessed" the man was whose sins are forgiven.
"Blessed" can be translated "Happy." Happy is the man whose sin the LORD
does not count against him. However, he also described his own personal
testimony of not confessing his sin. He shared that when he was silent, his
bones wasted away, probably referring to physical sickness from his sin (cf. 1
Cor 11:30). He groaned, meaning he was depressed. His strength was sapped.
He dealt with both physical and emotional weakness when he had unrepentant
sin in his life. Sin takes away our ability to live a joyful life. It takes away our
ability to celebrate. Confession and forgiveness of sin are necessary in order to
truly celebrate God.

This reminds us that true joy and celebration comes from a right
relationship with God (cf. Phil 4:4, Psalm 1:1). We cannot have a right
relationship with God while we are in sin. Therefore, confession is necessary.
The person who chooses to abide in sin and live in rebellion towards God can
know nothing of true joy or true celebration. Our joy and peace are in the Lord
and come from him (cf. Eph 2:14, Gal 5:22). We must continually seek
forgiveness to live the life of celebration God desires for us.

First John 1:9 says this: "But if we confess our sins, he is faithful and
righteous, forgiving us our sins and cleansing us from all unrighteousness." We
do not need to make a sin offering like Israel did to have our sins forgiven. All
we need to do is confess our sins to God, turn away from them, and God will
forgive and restore us to a right relationship with him, so we can have joy.

Application Question: In what ways have you experienced the loss of joy and
strength because of sin, as David did (Psalm 32:2-5)? In what ways have you
experienced joy, when you have experienced the forgiveness of God?

Christians Practice the Discipline of Celebration by Claiming God's Promises

They went over the Fountain Gate and continued directly up the steps
of the City of David on the ascent to the wall. They passed the house
of David and continued on to the Water Gate toward the east. The
second choir was proceeding in the opposite direction. I followed them,
along with half the people, on top of the wall, past the Tower of the
Ovens to the Broad Wall, over the Ephraim Gate, the Jeshanah Gate,

272

the Fish Gate, the Tower of Hananel, and the Tower of the Hundred, to the Sheep Gate. They stopped at the Gate of the Guard.
Nehemiah 12:37-39

Interpretation Question: What does walking around the walls of Jerusalem symbolize in Nehemiah 12:37-39, as seen throughout Scripture?

The next thing we must notice is that Israel dedicated the wall in part by walking around it in both directions. By walking around the wall, they were claiming that God did the work and claiming God's promise that he would give them the land (cf. Gen 12:7, 17:8).

We have seen this symbolic walking in several passages in the Bible. In Genesis 13:14-17, God called Abraham to lift his eyes to survey the land and to walk through it, for all of it had been given to him. In Joshua 1:3, Joshua was told that every place his foot touched was his. Furthermore, Joshua and Israel were called to walk around Jericho seven times, which symbolized God giving them that city, right before the walls of the city fell down and they conquered it (Josh 6).

Walking around the land of Jerusalem symbolically demonstrated their claiming of God's covenant promise to eternally give the land to the nation of Israel. It was them saying, "Lord, we believe you! We recognize this victory of building the wall came from you, and we are claiming your promise of this land!"

Claiming God's promises is necessary for us to live a life of celebration as well. Many Christians live without joy and celebration because they refuse to take hold of God's promises.

Application Question: What types of promises has God given us which will help us to live a life of joy and celebration?

It has been said that there are over 3000 promises in the Scripture, and we must claim them by faith and be obedient to them in order to live a life of celebration. Here are a few to consider:

> You will keep in perfect peace him whose mind is steadfast, because he trusts in you.
> Isaiah 26:3 (NIV 1984)

> How blessed is the one who does not follow the advice of the wicked, or stand in the pathway with sinners, or sit in the assembly of scoffers! Instead he finds pleasure in obeying the Lord's commands; he meditates on his commands day and night. He is like a tree planted by

flowing streams; it yields its fruit at the proper time, and its leaves never fall off. He succeeds in everything he attempts.
Psalm 1:1-3

Do not be anxious about anything. Instead, in every situation, through prayer and petition with thanksgiving, tell your requests to God. And the peace of God that surpasses all understanding will guard your hearts and minds in Christ Jesus.
Philippians 4:6-7

These are all promises of God we must take hold of by faith. By keeping our mind on God regardless of the circumstances, we can have the Lord's peace. By separating from the sinful influence of the ungodly and delighting in God's Word day and night, we will prosper in everything that we do. Instead of worrying, we must refuse to be anxious and instead choose to live a lifestyle of prayer with thanksgiving, and God's peace will guard our hearts. Like Israel, we must take these steps by faith to receive God's promises. The Christian life should be a continual unwrapping of God's promises, as we walk by faith in them.

We can't live a life of worship—a life of joy—unless we are taking the promises of God and claiming them. Yes, the nations around Israel were daunting. How could they keep the land and protect the land with such daunting adversaries? All they could do was obediently trust God's Word, and God would do the rest. It is the same for us.

We each have enemies in our lives that threaten to steal our joy and life of celebration. But, we must claim God's promises so that we can celebrate even in the presence of our enemies. David said this: "You prepare a feast before me in plain sight of my enemies. You refresh my head with oil; my cup is completely full" (Psalm 23:5). Amen, let it be so.

Application Question: What are your favorite promises in Scripture? Which promises do you feel God is calling you to stand on and claim right now so that you can celebrate, even in the midst of your enemies?

Christians Practice the Discipline of Celebration by Investing in the House of God

Then the two choirs that gave thanks took their stations in the temple of God. I did also, along with half the officials with me, and the priests— Eliakim, Maaseiah, Miniamin, Micaiah, Elioenai, Zechariah, and

Hananiah, with their trumpets—and also Maaseiah, Shemaiah, Eleazar, Uzzi, Jehohanan, Malkijah, Elam, and Ezer. The choirs sang loudly under the direction of Jezrahiah. And on that day they offered great sacrifices and rejoiced, for God had given them great joy. The women and children also rejoiced. The rejoicing in Jerusalem could be heard from far away.
Nehemiah 12:40-43

What else can we learn about a life of celebration from Israel's celebration?

We see that after they walked around the wall with two groups going in opposite directions (v. 38), they went into the "temple of God" (v. 40). They gave "great sacrifices" and rejoiced with "great joy" (v. 43). This seems to be the pinnacle of their celebration. The sound of their corporate rejoicing was so loud it could be heard from far away.

Yes, in the same way, our joy is the greatest when we have invested in the house of God, which is his church—God's people (cf. 1 Peter 2:5). Why do I call it an "investment"? It's an investment because of how the Israelites gave. It says that they gave "great sacrifices" (v. 43). This means that they gave their best to the Lord at the temple.

Similarly, I believe many people struggle with living a life of celebration because they are not really invested in their church. They are not invested in the people of God.

They come to church on Sunday but never take time to get involved in people's lives through small groups or other ministries. There is no "great sacrifice" in their corporate worship. Too many people in the church think that their appearance on Sunday is some great sacrifice to God. They say, "Lord, I got up and made it to church. Aren't you happy?"

But we must remember that God wants our best. He wants us to invest in him and his people. Listen to what God said to Israel in Malachi 1 about their sacrifices:

"A son naturally honors his father and a slave respects his master. If I am your father, where is my honor? If I am your master, where is my respect? The Lord who rules over all asks you this, you priests who make light of my name! But you reply, 'How have we made light of your name?' You are offering improper sacrifices on my altar, yet you ask, 'How have we offended you?' By treating the table of the Lord as if it is of no importance! For when you offer blind animals as a sacrifice, is that not wrong? And when you offer the lame and sick, is that not wrong as well? Indeed, try offering them to your governor! Will he be pleased with you or show you favor?" asks the Lord who rules over all.

But now plead for God's favor that he might be gracious to us. "With this kind of offering in your hands, how can he be pleased with you?" asks the Lord who rules over all.
Malachi 1:6-9

In this text, Israel was rejected by God because they gave him their leftovers. They gave the lamb with one eye and a broken leg, and God said that he wouldn't accept it.

Similarly, many Christians don't offer God their best; they don't truly invest. They give him the scraps of their day, the scraps of their time. They aren't committed to serving his people, the church. It is good to remember the correspondence between the sheep and Jesus in Matthew 25. The sheep said to Jesus, "When did we feed you; when did we clothe you?" Christ responded, "When you did it to the least of these, you did it to me" (v. 37 and 40, paraphrased). Whatever we do to God's people, we do to him.

Israel's celebration and joy were marked by the "great sacrifices" they gave God in the temple. Many of the Old Covenant sacrifices were not only offered to God but eaten by both the offerer and the priests. They were communal meals that not only blessed God but others. They gave God their best and so must we, as we invest in the church—his people.

Are you investing in the people of God? Israel had their greatest joy as they offered their best to the Lord in his house.

One of the ways you invest in something is by giving the best of your time, the best of your money, and the best of your energy. Are you doing that with the house of God, God's people?

God promises that whatever you give, he will give back to you. Jesus said this: "Give, and it will be given to you: A good measure, pressed down, shaken together, running over, will be poured into your lap. For the measure you use will be the measure you receive" (Luke 6:38). Proverbs 11:25 in the New Living Translation says, "Those who refresh others shall themselves be refreshed." God will give you a life of tremendous joy, as you give your best to him and his people. He will enable you to live a life of celebration—a life of joy.

Application Question: What are some practical ways that we can invest in the house of God (the people of God) to live a life of celebration? In what ways have you experienced an enriched joy through this practice?

Christians Practice the Discipline of Celebration by Being Devoted to the Word of God

On that day the book of Moses was read aloud in the hearing of the people. They found written in it that no Ammonite or Moabite may ever enter the assembly of God, for they had not met the Israelites with food and water, but instead had hired Balaam to curse them. (Our God, however, turned the curse into blessing.) When they heard the law, they removed from Israel all who were of mixed ancestry.
Nehemiah 13:1-3

When Nehemiah 13:1 says "on that day," it seems to be referring to the day they dedicated the wall. The dedication of the wall included reading Scripture and obeying it. As they were investing in the house of God, they found that the Scripture forbade having an Ammonite or Moabite in the temple. These nations were antagonistic towards Israel while they were traveling in the wilderness after leaving Egypt. Therefore, the Jews, in obedience, excluded anybody from foreign descent.

It must be noted that part of their celebration was being devoted to Scripture as they read and obeyed it. This must be true for us as well. If we are going to lead our lives and the people we serve in celebration, we must lead them to honor the Word of God and to submit to it.

Certainly, we see this throughout the Scripture. David, in writing the hymnal of Israel, began the Psalms encouraging the people to meditate on the law of the Lord day and night (Psalm 1:2). Similarly, in Psalm 19:7-8 (NIV 1984) he said this:

The law of the LORD is perfect, reviving the soul. The statutes of the LORD are trustworthy, making wise the simple. The precepts of the LORD are right, giving joy to the heart. The commands of the LORD are radiant, giving light to the eyes.

David championed many of the benefits of honoring the Word of God. He taught that the Word of God revives the soul, makes people wise, gives joy to the heart, and gives light to the eyes (gives us direction). The law of the Lord is truly perfect; its benefits are legion. If we are going to live lives of celebration, they must be lives devoted to Scripture. The law of the Lord revives the soul and brings joy to the heart.

Are you living a life devoted to Scripture? Are you exhorting those you lead to do the same? Consider what Paul told his disciple Timothy: "Until I come, give attention to the public reading of scripture, to exhortation, to teaching" (1 Timothy 4:13). Let us apply this exhortation to our own lives and also to those we lead. Certainly, not all are called to preach, but we are all called to teach as we make disciples of all nations. In order to live a life of celebration, we must be devoted to Scripture.

Application Question: In what ways have you experienced joy by being in the Word of God, obeying it, and sharing it with others? How can you more effectively use Scripture to live a life of celebration?

Conclusion

How do we live a life of celebration? Christians practice the discipline of celebration by:

- planning daily and special times of celebration
- dedicating everything to God
- leading with joy
- participating in corporate worship
- giving thanks in everything
- continually confessing our sins
- claiming the promises of God
- investing in the house of God
- and by being devoted to the Word of God

Application Question: In what ways has God challenged you to live a life of celebration in order to increase your joy and the joy of others?

Signs of Spiritual Decay

....During all this time I was not in Jerusalem, for in the thirty-second year of King Artaxerxes of Babylon, I had gone back to the king. After some time I had requested leave of the king, and I returned to Jerusalem. Then I discovered the evil that Eliashib had done for Tobiah by supplying him with a storeroom in the courts of the temple of God. I was very upset, and I threw all of Tobiah's household possessions out of the storeroom. Then I gave instructions that the storerooms should be purified, and I brought back the equipment of the temple of God, along with the grain offering and the incense...
Nehemiah 13:4-31 (NET)

What are signs of spiritual decay in our lives or others and how should we confront it?

After seeing the revival that happened in Israel, we also see how prone they were to fall back into sin and compromise. Some have compared the spiritual life to walking upstream; if you are not fighting to move forward, then you are, by default, going backwards.

At this point in the final chapter of Nehemiah, Nehemiah returned to Persia for some unspecified amount of time.[47] Some commentators think his second term as governor began approximately nine years after he left.[48] While Nehemiah was gone, it is possible that Ezra had died "(in 13:13, Zadok is called 'the' scribe, perhaps indicating that Ezra no longer held that post)."[49] When Nehemiah returned, Israel had reneged on the majority of its commitments to God, which they made in chapter 10.

This may seem like a surprise after all God had done for them and their seemingly genuine repentance; however, this not only happened with Israel, it commonly happens to us individually and corporately. If we are not fighting to move forward, then we are sliding backwards. It is for this reason that we must be tenacious in seeking to practice a holy life and also fighting for holiness in our churches. There is a continual inertia drawing us and others towards spiritual decay.

279

Certainly, we see this in our churches and Christian communities. Why are so many of our churches in disarray? Statistics say that around 75% of youth fall away from the faith in college and never return.[50] Seventeen hundred pastors leave the ministry every month in America.[51] We have churches making all kinds of moral compromises as they disregard Scripture. We are seeing a very rapid spiritual decay happening in the church.

As we consider Nehemiah 13, it can seem a little depressing after such a great revival. And, it also can be depressing as we consider the decline of Christianity happening in so many parts of the world; however, there is hope. We see hope in a man who was zealous for the Lord named Nehemiah.

Four times he prays for God to remember his works in this chapter. He is a man who wants to please God. Yes, there is hope for us individually and as a church as well. God still uses people like Nehemiah, people like John the Baptist, godly leaders who are zealous to turn communities and individuals back to God.

In this text, Nehemiah is a type of Christ. As Christ went into the temple, he pulled out a whip, turned over tables, and harshly rebuked the leaders of Israel. Scripture says of Christ that zeal for the house of God consumed him (John 2:17). Nehemiah was the same. He threw a man out of the temple who was defiling it, rebuked the leaders for their lack of faithfulness in giving, locked people out of the city who were abusing the Sabbath, and pulled out the hairs of those who married foreign women in order to turn them back to God. Nehemiah was a man consumed with seeing God's glory in Israel.

In the same way, God is calling for people in this generation to be zealous for personal holiness and also holiness in the church. He is looking to raise people who are consumed with zeal for the house of God (cf. 2 Chronicles 16:9).

In this text, we will consider common signs of spiritual decay not only in the church but in our spiritual lives. Godly leaders must be able to spiritually diagnose their people, their society, and even their own lives. They must be able to diagnose so they can participate in the restoration process. In this text, we will not only see common signs of spiritual decay but also steps to restoration—to restore our churches and our lives.

Big Question: What signs of spiritual decay do we see happening to Israel in Nehemiah 13; how does Nehemiah confront them, and how should we apply these truths as leaders to our spiritual lives and our ministries?

Compromised Leadership Is a Sign of Spiritual Decay

But prior to this time, Eliashib the priest, a relative of Tobiah, had been appointed over the storerooms of the temple of our God. He made for himself a large storeroom where previously they had been keeping the grain offering, the incense, and the vessels, along with the tithes of the grain, the new wine, and the olive oil as commanded for the Levites, the singers, the gate keepers, and the offering for the priests.
Nehemiah 13:4-5

Most versions seem to translate verse 4 and 5 a little differently than the NET. The ESV says, "*Now before this, Eliashib the priest, who was appointed over the chambers of the house of our God, and who was related to Tobiah, prepared for Tobiah a large chamber where they had previously put the grain offering...*" Here, Nehemiah begins to introduce us to the compromises that were happening within Israel. They broke all the commitments they made in chapter 10. It is no surprise that when he started to list their sins, he started with the leadership of Israel. The High Priest was disrespecting God by allowing an Ammonite official into the temple (cf. Neh 2:10, 13:1, 28). He had given Tobiah, who had previously persecuted the Jews, a room in God's house.

This is how moral compromise often begins in the people of God—it begins with the leadership. The leadership starts to compromise by disobedience and disregard for the teachings of the Word of God, which eventually affects all the people. Have we not seen the effects of bad leadership throughout Scripture?

Interpretation Question: In what ways have we seen the negative effects of bad leadership throughout Scripture?

Solomon compromised by marrying pagan women in disobedience to the law, and consequently, all of Israel was led astray into worshiping idols. The book of Kings shows us a pattern of Israel's stumbles. They would have a good king and, therefore, start following God. And then they would have a bad king and, consequently, stumble away from him. For every Josiah, Asa and Jehoshophat, there was a Jereboam, Jehu, and Ahab, the wicked kings of Israel who led the nation astray.

During this time period, not only were the kings corrupt but so were the priests. In fact, right before God judged Israel by Assyria, God rebuked the priests through the prophet Hosea.[52] Listen to what he said:

The more the priests increased, the more they sinned against me; they exchanged their Glory for something disgraceful. They feed on the sins of my people and relish their wickedness. And it will be: Like people,

like priests. I will punish both of them for their ways and repay them for their deeds.
Hosea 4:7-9 (NIV 1984)

The priests were sinning just like the people. In fact, they enjoyed the sins of the people and made a profit off of them. God promised he would punish the priests and the people together for their compromise.

Theological and moral compromises amongst the leadership of churches or ministries typically precede people going astray. In fact, when Christ appeared in the Gospels, Israel was being run by the Pharisees and Sadducees who were corrupting the teachings of Scripture and leading people astray as well. In the Gospels, Christ spent a significant amount of time correcting and rebuking the leadership of the people.

Application Question: Why is the leadership of the church so important?

Consider what Christ said: "A disciple is not greater than his teacher, nor a slave greater than his master. It is enough for the disciple to become like his teacher, and the slave like his master" (Matthew 10:24-25). The people can go no farther than their leaders. The leaders create the ceiling for the church.

When we look at the state of our churches, it is often a reflection of its leaders. When we have leadership that does not preach the Word, leadership that is not on fire for God, leadership that does not run their household well, it is no surprise that the light in the church is so dim.

Paul described the church in the last days in a similar manner. He said that the church would not be able to stand sound doctrine and, therefore, would heap up many teachers to itch their ears and to say what they wanted to hear (2 Tim 4:3-4).

Interpretation Question: Why was the High Priest compromising? What could be some of the reasons?

We are not sure why the High Priest compromised; it could be many reasons:

1.   Maybe, he had liberal doctrine.

Even though they had just read that Moabites and Ammonites could not enter the temple (cf. Neh 13:1), maybe he thought the Scripture was antiquated, full of errors, and not relevant. Maybe he thought God was not the author of "every" portion of Scripture, and therefore he could pick and choose what was of God. We see that happening in many churches today, and consequently, instead of submitting to the Word of God, they stand in judgment over it. They take liberty to decide what God said and did not say. They say, "God didn't really create the earth as seen in Genesis; it was created through the evolutionary process." "Jonah wasn't really swallowed by a big fish." "Jesus didn't really turn water into wine." They choose what is of God and not of God, and therefore, they choose what not to submit to.

Eliashib might have rebelled because of his doctrine which, no doubt, would have also negatively affected the people.

2.   Maybe, he was a people pleaser—meaning he wanted the applause of the people instead of God.

Potentially, it was the Israelites clamoring for more liberality and for him to stop being so narrow-minded. Later in this chapter, we see that many of the people married foreigners and their children couldn't speak Hebrew (v. 23-24). Maybe he wouldn't stand up for God.

As mentioned previously, Paul declared that this would happen in the last days. People would heap up many teachers that would itch their ears and make them feel good. Many ministers won't preach strong doctrine or hold the church accountable for fear of losing their jobs, status, or numbers in the church. Today, we have many leaders in the church who are "men of men" instead of "men of God."

3.   Maybe, he was simply a hypocrite.

He might have been preaching the truth but not practicing it in the temple. In that case, he would have been a hypocritical leader.

Whatever the reason, we can be sure that his actions contributed to the sins of the people. As we look at the rest of the text, we see that the people are living in great compromise as well. Like priest, like people; we see this happening all around us, and therefore, decay has crept into many of our churches.

Leaders of the church must ask themselves, "Are we setting the example?" (1 Peter 5:3). It is the leaders who set the spiritual ceiling for the congregation. It is enough for a student to be like his teacher. If the pastor, elders, and teachers are no longer growing in zeal for Christ, how can they expect it from the congregation? If the leadership in the church is no longer growing in the knowledge of Scripture, how can they expect it from the congregation? The leadership sets both the ceiling and the direction of the congregation.

283

Let this challenge us as we serve in any form of leadership to never be lacking in zeal or obedience and to always be abounding in the work of the Lord (cf. 1 Cor 15:58). But also let this challenge us to pray daily for the leadership of our local church and churches around the world. It is enough for a disciple to be like his teacher.

Application Question: In what ways have you seen both the positive and negative effects of leadership in the church? How can the church better support our leaders in order to encourage their continual growth in the Lord?

Misuse of Finances Is a Sign of Spiritual Decay

> I also discovered that the grain offerings for the Levites had not been provided, and that as a result the Levites and the singers who performed this work had all gone off to their fields.
> Nehemiah 13:10

Nehemiah 13:10 says the Israelites stopped supporting the Levites who maintained the temple and taught the people. Because they were not being supported they moved back to their fields to earn a living. Listen to what Nehemiah said: "I also discovered that the grain offerings for the Levites had not been provided, and that as a result the Levites and the singers who performed this work had all gone off to their fields."

Most commentators say that Malachi was prophesying during this period of time.[53] God said through the prophet in Malachi 3:8 that the people had robbed God through their tithes and offerings. They had stopped giving to God.

Similarly, this is a common sign of spiritual decay with us. Whatever we really love, we put our money into. If we really love books, movies, food, or anything else, one can tell by looking at our bank statements.

In the same way, when God is no longer our priority, we will find it harder to support his work with our finances. This is what was happening with Israel. God had ceased to be their priority, and therefore, they stopped giving to his work. Similarly, when they were on fire for God, their offerings were great. Remember the giving in the previous chapter:

> And on that day they offered great sacrifices and rejoiced, for God had given them great joy. The women and children also rejoiced. The rejoicing in Jerusalem could be heard from far away. On that day men were appointed over the storerooms for the contributions, first fruits,

284

and tithes, to gather into them from the fields of the cities the portions prescribed by the law for the priests and the Levites, for the people of Judah took delight in the priests and Levites who were ministering. Nehemiah 12:43-44

When they were on fire for God, they gave great sacrifices with joy. Similarly, when we are on fire for God, we also give joyfully, but when our relationship with God cools, we start to give less or the giving ceases all together.

I have seen this personally in my own life. I remember being in college on a full basketball scholarship, without any real financial needs. I was growing in God—knowing his voice more and enjoying his presence. With that came a growing desire to give to him, simply because I loved him. But the problem was I didn't make any money. My scholarship provided all my needs, but it didn't provide any spending money. So, I remember getting a part-time job just because I wanted to have something to give, not only to God but also to others who had needs. This is a natural occurrence. When you are growing in love with someone, you naturally want to give, not only financially, but you want to share in all good things with that person.

I experienced this with my daughter, especially when she was a baby. I remember going to the store to buy groceries, and without a real need, I went straight to the baby section. I was thinking, "What can I buy for my daughter?" There was great joy in buying things for her. I got new diapers and a special no-throw-up formula. I got some scented baby bath liquid that would help put her to sleep (which my wife swiftly threw away, saying something about "chemicals"). I bought a bunch of stuff that at that stage of life meant nothing to my daughter, and she couldn't even thank me for them. However, giving to her helped fulfill my joy. It's a natural thing to give when you really love someone and that includes giving to God.

Jesus said this about our treasures—our finances: "For where your treasure is, there your heart will be also" (Matthew 6:21). He taught that wherever one puts his money, it will show where his heart really is.

In fact, what a person spends his money on is often an indicator of his spiritual health—including his salvation. Let's look at John the Baptist when he called Israel to bear fruits worthy of repentance or to prove their salvation (cf. Lk 3:8). He said:

So the crowds were asking him, "What then should we do?" John answered them, "The person who has two tunics must share with the person who has none, and the person who has food must do likewise." Tax collectors also came to be baptized, and they said to him,

285

"Teacher, what should we do?" He told them, "Collect no more than you are required to." Then some soldiers also asked him, "And as for us—what should we do?" He told them, "Take money from no one by violence or by false accusation, and be content with your pay." Luke 3:10-14

To the wealthy who had two tunics (or jackets), he said, "Share." To the tax collectors, he said, "Collect no more than you are required to." To the soldiers, he said, "Take money from no one by violence or by false accusation, and be content with your pay."

Isn't that interesting? Every fruit that had to do with true repentance, which really means true salvation, was shown in their finances. How people handle their money shows whether they truly love God. It shows where their relationship with God is.

What does the way you use your finances say about your relationship with God? The decay in Israel's spiritual life was shown in their lack of giving to the Lord.

Consider what Paul teaches about our giving in 2 Corinthians 8:7: "But as you excel in everything—in faith, in speech, in knowledge, and in all eagerness and in the love from us that is in you—make sure that you excel in this act of kindness too."

He says as believers, we should seek to grow in our giving to the Lord. It should be abounding. This makes perfect sense because giving is an indicator of our love for God. Since our love for God should always be growing, by necessity, so should our giving. Therefore, when our desire to give is less, it is a sign of spiritual decay. That's what happened with Israel and that's what happens with us.

What does your giving say about your heart? How is God calling you to excel in giving?

Application Question: What do you spend most of your money on? What does that say about your heart?

A Decrease in Time Given to Worship Is a Sign of Spiritual Decay

In Nehemiah 13:15-16, we also see that the people stopped practicing the Sabbath. Look at what it says:

In those days I saw people in Judah treading winepresses on the Sabbath, bringing in heaps of grain and loading them onto donkeys, along with wine, grapes, figs, and all kinds of loads, and bringing them to Jerusalem on the Sabbath day. So I warned them on the day that they sold these provisions. The people from Tyre who lived there were bringing fish and all kinds of merchandise and were selling it on the Sabbath to the people of Judah—and in Jerusalem, of all places!

The Sabbath originally was meant to be a time of rest, where the Israelites focused on God instead of work or other things. However, at this point, many people no longer practiced the Sabbath but instead compromised with the world, as they bought and sold on the Sabbath day. Instead of focusing on God and worshiping him, they focused on their work and making money instead.

No doubt, Israel had excuses. If everybody was working and they closed their businesses, they would lose money and customers. They could rationalize it.

It's the same for us. It's easy to rationalize missing church, small group, or our personal Bible study, but that doesn't make it right. "I've got school." "I've got work." "If I don't work, how am I going to pay my bills? I can't commit to church or small group." "I got home from work late; I can't go to church tomorrow." We have all types of excuses that keep us from worshiping, keep us from reading our Bible or serving the church. This was a sign of spiritual decay with Israel, and it's the same for us.

I don't believe we are under the Sabbath as a law because Christ is our Sabbath (cf. Col 2:16-17), but the principle is the same. Typically, when there is moral decline in our life, we will find that there has also been a decline in our time given to worshipping God.

The signals of this are hard to miss. Some people may stop going to church all together and others become sporadic. They stop going to small group and start missing their daily quiet times. Many never commit to any type of consistent worship. These are all signs of spiritual decay. You must be fighting to grow or your relationship with God and your holiness will decline. Paul said, "train yourself for godliness" (1 Timothy 4:7). Without disciplining ourselves to worship, we cannot be godly people.

How is your daily and weekly commitment to worship? What does it say about your relationship with God?

It should also be noted that what we give our time to in lieu of worship shows our idolatry. The Israelites were making wealth an idol over God. They would shop, buy, and sell on the Sabbath instead of worshiping the Lord. Materialism had become their idol.

287

What is keeping you out of worship? Is it work? Is it friends? Is it rest? What is keeping you from finding your Sabbath in Christ? Whatever you do instead of worshiping the Lord or spending time with him shows the idols in your heart.

Application Question: What are common things that cause you to neglect the worship of God? How is God calling you to put him first?

Worldly Relationships Are a Sign of Spiritual Decay

In Nehemiah 13:23-24, we see that the Israelites also compromised by marrying pagan women. Nehemiah said this:

> Also in those days I saw the men of Judah who had married women from Ashdod, Ammon, and Moab. Half of their children spoke the language of Ashdod (or the language of one of the other peoples mentioned) and were unable to speak the language of Judah. Nehemiah 13:23-24

This compromise was so bad that many of the children couldn't even speak Hebrew, which meant they couldn't read the Holy Scriptures or understand the teaching of the priests and Levites.

When we compromise with the world, not only does it affect us, but it affects those close to us, like our children. They will grow up speaking and thinking like the world, instead of speaking and thinking like God.

God gave strict rules against marrying foreigners in the Old Testament because of the tendency of being drawn to worship other gods. Solomon compromised in this area and, essentially, turned the nation of Israel away from God, eventually leading to their exile. This dangerous compromise had previously almost destroyed Israel. The marrying of a foreigner itself probably wasn't sin, for Ruth and Rahab were both foreigners. However, they had committed to worshiping Yahweh and were, eventually, placed in the lineage of Christ.

In the New Testament, we similarly have clear admonitions and prohibitions against marrying an unbeliever. Look at what Paul says to the widows in 1 Corinthians 7:39: "A wife is bound as long as her husband is living. But if her husband dies, she is free to marry anyone she wishes (only someone in the Lord)."

A widow was free to marry anyone, but the person had to belong to the Lord. It had to be someone who was serving God. Similarly, Paul declared

288

how he had the right to take a "believing wife," which implies he didn't have a right to take one who didn't believe. Look at what he said in 1 Corinthians 9:5: "Do we not have the right to the company of a believing wife, like the other apostles and the Lord's brothers and Cephas?"

However, this call to separation does not just apply to marriage but to all intimate relationships with the world. Second Corinthians 6:14 (NIV 1984) says this: "Do not be yoked together with unbelievers. For what do righteousness and wickedness have in common? Or what fellowship can light have with darkness?"

Paul used an analogy from the Old Testament law about not yoking two different animals together, such as an ox and a donkey in Deuteronomy 22:10. Many believe this work-related law had to do with their inability to plow a straight line. The ox and donkey have different natures and different temperaments. The ox is so strong it would pull the donkey in a different direction, and therefore, the work would be unproductive.

In the same way, Christians are not to be in any worldly relationships that keep them from walking a straight line with Christ—that pull them away from God and hinder them from being productive in serving him. Certainly, this applies to marriage, but it also applies to friendship, work, and everything else.

One seminary professor said where a person will be in ten years will mostly be affected by the books they read and the company they kept.[54] What do your most intimate relationships say about your relationship with God and your future? Solomon said something similar. Proverbs 13:20 says, "The one who associates with the wise grows wise, but a companion of fools suffers harm."

Now, certainly we are called to minister to the world and to love them, but we are not called to be "yoked" with them. Christ ate and drank with the world in hopes of winning them to God. He befriended them, prayed for them, and served them, but, when you look at his most intimate relationships, it shows that his most intimate relationships were with believers.

It has often been said that Christ had five rings of fellowship around him. He had the three apostles: Peter, James and John—his most intimate friends. He took them up on the Mount of Transfiguration when he didn't take others. He took them to pray before his death. Then Christ had the nine other apostles who were always with him. He had the seventy-two (cf. Lk 10:1). And he had other followers outside of that, and then he had the world.

His most intimate relationships were not with those going a different direction. He was a friend of sinners, but his deepest friendships were with those who were following God. Christ said this: "Who are my mother, brother, and sister but those who obey God?" (Matt 12:50, paraphrase). You are affected by your most intimate relationships. Amos said this: "Can two walk together unless they are agreed?" (Amos 3:3 NIV 1984).

Your most intimate relationships not only affect your ministry, but they also reflect who you are. They reflect what is inside you and what you agree with.

What do your most intimate relationships say about your relationship with God? Are your closest relationships with those who will pull you closer to the Lord or farther away from him? Friendship with the world is a sign of spiritual decay (cf. James 4:4).

Application Question: What is the balance of being salt and light in the world and also being separate from the world? Do you have any relationships that commonly pull you away from God? How is God calling you to remedy that?

How to Fix Spiritual Decay

We just looked at signs of spiritual decay in the life of a community or an individual believer. We can discern spiritual decay by looking at our leaders, our use of finances, our time given to worship, and our relationships.

What should we do if we see areas of decay in our life or in the church? How can we fix it? What can we learn from Nehemiah who is a type of Christ, as he zealously sought to turn the nation back to God?

Application Question: How can we fix spiritual decay, as demonstrated through Nehemiah?

1. We must become aware of areas of sin.

In this chapter, we commonly see how Nehemiah saw or was informed about the sins happening in Israel. Look at the passages below:

> and I returned to Jerusalem. Then I discovered the evil that Eliashib had done for Tobiah by supplying him with a storeroom in the courts of the temple of God.
> Nehemiah 13:7

> I also discovered that the grain offerings for the Levites had not been provided, and that as a result the Levites and the singers who performed this work had all gone off to their fields.
> Nehemiah 13:10

290

> Also in those days I saw the men of Judah who had married women
> from Ashdod, Ammon, and Moab.
> Nehemiah 13:23

Similarly, if we are going to fix areas of compromise in our lives or
others, we must be aware of it. This is the first step. The problem with many
individuals and communities is the fact that they don't even know they have a
problem. They are unaware of the idolatry in their hearts. They are unaware of
their sin or don't think the sin in their lives or their community is a big problem.
Therefore, they don't seek to remedy it.

Application Question: What are ways that we can better discern areas of sin or
compromise in ourselves and others?

- We must be people of the Word of God.

This is implied in verses 1-3. The Israelites were reading the Scripture
on the day they dedicated the wall (cf. Nehemiah 12), and they learned they
were forbidden to allow Ammonites and Moabites to enter the temple, leading
them to repent. Look at what it says:

> On that day the book of Moses was read aloud in the hearing of the
> people. They found written in it that no Ammonite or Moabite may ever
> enter the assembly of God, for they had not met the Israelites with food
> and water, but instead had hired Balaam to curse them. (Our God,
> however, turned the curse into blessing.) When they heard the law,
> they removed from Israel all who were of mixed ancestry.
> Nehemiah 13:1-3

In the same way, we must constantly be in the Word if we are going to
recognize sin. It is like a mirror that reveals our sin and compromise (cf. James
1:22-25) and the sin of others.

- We must have accountability relationships where people have the right
  to speak into our lives.

This is what we see with Nehemiah. Nehemiah came back to Israel
and pointed out all the wrong things being committed within her. David had
Nathan. Nathan, as a prophet, would confront David when he was in sin, no

matter how uncomfortable it must have felt. Similarly, we should have people that we allow and invite to be prophetic in our life.

These accountability relationships include sometimes asking questions like: "How is your spiritual life going?" "How is your marriage going?" "How is your time in the Word of God?" If we are going to be part of the solution, we must be aware of the problem.

Who is your Nehemiah? Who has the right to speak into your life?

- We should pray for God to point sin out in our lives and our communities.

Listen to how David prayed: "Examine me, and probe my thoughts! Test me, and know my concerns! See if there is any idolatrous tendency in me, and lead me in the reliable ancient path!" (Psalm 139:23-24).

David sought for God to reveal things in his life that were not right. We must continually bring ourselves before God as well and ask him to show us areas of compromise so we can become more like him.

- We must spend time with the people we lead and get to know them in order to discern how we can help them.

The good shepherd knows his sheep by name (John 10:3, 14). We must spend time with them. We must be with them in times of celebration, in times of mourning, and in everyday activities. We must know them. As we know them, we will better discern areas of compromise in their lives and how to minister to those areas.

What else should we do to help fix spiritual decay in our lives and others'?

2.   We must develop a righteous anger that leads us to confront sin.

Nehemiah 13:8 says, "I was very upset, and I threw all of Tobiah's household possessions out of the storeroom."

Nehemiah became very displeased when he heard about Tobiah being in the temple. However, not only was he displeased, he went into the apartment, threw everything outside, and then filled it with the offerings and the other things of God.

His anger also led him to confront many of the other people. Consider these texts:

So I registered a complaint with the leaders, asking "Why is the temple of God neglected?" Then I gathered them and reassigned them to their positions.
Nehemiah 13:11

So I registered a complaint with the nobles of Judah, saying to them, "What is this evil thing that you are doing, profaning the Sabbath day?
Nehemiah 13:17

So I entered a complaint with them. I called down a curse on them, and I struck some of the men and pulled out their hair.
Nehemiah 13:25

Now one of the sons of Joiada son of Eliashib the high priest was a son-in-law of Sanballat the Horonite. So I banished him from my sight.
Nehemiah 13:28

Not only did his anger lead to rebuking the people, but also to beating the men who had compromised by marrying the pagan women. He beat them and pulled out their hair (v. 25). When he said that he pulled out their hair, he was probably referring to the hair on their beards. By pulling out the hair on their beards, he was probably disrespecting their Jewishness. Jews were called to be holy, and one of the ways they represented that was by the males growing beards. Essentially, he was saying, "You are not following God! You are not a Jew!"

Another outlet of his righteous anger was running the High Priest's son away from the temple for also marrying a pagan (v. 28). This man had defiled the priesthood. God gave specific commandments for a priest's wife. She had to be a Jew and a virgin (Leviticus 21). Therefore, the High Priest's son was disobeying God and consequently leading others to do the same.

Now many of us struggle with what Nehemiah did, and it may even seem unkind. However, this is exactly how Scripture calls us to handle sin, especially our own. Listen to what Jesus said:

If your right eye causes you to sin, tear it out and throw it away! It is better to lose one of your members than to have your whole body thrown into hell. If your right hand causes you to sin, cut it off and throw it away! It is better to lose one of your members than to have your whole body go into hell.
Matthew 5:29-30

Christ said you must be drastic in trying to get rid of sin in your life. If you struggle with lust, get rid of whatever is leading you into sin. Get rid of the TV; turn off your Internet connection. If it's a friendship or a relationship leading you into sin, be willing to separate yourself from it. John Owen said, "Be killing sin or it will be killing you." We must be drastic in seeking to get rid of sin in our lives.

But this is not just for individuals, it is also needed in the church when there is unrepentant sin. Look at what Paul said to the Corinthians:

> hand this man over to Satan for the destruction of the flesh, so that his spirit may be saved in the day of the Lord. Your boasting is not good. Don't you know that a little yeast affects the whole batch of dough?
> 1 Corinthians 5:5-6

In this context, a believer was having sex with his father's wife. Paul told them to kick this person out of the church (hand over to Satan) because the yeast of this person's sin would spread. It would spread like a deadly cancer. Paul commanded them to not even eat with a professing believer who was living in unrepentant sin (1 Cor 5:11).

In the same way that it is not cruel or unloving for a doctor to cut cancer out of a patient to save his life, it is not cruel or unloving for the church to do the same with sin. We must lovingly help our friends get rid of habitual sins. At times, we must even separate ourselves from those who will not repent. Although this may be hard, we must do this in order to become holy and to help others become holy.

Because the church does not often practice this, it has become more and more compromising and less effective for the kingdom of God.

Yes, we must be wise as serpents and gentle as doves (Matt 10:16). There is a place for tact, but I think the church has too much wisdom and too much tact, which often means that we do nothing. There is a place for this in the wise plan of God. It is those who are righteously angry who do something about abortion. It is those who are righteously angry who do something about trafficking. It is those who are righteously angry who say this is not right and who fight for justice. It is the righteously angry who mourn, weep, and pray for the God of heaven to move on our behalf. We need to be forceful men and women who advance the kingdom of God (Matthew 11:12).

3. We must be people who truly desire to please God.

Nehemiah 13:14 says, "Please remember me for this, O my God, and do not wipe out the kindness that I have done for the temple of my God and for its services!"

Four times Nehemiah prays that God would remember him. This reflects the reason that Nehemiah was so zealous. It was because he truly wanted God's approval and favor over his life. When one is living for the world's approval instead of God's, it will be easy to compromise and not respond to sin.

We must be people who truly desire to see God pleased with our lives. The fact that this is repeated four times demonstrates how great of a priority this was for Nehemiah, and it must be for us as well.

4. We must be people with perseverance.

Another thing clearly demonstrated in this text is Nehemiah's great perseverance. He had already challenged Israel about all these things in the previous chapters. He had already helped them get rid of the compromise with foreigners. He had helped restore the Sabbath. In fact, in chapter 10, Israel made commitments to be faithful in all these areas, but now they had compromised again.

It is no different for us when battling with sin in our lives or others. For many Christians, Satan will get them so discouraged at their failures that they just give up and wallow in their sin. Similarly, others will give up on trying to help people all together. They say to themselves, "This is impossible."

Again, statistically 1,700 pastors leave the ministry each month. No doubt, a major reason for this is discouragement. They feel like they are not making a change, that people are stuck in their ways, and the church is not growing. Therefore, they get discouraged and quit.

However, when God rewards his servants in the Parable of the Talents, he doesn't reward them because they were successful; he rewards them because they were "faithful." He says, "Well done good and faithful slave!" (Matt 25:21). In the same way, we must be faithful in battling sin, faithful in battling compromise in our lives and the lives of others in order to honor God. We must be people of perseverance if we are going to get rid of sin.

Galatians 6:9 says, "So we must not grow weary in doing good, for in due time we will reap, if we do not give up."

Application Question: Do you have any people who are allowed to speak prophetically in your life? In what ways is God calling you to be an agent of change like Nehemiah in the lives of others?

Conclusion

In this text, we see common signs of decay in the lives of the people of God. What are signs of compromise amongst the people of God?

1. Compromised leadership
2. Misuse of money
3. A decrease in time given to worship—Sabbath
4. Worldly relationships

In what ways is God calling you to fix areas of compromise in your life or others? How is God calling you to be like Nehemiah, a type of Christ, who zealously confronted sin?

Application Question: What are the primary leadership lessons you learned from the book of Nehemiah and how is God challenging you to implement them into your life to become more of a godly leader?

Study Group Tips

Leading a small group using the Bible Teacher's Guide can be done in various ways. One format for leading a small group is the "study group" model, where each member prepares and shares in the teaching. This appendix will cover tips for facilitating a weekly study group.

1. Each week the members of the study group will read through a select chapter of the guide, answer the reflection questions (see Appendix 2), and come prepared to share in the group.

2. Prior to each meeting, a different member can be selected to lead the group and share Question 1 of the reflection questions, which is to give a short summary of the chapter read. This section of the gathering could last from five to fifteen minutes. This way, each member can develop their gift of teaching. It also will make them study harder during the week. Or, each week the same person could share the summary.

3. After the summary has been given, the leader for that week will facilitate discussions through the rest of the reflection questions and also ask select review questions from the chapter.

4. After discussion, the group will share prayer requests and pray for one another.

The strength of the study group is the fact that the members will be required to prepare their responses before the meeting, which will allow for easier discussion. In addition, each member will be given the opportunity to teach, which will further equip their ministry skills. The study group model has distinct advantages.

298

Reflection Questions

Writing is one of the best ways to learn. In class, we take notes and write papers, and all these methods are used to help us learn and retain the material. The same is true with the Word of God. Obviously, all of the authors of Scripture were writers. This helped them better learn the Scriptures and also enabled them to more effectively teach it. In studying God's Word with the Bible Teacher's Guide, take time to write so you can similarly grow both in your learning and teaching.

1. How would you summarize the main points of the text/chapter? Write a brief summary.

2. What stood out to you most in the reading? Did any of the contents trigger any memories or experiences? If so, please share them.

3. What follow–up questions did you have about the reading? What parts did you not fully agree with?

4. What applications did you take from the reading, and how do you plan to implement them into your life?

5. Write several commitment statements: As a result of my time studying God's Word, I will . . .

6. What are some practical ways to pray as a result of studying the text? Spend some time ministering to the Lord through prayer.

Walking the Romans Road

How can a person be saved? From what is he saved? How can someone have eternal life? Scripture teaches that after death each person will spend eternity either in heaven or hell. How can a person go to heaven?

Paul said this to Timothy:

> You, however, must continue in the things you have learned and are confident about. You know who taught you and how from infancy you have known the holy writings, which are able to give you wisdom for salvation through faith in Christ Jesus.
> 2 Timothy 3:14-15

One of the reasons God gave us Scripture is to make us wise for salvation. This means that without it nobody can know how to be saved.

Well then, how can a people be saved and what are they being saved from? A common method of sharing the good news of salvation is through the Romans Road. One of the great themes, not only of the Bible, but specifically of the book of Romans is salvation. In Romans, the author, Paul, clearly details the steps we must take in order to be saved.

How can we be saved? What steps must we take?

Step One: We Must Accept that We Are Sinners

Romans 3:23 says, "For all have sinned and fall short of the glory of God." What does it mean to sin? The word sin means "to miss the mark." The mark we missed is looking like God. When God created mankind in the Genesis narrative, he created man in the "image of God" (1:27). The "image of God" means many things, but probably, most importantly it means we were made to be holy just as he is holy. Man was made moral. We were meant to reflect God's holiness in every way: the way we think, the way we talk, and the way we act. And any time we miss the mark in these areas, we commit sin.

Furthermore, we do not only sin when we commit a sinful act such as: lying, stealing, or cheating. Again, we sin anytime we have a wrong heart motive. The greatest commandments in Scripture are to "Love the Lord your God with all your heart and to love your neighbor as yourself" (Matt 22:36-40, paraphrase). Whenever we don't love God supremely and love others as ourselves, we sin and fall short of the glory of God. For this reason, man is always in a state of sinning. Sadly, even if our actions are good, our heart is bad. I have never loved God with my whole heart, mind, and soul and neither has anybody else. Therefore, we have all sinned and fall short of the glory of God (Rom 3:23). We have all missed the mark of God's holiness and we must accept this.

What's the next step?

Step Two: We Must Understand We Are Under the Judgment of God

Why are we under the judgment of God? It is because of our sins. Scripture teaches God is not only a loving God, but he is a just God. And his justice requires judgment for each of our sins. Romans 6:23 says, "For the payoff of sin is death."

A wage is something we earn. Every time we sin, we earn the wage of death. What is death? Death really means separation. In physical death, the body is separated from the spirit, but in spiritual death, man is separated from God. Man currently lives in a state of spiritual death (cf. Eph 2:1-3). We do not love God, obey him, or know him as we should. Therefore, man is in a state of death.

Moreover, one day at our physical death, if we have not been saved, we will spend eternity separated from God in a very real hell. In hell, we will pay the wage for each of our sins. Therefore, in hell people will experience various degrees of punishment (cf. Lk 12:47-48). This places man in a very dangerous predicament—unholy and therefore under the judgment of God.

How should we respond to this? This leads us to our third step.

Step Three: We Must Recognize God Has Invited All to Accept His Free Gift of Salvation

Romans 6:23 does not stop at the wages of sin being death. It says, "For the payoff of sin is death, but the gift of God is eternal life in Christ Jesus our Lord." Because God loved everybody on the earth, he offered the free gift of eternal life, which anyone can receive through Jesus Christ.

Because it is a gift, it cannot be earned. We cannot work for it. Ephesians 2:8-9 says, "For by grace you are saved through faith, and this is not from yourselves, it is the gift of God; it is not from works, so that no one can boast."

Going to church, being baptized, giving to the poor, or doing any other righteous work does not save. Salvation is a gift that must be received from God. It is a gift that has been prepared by his effort alone.

How do we receive this free gift?

Step Four: We Must Believe Jesus Christ Died for Our Sins and Rose from the Dead

If we are going to receive this free gift, we must believe in God's Son, Jesus Christ. Because God loved us, cared for us, and didn't want us to be separated from him eternally, he sent his Son to die for our sins. Romans 5:8 says, "But God demonstrates his own love for us, in that while we were still sinners, Christ died for us." Similarly, John 3:16 says, "For this is the way God loved the world: He gave his one and only Son, so that everyone who believes in him will not perish but have eternal life." God so loved us that he gave his only Son for our sins.

Jesus Christ was a real, historical person who lived 2,000 years ago. He was born of a virgin. He lived a perfect life. He was put to death by the Romans and the Jews. And he rose again on the third day. In his death, he took our sins and God's wrath for them and gave us his perfect righteousness so we could be accepted by God. Second Corinthians 5:21 says, "God made the one who did not know sin to be sin for us, so that in him we would become the righteousness of God." God did all this so we could be saved from his wrath.

Christ's death satisfied the just anger of God over our sins. When God saw Jesus on the cross, he saw us and our sins and therefore judged Jesus. And now, when God sees those who are saved, he sees his righteous Son and accepts us. In salvation, we have become the righteousness of God.

If we are going to be saved, if we are going to receive this free gift of salvation, we must believe in Christ's death, burial, and resurrection for our sins (cf. 1 Cor 15:3-5, Rom 10:9-10). Do you believe?

Step Five: We Must Confess Christ as Lord of Our Lives

Romans 10:9-10 says,

> Because if you confess with your mouth that Jesus is Lord and believe in your heart that God raised him from the dead, you will be saved. For

with the heart one believes and thus has righteousness and with the mouth one confesses and thus has salvation.

Not only must we believe, but we must confess Christ as Lord of our lives. It is one thing to believe in Christ but another to follow Christ. Simple belief does not save. Christ must be our Lord. James said this: "...Even the demons believe that – and tremble with fear" (James 2:19), but the demons are not saved—Christ is not their Lord.

Another aspect of making Christ Lord is repentance. Repentance really means a change of mind that leads to a change of direction. Before we met Christ, we were living our own life and following our own sinful desires. But when we get saved, our mind and direction change. We start to follow Christ as Lord.

How do we make this commitment to the lordship of Christ so we can be saved? Paul said we must confess with our mouth "Jesus is Lord" as we believe in him. Romans 10:13 says, "For everyone who calls on the name of the Lord will be saved."

If you admit that you are a sinner and understand you are under God's wrath because of them; if you believe Jesus Christ is the Son of God, that he died on the cross for your sins, and rose from the dead for your salvation; if you are ready to turn from your sin and cling to Christ as Lord, you can be saved.

If this is your heart, then you can pray this prayer and commit to following Christ as your Lord.

> *Dear heavenly Father, I confess I am a sinner and have fallen short of your glory, what you made me for. I believe Jesus Christ died on the cross to pay the penalty for my sins and rose from the dead so I can have eternal life. I am turning away from my sin and accepting you as my Lord and Savior. Come into my life and change me. Thank you for your gift of salvation.*

Scripture teaches that if you truly accepted Christ as your Lord, then you are a new creation. Second Corinthians 5:17 says, "So then, if anyone is in Christ, he is a new creation; what is old has passed away – look, what is new has come!" God has forgiven your sins (1 John 1:9), he has given you his Holy Spirit (Rom 8:15), and he is going to disciple you and make you into the image of his Son (cf. Rom 8:29). He will never leave you nor forsake you (Heb 13:5), and he will complete the work he has begun in your life (Phil 1:6). In heaven, angels and saints are rejoicing because of your commitment to Christ (Lk 15:7).

Praise God for his great salvation! May God keep you in his hand, empower you through the Holy Spirit, train you through mature believers, and use you to build his kingdom! "He who calls you is trustworthy, and he will in fact do this" (1 Thess 5:24). God bless you!

Coming Soon

Praise the Lord for your interest in studying and teaching God's Word. If God has blessed you through the BTG series, please partner with us in petitioning God to greatly use this series to encourage and build his Church. Also, please consider leaving an Amazon review and signing up for free book promotions. By doing this, you help spread the "Word." Thanks for your partnership in the gospel from the first day until now (Phil 1:4-5).

Available:
First Peter
Theology Proper
Building Foundations for a Godly Marriage
Colossians
God's Battle Plan for Purity
Nehemiah
Philippians
The Perfections of God
The Armor of God
Ephesians
Abraham
Finding a Godly Mate
1 Timothy
The Beatitudes
Equipping Small Group Leaders
2 Timothy
Jacob

Coming Soon:
The Sermon on the Mount

About the Author

Greg Brown earned his MA in religion and MA in teaching from Trinity International University, a MRE from Liberty University, and a PhD in theology from Louisiana Baptist University. He has served over fourteen years in pastoral ministry and currently serves as chaplain and professor at Handong Global University, teaching pastor at Handong International Congregation, and as a Navy Reserve chaplain.

Greg married his lovely wife, Tara Jayne, in 2006, and they have one daughter, Saiyah Grace. He enjoys going on dates with his wife, playing with his daughter, reading, writing, studying in coffee shops, working out, and following the NBA and UFC. His pursuit in life, simply stated, is "to know God and to be found faithful by Him."

To connect with Greg, please follow at http://www.pgregbrown.com.

310

Notes

[1] Longman III, Tremper. Introducing the Old Testament: A Short Guide to Its History and Message. Zondervan. Kindle Edition.

[2] MacArthur, John (2003-08-21). The MacArthur Bible Handbook (Kindle Locations 3456-3457). Thomas Nelson. Kindle Edition.

[3] MacArthur, John (2003-08-21). The MacArthur Bible Handbook (Kindle Location 3454). Thomas Nelson. Kindle Edition.

[4] MacArthur, John (2003-08-21). The MacArthur Bible Handbook (Kindle Location 3456). Thomas Nelson. Kindle Edition.

[5] MacArthur, John (2003-08-21). The MacArthur Bible Handbook (Kindle Locations 3464-3465). Thomas Nelson. Kindle Edition.

[6] MacArthur, John (2003-08-21). The MacArthur Bible Handbook (Kindle Location 3468). Thomas Nelson. Kindle Edition.

[7] MacArthur, John (2003-08-21). The MacArthur Bible Handbook (Kindle Location 3479). Thomas Nelson. Kindle Edition.

[8] MacArthur, John (2003-08-21). The MacArthur Bible Handbook (Kindle Location 3480). Thomas Nelson. Kindle Edition.

[9] MacArthur, John (2003-08-21). The MacArthur Bible Handbook (Kindle Location 3556). Thomas Nelson. Kindle Edition.

[10] Guzik, D. (n.d.). Nehemiah Overview - David Guzik Commentary on the Bible. Retrieved January 11, 2015, from http://www.studylight.org/commentaries/guz/view.cgi?bk=15&ch=1

[11] Swindoll, Charles (1998-12-03). Hand Me Another Brick (p. 9). Thomas Nelson. Kindle Edition.

[12] Getz, Gene (1995-06-22). Men of Character: Nehemiah (Kindle Locations 472-473). B&H Publishing Group. Kindle Edition.

[13] Constable, T. (n.d.). Notes on Nehemiah. Retrieved January 11, 2015, from http://www.soniclight.com/constable/notes/pdf/nehemiah.pdf

[14] Boice, J. M. (2005). Nehemiah: An expositional commentary (24). Grand Rapids, MI: BakerBooks.

[15] Cole, Steven. "Lesson 2: The Realities of Serving God (Nehemiah 2:1-20)". Retrieved 1/15/15 from https://bible.org/seriespage/lesson-2-realities-serving-god-nehemiah-21-20

[16] Cole, Steven. "Lesson 2: The Realities of Serving God (Nehemiah 2:1-20)". Retrieved 1/15/15 from https://bible.org/seriespage/lesson-2-realities-serving-god-nehemiah-21-20

[17] Getz, Gene (1995-06-22). Men of Character: Nehemiah (Kindle Locations 739-740). B&H Publishing Group. Kindle Edition.

[18] Swindoll, Charles (1998-12-03). Hand Me Another Brick (p. 48). Thomas Nelson. Kindle Edition.

[19] Kidner, D. (1979). *Ezra and Nehemiah: An Introduction and Commentary* (Vol. 12, p. 88). Downers Grove, IL: InterVarsity Press.

[20] MacArthur, J., Jr. (Ed.). (1997). *The MacArthur Study Bible* (electronic ed., p. 661). Nashville, TN: Word Pub.

[21] Kidner, D. (1979). *Ezra and Nehemiah: An Introduction and Commentary* (Vol. 12, p. 92). Downers Grove, IL: InterVarsity Press.

[22] Getz, Gene (1995-06-22). Men of Character: Nehemiah (Kindle Locations 1038-1039). B&H Publishing Group. Kindle Edition.

[23] Wiersbe, W. W. (1996). *Be Determined* (p. 41). Wheaton, IL: Victor Books.

[24] *Swindoll, Charles (1998-12-03). Hand Me Another Brick (p. 98). Thomas Nelson. Kindle Edition.*

[25] Swindoll, Charles (1998-12-03). Hand Me Another Brick (p. 98). Thomas Nelson. Kindle Edition.

[26] "40% of Pastors Admit to Having Extramarital Affair!" retrieved 12/31/14, from https://www.standingstoneministry.org/40-of-pastors-admit-to-having-extramarital-affair/

[27] Kidner, D. (1979). *Ezra and Nehemiah: An Introduction and Commentary* (Vol. 12, p. 108). Downers Grove, IL: InterVarsity Press.

[28] Getz, Gene (1995-06-22). Men of Character: Nehemiah (Kindle Location 2841). B&H Publishing Group. Kindle Edition.

[29] Wiersbe, W. W. (1996). *Be Determined*. "Be" Commentary Series (77). Wheaton, IL: Victor Books.

[30] "Integrity" retrieved 11/14/2014, from http://dictionary.reference.com/browse/integrity

[31] MacArthur, J., Jr. (Ed.). (1997). *The MacArthur Study Bible* (electronic ed., p. 668). Nashville, TN: Word Pub.

[32] Kidner, D. (1979). *Ezra and Nehemiah: An Introduction and Commentary* (Vol. 12, p. 112). Downers Grove, IL: InterVarsity Press.

[33] MacArthur, J., Jr. (Ed.). (1997). *The MacArthur Study Bible* (electronic ed., p. 669). Nashville, TN: Word Pub.

[34] Boice, J. M. (2005). *Nehemiah: an expositional commentary* (p. 84). Grand Rapids, MI: BakerBooks.

[35] Kidner, D. (1979). *Ezra and Nehemiah: An Introduction and Commentary* (Vol. 12, p. 115). Downers Grove, IL: InterVarsity Press.

[36] Boice, J. M. (2005). *Nehemiah: an expositional commentary* (p. 93). Grand Rapids, MI: BakerBooks.

[37] Holmes, Leslie. "Up to 1500 Pastors a Month Need to Read this Column" retrieved 11/21/14, from http://www.preaching.com/resources/articles/11682911/

[38] Terpstra, Charles. "The Reformation: A Return to the Primacy of Preaching." retrieved 1/9/15, from http://www.prca.org/resources/publications/pamphlets/item/639-the-reformation-a-return-to-the-primacy-of-preaching

[39] Terpstra, Charles. "The Reformation: A Return to the Primacy of Preaching." retrieved 1/9/15, from http://www.prca.org/resources/publications/pamphlets/item/639-the-reformation-a-return-to-the-primacy-of-preaching

[40] MacArthur, J., Jr. (Ed.). (1997). *The MacArthur Study Bible* (electronic ed., p. 671). Nashville, TN: Word Pub.

[41] Guzik, D. (n.d.). Nehemiah Overview - David Guzik Commentary on the Bible. retrieved 1/9/15, from http://www.studylight.org/commentaries/guz/view.cgi?bk=15&ch=9

[42] Wiersbe, W. W. (1996). *Be Determined* (p. 123). Wheaton, IL: Victor Books.

[43] Wiersbe, W. W. (1996). *Be Determined*. "Be" Commentary Series (126). Wheaton, IL: Victor Books.

[44] MacArthur, John (2003-08-21). The MacArthur Bible Handbook (Kindle Locations 6969-6970). Thomas Nelson. Kindle Edition.

[45] Kidner, D. (1979). *Ezra and Nehemiah: An Introduction and Commentary* (Vol. 12, p. 132). Downers Grove, IL: InterVarsity Press.

[46] Foster, Richard J. (2009-03-17). Celebration of Discipline (Kindle Locations 2931-2932). HarperCollins. Kindle Edition.

[47] The Moody Bible Commentary (Kindle Locations 26193-26194). Chicago: Moody Publishers. Kindle Edition.

[48] MacArthur, John (2003-08-21). The MacArthur Bible Handbook (Kindle Location 3464). Thomas Nelson. Kindle Edition.

[49] Cole, Steven. "Lesson 13: The Problem of Permissiveness (Nehemiah 13:1-31)". Retrieved 1/15/15 from https://bible.org/seriespage/lesson-13-problem-permissiveness-nehemiah-131-31

[50] Turek, Frank. "Youth Exodus Problem". retrieved 1/11/15, from http://crossexamined.org/youth-exodus-problem/

[51] "Statistics in Ministry". retrieved 1/11/15, from http://www.pastoralcareinc.com/statistics/

[52] MacArthur, John (2003-08-21). The MacArthur Bible Handbook (Kindle Locations 5841-5842). Thomas Nelson. Kindle Edition.

[53] MacArthur, John (2003-08-21). The MacArthur Bible Handbook (Kindle Locations 6969-6970). Thomas Nelson. Kindle Edition.

[54] Cole, Steven. "Lesson 13: The Problem of Permissiveness (Nehemiah 13:1-31)". Retrieved 1/15/15 from https://bible.org/seriespage/lesson-13-problem-permissiveness-nehemiah-131-31